全国英语专业博雅系列教材/总主编　丁建新

英国文学作品选读

主　编　李成坚
副主编　陈　平　何　敏

中山大学出版社
SUN YAT-SEN UNIVERSITY PRESS
·广州·

版权所有　翻印必究

图书在版编目（CIP）数据

英国文学作品选读/李成坚主编；陈平，何敏副主编. —广州：中山大学出版社，2014.8

（全国英语专业博雅系列教材/总主编　丁建新）

ISBN 978-7-306-04951-3

Ⅰ.①英…　Ⅱ.①李…②陈…③何…　Ⅲ.①英语—阅读教学—高等学校—教材②英国文学—作品—介绍　Ⅳ.①H319.4：I

中国版本图书馆 CIP 数据核字（2014）第 151051 号

出 版 人：	徐　劲
策划编辑：	熊锡源
责任编辑：	熊锡源
封面设计：	曾　斌
责任校对：	林彩云
责任技编：	何雅涛
出版发行：	中山大学出版社
电　　话：	编辑部 020 - 84111996，84113349，84111997，84110779
	发行部 020 - 84111998，84111981，84111160
地　　址：	广州市新港西路 135 号
邮　　编：	510275　　传　　真：020 - 84036565
网　　址：	http://www.zsup.com.cn　　E-mail：zdcbs@mail.sysu.edu.cn
印 刷 者：	广州中大印刷有限公司
规　　格：	787mm×960mm　1/16　14.75 印张　322 千字
版次印次：	2014 年 8 月第 1 版　2014 年 8 月第 1 次印刷
印　　数：	1～4000 册　　定　　价：35.00 元

如发现本书因印装质量影响阅读，请与出版社发行部联系调换

全国英语专业博雅系列教材编委会

总主编 丁建新（中山大学）

编 委 会

李洪儒（黑龙江大学）
司显柱（北京交通大学）
赵彦春（天津外国语大学）
田海龙（天津外国语大学）
夏慧言（天津科技大学）
李会民（河南科技学院）
刘承宇（西南大学）
施　旭（浙江大学）
辛　斌（南京师范大学）
杨信彰（厦门大学）
徐畅贤（湖南城市学院）
李玉英（江西师范大学）
李发根（江西师范大学）
肖坤学（广州大学）
宫　齐（暨南大学）
张广奎（广东财经大学）
温宾利（广东外语外贸大学）
杜金榜（广东外语外贸大学）
阮　炜（深圳大学）
张晓红（深圳大学）

博雅之辩（代序）

大学精神陷入前所未有的危机，许多人在寻找出路。

我们的坚持是，提倡博雅教育（Liberal Education）。因为大凡提倡什么，关键在于审视问题的症结何在，对症下药。而当下之困局，根源在于功利，在于忘掉了教育之根本。

博雅教育之理念，可以追溯至古罗马人提倡的"七艺"：文法、修辞、辩证法、音乐、算术、几何、天文学。其目的在于培养人格完美的自由思考者。在中国教育史上，博雅的思想，古已有之。中国儒家教育的传统，强调以培养学生人格为核心。儒家"六艺"，礼、乐、射、御、书、数，体现的正是我们所讲的博雅理念。"学识广博，生活高雅"，在这一点上，中国与西方，现代与传统，并无二致。

在古罗马，博雅教育在于培育自由的人格与社会精英。在启蒙时代，博雅教育意指解放思想，破除成见。"什么都知道一点，有些事情知道得多一点"，这是19世纪英国的思想家约翰·斯图亚特·密尔（John Stuart Mill）对博雅的诠释。同一时期，另外一位思想家，曾任都柏林大学校长的约翰·亨利·纽曼（John Henry Newman）在《大学理念》一书中，也曾这样表述博雅的培养目标："如果必须给大学课程一个实际目标，那么，我说它就是训练社会的良好成员。它的艺术是社会生活的艺术，它的目的是对世界的适应……大学训练旨在提高社会的精神格调，培养公众的智慧，纯洁一个民族的趣味"。

博雅教育包括科学与人文，目标在于培养人的自由和理性的精神，而不是迎合市场与风俗。教育的目标在于让学生学会尊重人类生活固有的内在价值：生命的价值、尊严的价值、求知的价值、爱的价值、相互尊重的价值、自我超越的价值、创新的价值。提倡博雅教育，就是要担当这些价值守护者的角色。博雅教育对于我们来说，是一种素质教育、人文教育。人文教育关心人类的终极目标，不是以"有用"为标准。它不是"万金油"，也无关乎"风花雪月"。

在美国，专注于博雅教育的大学称为"文理学院"，拒绝职业性的教育。在中国香港，以博雅教育为宗旨的就有岭南大学，提倡"全人教育"；在台湾大学，博雅教育是大学教育的基础，课程涉及文学与艺术、历史思维、世界文明、道德与哲学、公民意识与社会分析、量化分析与数学素养、物质科学、生命科学等八大领域。在欧洲，博雅教育历史中的七大范畴被分为"三道"（初级）与"四道"（高级）。前者包括语法、修辞与辩证法，后者包括算术、几何、天文与音乐。在中国大陆的中山大学，许多有识之士也提倡博雅之理念，让最好的教授开设通识课程，涉及现代学科之环境、生物、地理等各门。同时设立"博雅学院"，学拉丁，读古典，开风气之先。

外语作为一门人文性很强的学科，尤其有必要落实博雅之理念。对于我们来说，最好的"应用型"教育在于博雅。早在20世纪20～40年代，在水木清华的外文系，吴宓先生提倡"语""文"并重，"中""西"兼修，教学上提倡自主学习与互动研究。在《西洋文学系学程总则》中，吴宓明确了"博雅之士"的培养目标：

> 本系课程编写的目的为使学生：（甲）成为博雅之士；（乙）了解西洋文明之精神；（丙）熟读西方文学之名著，谙悉西方思想之潮流，因而在国内教授英、德、法各国语言文字及文学，足以胜任愉快；（丁）创造今日之中国文学；（戊）汇通东西方之精神而互为介绍传布。

博雅之于我们，不仅仅是理念，更重要的是课程体系，是教材，是教法，是实践，是反应试教育，是将通识与专业熔于一炉。基于这样的理念，我们编写了这套丛书。希望通过这样的教育，让我们的学生知道人之为人是有他内在的生活意义，告诉我们的学生去求知，去阅读，去思考，去创造，去理解世界，去适应社会，去爱，去相互尊重，去审美，去找回精神的家园。

无需辩驳，也不怕非议。这是我们的坚守。

中山大学外国语学院　教授、博士生导师
中山大学语言研究所　所长
丁建新
2013 年春天

序　言

　　文学是人类文化和文明的延续，是生命情感的表达和交流，充满艺术特质的美学表现。文学即人学。历经岁月的洗涤、传世流传的经典文学作品是人类价值建构和精神生长的过程，是人类生存意义的自我确证。因此，阅读一部文学作品，透过作家独特的心灵诉求和审美经验的表达，管窥一个时代的社会风貌和精神气质，使读者发问最为根本的人生命题：人到底需要什么样的生活？人该怎么生活？文学根本上就是一种内省、一种探索、一种超越。

　　英国文学具有悠久的历史。从以《贝奥武夫》为代表的盎格鲁－撒克逊时期的口头文学传统，到14世纪末乔叟在其《坎特伯雷故事集》开启的伦敦方言创作，到16世纪高歌人文主义的文艺复兴文学巨匠，如莎士比亚、马洛、斯宾塞、弥尔顿，英格兰在经济发展、国力强盛和政治变革后，迎来了其民族意识的觉醒和民族文化的自觉。自18世纪英国步入工业革命，科学的发展、技术的革新不仅更新了西方人对于自然和宇宙的认知，而且彻底改变了西方人的生活方式。文学上，现实主义、浪漫主义、批判现实主义、唯美主义、现代主义各种流派纷呈，真实而生动地记载了英国的社会发展和生活图景，敏感而深刻地捕捉了物质繁荣下的心理现实和精神需求。因此，英国文学历史根本上折射出民族发展的历史，透过英国经典文学作品，细品英国人的精神历程和审美趣味之余，更深层次上，是他山之石的文化借鉴功能的实现。

　　本书按照文学文类，分为诗歌编、小说编和戏剧编。三个部分都强调对文学经典的原文阅读，以求达到对英语语言的质感把握。为帮助教师和学生更好地使用本教材，每编包含对英国诗歌、小说和戏剧发展的宏观概况，力图呈现英国文学的整体面貌，使学生形成较为完整的文学历史感。文本后则有注释、问题与思考、名言录及相关文类的重要术语概念解释，以求更有效地指导教与学。本教材所选材料可满足64学时教学的需要，也方便教师在具体教学实践中，做出弹性选择。

　　本教材总体设计和诗歌编由李成坚负责，陈平负责小说编，何敏负责戏剧编。全书由李成坚统稿。硕士研究生李缘、温婷参与了本教材的校对工作。

I

本教材作为电子科技大学"十二五"规划教材,得到学校教务处的经费资助;出版过程中,得到中山大学外语学院丁建新教授的认可和中山大学出版社熊锡源老师的鼎力支持,在此一并表达感谢。

限于作者的学术水平,错误与不妥之处在所难免,敬请读者批评指正。

李成坚
2014 年 3 月

目　录

第一章　英国诗歌选编

导　言 …………………………………………………………… 3
1　Sonnet 18 ………………………………… by William Shakespeare　5
2　Spring, the Sweet Spring …………………………… by Thomas Nashe　7
3　Valediction: Forbidding Mourning …………………… by John Donne　8
4　On His Blindness ……………………………………… by John Milton　11
5　An Essay on Criticism ………………………………… by Alexander Pope　13
6　Elegy Written in a Country Churchyard ……………… by Thomas Gray　15
7　The Tiger ……………………………………………… by William Blake　17
8　A Red, Red Rose ……………………………………… by Robert Burns　19
9　I Wandered Lonely as a Cloud ………………… by William Wordsworth　21
10　Ode to West Wind …………………………………… by Percy Shelley　23
11　The Isles of Greece …………………………………… by George Byron　28
12　The First Looking into Chapman's Homer …………… by John Keats　35
13　The Eagle ……………………………………………… by Alfred Tennyson　37
14　My Last Duchess ……………………………………… by Robert Browning　38
15　The Dover Beach ……………………………………… by Mathew Arnold　42
16　In the Station of Metro ……………………………… by Ezra Pound　45
17　The Love Song of J Alfred Prufrock ………………… by T. S. Eliot　46
18　Church Going ………………………………………… by Philip Larkin　52
19　Hawk Roosting ………………………………………… by Ted Hughes　56
20　Clearances ……………………………………………… by Seamus Heaney　58
诗歌术语 ………………………………………………………… 59
　1. Aestheticism ………………………………………………… 59
　2. Alliteration ………………………………………………… 59
　3. Assonance …………………………………………………… 59
　4. Blank verse ………………………………………………… 59
　5. Byronic ……………………………………………………… 60
　6. Dramatic monologue ………………………………………… 60
　7. Elegy ………………………………………………………… 60
　8. Epic ………………………………………………………… 60

2　英国文学作品选读

9. Heroic couplet ········· 60
10. Iambic pentameter ········· 60
11. Imagism ········· 61
12. Lake poets ········· 61
13. Lyric ········· 61
14. Metaphysical poetry ········· 62
15. Ode ········· 62
16. Rhyme ········· 62
17. Rhythm ········· 63
18. Soliloquy ········· 63
19. Sonnet (Italian sonnet, English sonnet ········· 63
20. Tone ········· 63

第二章　英国小说选编

导　言 ········· 67
1　Robinson Crusoe ········· by Daniel Defoe　70
2　Gulliver's Travels ········· by Jonathan Swift　78
3　Pride and Prejudice ········· by Jane Austin：83
4　David Copperfield ········· by Charles Dickens　89
5　Jane Eyre and ········· by Charlotte Bronte sisters　103
6　Wuthering Heights ········· by Emily Bronte　108
7　Tess of the D'Urbervilles ········· by Thomas Hardy　111
8　Araby ········· by James Joyce　114
9　Mrs. Dalloway ········· by Virginia Woolf　120
10　Sons and Lovers ········· by D. H. Lawrence　128

小说术语 ········· 154
1. Allegory ········· 154
2. Analepsis ········· 154
3. Antagonist ········· 154
4. Anti-hero (anti-heroine. ········· 154
5. Bildungsroman ········· 154
6. Context ········· 154
7. Dialogue ········· 154
8. Embedded narrative ········· 154
9. First-person narrative ········· 154
10. Focalization ········· 154
11. Intertextuality ········· 155
12. Leitmotif ········· 155

13. Metafiction ……………………………………………… 155
14. Prolepsis ………………………………………………… 155
15. Third-person narrative ………………………………… 155
16. Narratology ……………………………………………… 155

第三章　英国戏剧选编

导　言 ………………………………………………………… 159
1　The Tragical History of the Life and Death of Doctor Faustus
　　……………………………………… *by Christopher Marlowe* 161
2　Hamlet ……………………………………… *by William Shakespeare* 167
3　The Merchant of Venice …………………… *by William Shakespeare* 170
4　Samson Agonistes ………………………………… *by John Milton* 171
5　The Importance of Being Earnest ………………… *by Oscar Wilde* 175
6　Major Barbara ……………………………… *by George Bernard Shaw* 183
7　Riders To the Sea …………………………………… *by J. M. Synge* 188
8　Waiting for Godot ………………………………… *by Samuel Beckett* 198
9　Look Back in Anger ………………………………… *by John Osborne* 205
戏剧术语 ……………………………………………………… 221
　1. Antagonist ………………………………………………… 221
　2. Character ………………………………………………… 221
　3. Comedy …………………………………………………… 221
　4. Diction …………………………………………………… 221
　5. Drama …………………………………………………… 222
　6. Melodrama ……………………………………………… 222
　7. Music …………………………………………………… 222
　8. Plot ……………………………………………………… 222
　9. Protagonist ……………………………………………… 222
　10. Spectacle ……………………………………………… 223
　11. Thought ………………………………………………… 223
　12. Tragedy ………………………………………………… 223
　13. Tragicomedy …………………………………………… 223

第一章　英国诗歌选编

导　言

　　诗歌是文学样式中最古老的形式。它起源于上古的社会生活，是因劳动生产、两性相恋、原始宗教等而产生的一种有韵律、富于感情色彩的语言形式。从最初的口头文学到书面形式，诗歌以叙事或抒情的形式，以高度凝练的语言，展现人的体验、情绪、见闻、想象力和文采。因而，诗歌是最古老同时也是最具文学特性的文体。

　　何谓诗？自古以来，对诗歌的定义莫衷一是。古希腊哲人西蒙尼德斯云："诗是有声之画，画是无声之诗"，突出了诗歌的意象和声效；19 世纪英国浪漫主义诗人华兹华斯曰："诗是强烈情感的自然流溢"，侧重诗歌的抒情性；同时代的柯勒律治则将诗定义为"诗是最佳的词以最佳的词序组合"，凸显了诗歌语言的精炼特质；20 世纪美国诗人弗罗斯特则以"诗歌是翻译中失去的东西"，强调了诗歌的独特音乐性；而中国历来有"诗言志"说，强调的是诗歌所呈现的思想境界。尽管诗歌的定义繁多各异，然而诗歌之所以为诗，应具有如下要素：凝练的语言、飞动的意象、丰沛的情感和鲜明的音乐性。阅读和欣赏诗歌因此可以磨练读者的判断力、丰富感情和美学体验。

　　英国是诗歌的国度，其诗歌是世界文学中历史最长、成就最高的民族诗歌之一。英国诗歌发展历史大约有 1500 多年，大致可分为三个阶段：

　　1. 古英语时期（公元 5～10 世纪）。其间，欧洲大陆不同部族的进入，多语言和文化的深度融合，形成非英格兰本土的题材和背景的口头文学，直至公元 10 世纪，才出现书面形式的文学留存。由于时间的久远和连年的战事，大量古英语时期的诗歌流失，仅 3 万多行诗保存在 4 个中世纪的抄本之中。这一时期的代表作为史诗《贝奥武夫》。该诗以丹麦为故事场景，描述了英雄贝奥武夫与海怪搏斗的精彩过程。该诗以 3000 多行的鸿篇巨制、以磅礴的英雄气概、典型的头韵法和丰富的比喻，展现了氏族时期人与自然力量之间的较量和抗争，是古英语时期最具艺术价值的文学作品。

　　2. 中古英语时期（公元 11～15 世纪）。尽管这一时期仍有外族人入侵（诺曼人 1066 年登陆，开启英国社会的封建社会时期），尽管这一时期法国文学鼎盛强势，但民族意识悄然在欧洲大陆萌芽，英国文学的本土意识也开始显现。乔叟的代表作《坎特伯雷故事集》便是英国本土文学的典型。被誉为英国文学之奠基人、英国诗歌之父的乔叟，在吸纳了法国文学和意大利文学精髓的基础上，以伦敦方言、以英国本土人物和题材（如巴斯妇）、以精妙的写实主义、以改良的英雄双韵体诗行形式，呈现出英国封建社会时期各个阶层的生活全景。论及对英国民族语言的普及贡献、诗歌形式的借鉴与探新和英国社会生活的艺术再现，乔叟都是中古英语时期的佼佼者。

3. 现代英语时期（16世纪至今），英国诗歌发展进入辉煌的发展阶段。近五百年来，英国诗歌历经了4次大的诗歌高潮：16～17世纪文艺复兴时期诗歌；18世纪新古典主义诗歌；19世纪浪漫主义诗歌和20世纪现代主义诗歌。每次高潮期都涌现出众多诗歌大家，如文艺复兴时期的莎士比亚、斯宾塞、西德尼、多恩和弥尔顿，18世纪的蒲柏，19世纪的华兹华斯、雪莱、拜伦、济慈、丁尼生、勃朗宁、阿诺德、哈代及20世纪的艾略特、叶芝、拉金、休斯等。本章中仅仅汲选了少量的精华，以窥现代英国诗歌繁荣之全貌。

诗歌的分类方式不一而足。就品种而言，诗歌可分为戏剧诗和抒情诗。戏剧诗，或又称为诗剧，是一种将诗和剧相结合的形式，做到了既高雅又普及。在文艺复兴时期，这一形式达到无后辈能及的巅峰，尽管20世纪现代派大师艾略特努力复兴诗剧形式。抒情诗又可再细分为史诗、民谣、悼亡诗、颂歌、田园诗等。就诗体而言，诗歌中有十四行体、斯宾塞体、英雄双韵体等。十四行体又分意大利体和英国体（亦称莎士比亚体）。无论是十四行体还是英雄双韵体，对英国而言都是舶来品。但从意大利体到莎士比亚体至弥尔顿的意大利改良体再至雪莱的变体，乔叟从法国引进的英雄双韵体至蒲柏手上臻于完美，英国诗歌的发展历史是一段诗歌形式力求更新和变革的历史。

再论诗歌语言和风格。16～17世纪的英国诗歌，现代英语中夹杂着古英语词或拉丁词，其诗风或田园甜美或庄重磅礴；18世纪新古典主义时期，以蒲柏为代表的诗人力求用词的精准和雅致，写就了不少家喻户晓的工整警句；19世纪的浪漫主义诗人，一反18世纪的诗风，倡导以质朴平实的口语入诗，借恣肆的想象力沉思自然、抗争命运；20世纪现代主义诗人则倡导语言的多义隐含，以艰涩的表义，展现人类精神的困境。

纵观英国诗歌的发展历程，其历史就是一段不断更新诗歌语言、不懈探索诗歌形式、表达不同时代精神和个体体验的历史。一个新的流派诞生，是对前一阶段文学样式的反驳，是一种新的陌生化效果的探索。然而新的手段和方式渐成一种普遍趋势，逐渐失去其新奇的效果时，就进入一种所谓"自动化"的阶段，最终又会被一种更新的陌生化效果所替代。尽管新的诗歌流派总是伴随着一个重大的历史时刻出现，就艺术发展的自身机制而言，诗歌史，乃至整个文学史的发展也是审美趣味不断更新的历史。

1 Sonnet 18

William Shakespeare

Shall I compare thee to a summer's day?[1]
Thou art[2] more lovely and more temperate:
Rough winds do shake the darling buds of May,[3]
And summer's lease hath all too short a date:[4]
Sometime too hot the eye of heaven[5] shines,
And often is his gold complexion dimmed;[6]
And every fair from fair sometime declines,[7]
By chance or nature's changing course untrimmed,[8]
But thy eternal summer shall not fade,
Nor lose possession of that fair thou ow'st,[9]
Nor shall death brag thou wander'st in his shade,
When in eternal lines to time thou grow'st:[10]
So long as men can breathe, or eyes can see,
So long lives this, and this gives life to thee.

【注释】

1. Shall...day: 诗人把爱人比作夏天。英国夏季气候宜人，故有此比。

2. thou art: you are; 古英语词 thou 是单数，复数为 ye，不像现代英语中单复数都是 you。

3. rough winds do shake the darling buds of May: 第一个音步为扬抑格（trochee）。rough 重读，音律上的变化强调了自然之美不如爱人之美，从此行起至第八行都以具体的形象支持第二行的断言。

4. lease:（房、土地等）租期; date: duration, 延续的时期。此行喻夏日苦短，不能久留。

5. the eye of heaven: 天之眼睛，即太阳。

6. gold complexion dimmed:（太阳）金色的容颜被罩上阴云。

7. every fair from fair sometimes declines: 此处两个 fair 都作名词，前者指美人，后者指美貌（同第 10 行）。

8. by chance...untrimmed: 倒装句，正常结构应作 untrimmed by chance or nature's changing course; untrimmed: 剥夺美丽的外表。

9. that fair thou ow'st: 你所占有的美貌。ow'st: owest。按: owe 即 own, 此系古义，和现在的"负债"之意恰好相反，如《暴风雨》(*Tempest*): This is no

mortal business, nor no sound / That the earth owes.

10. to time thou grow'st: 与时间同寿，喻亘古不变; to time: to all time。

Questions for discussion:

1. Do you think this poem is a love song? What's the theme of the poem?
2. What is humanism? How is the humanistic idea expressed in this poem?
3. What is sonnet? What's Shakespearian sonnet?

名言摘录

What a piece of work is a man, how noble in reason, how infinite in faculties, in form and moving, how express and admirable in action, how like an angle in apprehension, how like a god!

——*William Shakespeare (1564 – 1616)*

2 Spring, the Sweet Spring

Thomas Nashe

Spring, the sweet spring, is the year's pleasant king,
Then blooms each thing, then maids dance in a ring,
Cold doth[1] not sting, the pretty birds do sing:
Cuckoo, jug-jug, pu-we, to-witta-woo![2]

The palm and may[3] make country houses gay,
Lambs frisk[4] and play, the shepherds pipe all day,
And we hear aye birds tune this merry lay:[5]
Cuckoo, jug-jug, pu-we, to-witta-woo!

The fields breathe sweet, the daisies kiss our feet,
Young lovers meet, old wives a-sunning[6] sit,
In every street these tunes our ears do greet:
Cuckoo, jug-jug, pu-we, to witta-woo!

Spring, the sweet spring!

【注释】
1. doth: does.
2. Cuckoo: 布谷鸟叫声; jug-jug: 夜莺叫声; pu-we: 田鸠的叫声; to-witta-woo: 猫头鹰的叫声。
3. may: 山楂花。
4. frisk: 跳跃。
5. aye: (古) always; lay: song。
6. a-sunning: 晒太阳; 前缀 "a-" 表示动作在进行之中。

Questions for discussion:

1. How does the poet convey a vivid picture of spring? How can you trace the sweetness of spring?
2. Are there anything special in terms of sound effect?

3 A Valediction: Forbidding Mourning

John Donne

As virtuous men pass mildly away,[1]
And whisper to their souls to go,[2]
Whilst some of their sad friends do say
The breath goes now, and some say,[3] No;

So let us melt,[4] and make no noise,
No tear-floods, nor sigh-tempests move,[5]
'Twere[6] profanation of our joys
To tell the laity[7] our love.

Moving of th' earth[8] brings harms and fears,
Men reckon what it did, and meant;
But trepidation of the spheres,[9]
Though greater far, is innocent.

Dull sublunary[10] lovers' love
(Whose[11] soul is sense) cannot admit
Absence, because it doth remove
Those things which elemented[12] it.

But we by a love so much refined
That our selves[13] know not what it is,
Inter-assuréd of the mind,[14]
Care less, eyes, lips and hands to miss.[15]

Our two souls therefore, which are one,
Though I must go, endure not yet
A breach, but an expansion,[16]
Like gold to airy thinness beat.[17]

If they be two, they are two so
As stiff twin compasses are two;[18]

Thy soul, the fixed foot, makes no show
To move, but doth, if th' other do.

And though it in the center sit,[19]
Yet when the other far doth roam,
It leans, and hearkens after it,
And grows erect, as that comes home.

Such wilt thou be to me, who must
Like th' other foot, obliquely run;[20]
Thy firmness makes my circle just,[21]
And makes me end where I begun[22].

【注释】

1. as：和第 5 行的 so 呼应，即 Just as ... so ...; pass mildly away：静静地离开人世。

2. to go：有的版本在 to 之前加逗号。离别赠诗，起首论生离死别，实在是大胆新奇之笔。

3. the breath goes now：say 引起的直接引语，"已经咽气"。

4. melt：depart unobtrusively，"悄然死去"，应上文 pass mildly away。

5. No tear-floods, nor sigh-tempests move：move no tear-floods, nor sigh-tempests, 不使人悲泪双流，哀痛欷歔。

6. 'Twere：it were.

7. laity：（区别于僧侣、教士的）俗人。

8. moving of th'earth：地震。

9. trepidation of the spheres：天体的震颤。文艺复兴时期的一种假设，认为天体因震动而偏离正常的运动轨道，但地球上的人观察不到，故并不为之担忧。这种运动不像地震，被认为是无害的（innocent），虽然天体的颤抖要比地震猛烈得多（though greater far）。"天体震颤"一说在 950 年由托勒密天体学提出，以解释某些天象，其实只是地球在绕地轴旋转时发生抖动而引起的。

10. sublunary：below the moon，月亮下的，即尘世的，多变的。

11. whose：指 love。这种爱情的本质（soul）是感官之爱，故不能容忍别离（cannot admit absence）。

12. elemented：composed；此句意为感官之爱消除了爱的基本因素，使爱情空虚，故只能凭借感官得以生存。

13. our selves：我们的自我。

14. Inter-assuréd of the mind：彼此心心相印。

15. Care less, eyes, lips, and hands to miss：care less to miss eyes, lips, and hands.

16. endure...a breach, but an expansion：（由于我们心有灵犀一点通，）所以我们的心灵经受的不是背弃，而是扩展。

17. like gold to airy thinness beat：正常结构为 beat to airy thinness（别离时爱情的扩展）犹如黄金被延展成薄片。

18. as stiff twin compasses are two：像两脚圆规两只脚。把相恋的情人比作圆规，这是邓恩典型的奇思怪想（conceits），这一比喻常用来说明玄学派奇思的特点。

19. though it in the center sit：sit 为虚拟语气，早期英语 though 引导的从句中，动词用虚拟语气。

20. obliquely run：圆规活动的那只脚有所倾斜，故说 obliquely。

21. Thy firmness makes my circle just：你的坚定使我的圆圈更圆满；just：proper。

22. makes me end where I begun：我的活动首尾相连。表明走得很圆，圆是完美的象征。

Questions for discussion：

1. How do you think of the beginning of the poem on death? What's the intention of the poet before the separation from his wife?

2. How do you comment the image of gold to airy thinness? How does it work with the comparison of love?

3. The poem is characterized by its peculiar conceit and reasoning. Do you agree or disagree? State your reason(s).

名言摘录

No man is an island, entire of itself; every man is a piece of the continent, a part of the man...Any man's death diminishes me, because I am involved in mankind; and therefore never send to know for whom the bell tolls; it tolls for thee.

——*by John Donne* (*1608 – 1674*)

4 On His Blindness

John Milton

When I consider how my light is spent[1]
Ere half my days, in this dark world and wide,[2]
And that one talent which is death to hide,[3]
Lodged with me useless, though my soul more bent
To serve therewith my Maker,[4] and present
My true account, lest he returning chide;[5]
"Doth God exact day-labor, light denied?"[6]
I fondly ask; but Patience to prevent
That murmur, soon replies, "God doth not need
Either man's work or his own gifts; who best
Bear his mild yoke, they serve him best.[7] His state
Is kingly. Thousands[8] at his bidding speed
And post[9] o'er land and ocean without rest:
They also serve who only stand and wait."[10]

【注释】

1. light is spent: 光明燃尽，指双目失明。

2. ere half my days: 诗人于 1652 年双目失明，时年 42 岁，故说尚未到半生；ere: before; this dark world and wild: this dark and wild world, 当时王权复辟，许多革命志士惨遭迫害，形势险峻。弥尔顿因双目失明，才得幸免。他在《失乐园》第七卷中说：though fall'n on evil days, / On evil days though fall'n, and evil tongues; / In darkness, and with dangers compassed round, / And solitude; yet not alone, 其中 "not alone" 两字指诗人得到诗神的灵感，在黑暗中吟咏这首史诗，毫无寂寞之感。

3. one talent which is death to hide: 直到死亡才会消失的能力，指写作能力。诗人憾慨失明之苦，何能再事写作（下行 lodged with me useless）。《失乐园》（*Paradise Lost*）和《力士参孙》（*Samson Agonistes*）都是失明后创作的。此处 talent 语涉双关，既指 "能力"（ability），又指古希腊、罗马和中东等的钱币（译为 "泰伦"）。《新约·马太福音》XXV. 14 – 30 节中有一寓言：主人在外旅行前根据其仆人的能力分发泰伦，一仆人得五枚，另一人得三枚，最后一人得一枚。前两个仆人都以所得的钱挣得更多的钱，主人回来后如数交出。唯独取一枚者将钱埋在地里，一无所获，遭主人斥责。talent 引申为 "能力"，本此。which

is death to hide 借用的正是这一故事，对弥尔顿来说，埋藏他的 talent 无疑是死亡。

4. therewith：with that；Maker：上帝。

5. true account, lest he returning chide：承上寓言，意为想以这个泰伦为上帝服务，把账目结清，免得他回来责怪。诗人虽感失明后力不从心，但仍不甘沉沦，力图有所作为。由 when 引导的状语从句至此结束。

6. Doth God exact day-labor, light denied：上帝既不给我光明，是否还要逼我做日工？exact：强求。

7. who … him best：谁最能忍受上帝的宽松的枷锁，谁对上帝的服务最为周到。此句正常结构为 whoever best bear his mild yoke serve him best。

8. Thousands：the heavenly angels，成千上万的天使。

9. post：急速行走。

10. they also serve who only stand and wait：those who only stand and wait also serve，静候侍主也在为上帝效劳。末三行吐露了诗人失明后的哀怨之情，但又勉励自己要有耐心，静候历史使命，不能以残疾毕志。

Questions for discussion：

1. Compare with Shakespeare's sonnet 18. What is the difference between the sonnet and sonnet 18? Please tell the main features of Italian sonnet.

2. What's the significance of the ambiguity of the word "talent" in the poem?

名言摘录

Truth is compared … to a streaming fountain; if her waters flow not in a perpetual progression, they sicken into a muddy pool or conformity and tradition.

——*John Milton（1608 - 1674）*

5 An Essay on Criticism
(excerpt, Lines 289 – 304)

Alexander Pope

Some to conceit[1] alone their taste confine,
And glittering thoughts struck out[2] at every line;
Pleased with a work where nothing's just or fit,[3]
One glaring chaos[4] and wild heap of wit.
Poets, like painters, thus unskilled to trace
The naked nature and the living grace,
With gold and jewels cover every part,
And hide with ornaments their want of art.[5]
True wit is Nature to advantage dressed,[6]
What oft was thought, but ne'er so well expressed;[7]
Something whose truth convinced at sight we find,
That gives us back the image of our mind.
As shades more sweetly recommend[8] the light,
So modest plainness sets off sprightly wit;
For works may have more wit than does them good,[9]
As bodies perish through excess of blood.

【注释】

1. conceit：奇思怪想，指遣词诡异、怪癖晦涩的奇特比喻，奇思风格。此乃玄学派诗人多恩（Donne）首创。以下数行均系对玄学派诗风的讥评。此句倒装，正常结构为 Some confine their taste to conceit alone。

2. struck out：提出。

3. where nothing's just or fit：作品中所言不当，出格。

4. glaring chaos：强烈的混沌杂乱。wit：妙语；此词在本诗中有各种意义，可指 a clever remark or the man who makes it, a conceit, liveliness of mind, inventiveness, fancy, a genius, poetry itself 等。

5. want of art：技巧的贫乏。

6. True wit is Nature to advantage dressed：自然巧描摹，始见文思奇。wit：此处指把思想和文采加以结合的能力（the power of combining ideas with a pointed verbal effect）；dressed to advantage：描绘恰到好处。

7. What oft was thought, but ne'er so well expressed：所思虽常见，妙笔则空前。oft：often；ne'er：never. 这是常为引用的名句。蒲柏创作本诗的意旨也不是

想有所创见，他只是思前人之所未言，是不重创思而重表意。

8. recommend：衬托，使……更见可爱。

9. more wit than does them good：妙语过多，弄巧成拙。

Questions for discussion：

1. What main poetic principles does the poet put forward in this excerpt?

2. According to his own poetics, what attitude should Pope present towards the poem "Valediction" by John Donne? Please state the different aesthetic tastes between Pope and Donne.

3. Please point out the dominant features in the rhyme scheme.

名言摘录

The sound must be an echo to the sense.

——*by Alexander Pope（1688 – 1744）*

6 Elegy Written in a Country Churchyard

Thomas Gray

The curfew[1] tolls the knell of parting day,
The lowing herd wind slowly o'er the lea,[2]
The plowman homeward plods his weary way,
And leaves the world to darkness and to me.

Now fades the glimmering landscape on the sight,
And all the air a solemn stillness holds,[3]
Save where the beetle wheels[4] his droning flight,
And drowsy tinklings lull the distant folds;[5]

Save that from yonder ivy-mantled tower[6]
The moping[7] owl does to the moon complain
Of such as, wandering near her secret bower,
Molest her ancient solitary reign.[8]

Beneath those rugged elms,[9] that yew tree's shade,
Where heaves the turf[10] in many a moldering heap,
Each in his narrow cell[11] forever laid,
The rude forefathers of the hamlet[12] sleep.

The breezy call of incense-breathing Morn,[13]
The swallow twittering from the straw-built shed,
The cock's shrill clarion, or the echoing horn,[14]
No more shall rouse them from their lowly bed.[15]

For them no more the blazing hearth shall burn,
Or busy housewife ply her evening care;
No children run to lisp their sire's return,
Or climb his knees the envied kiss to share.[16]

Oft did the harvest to their sickle yield,
Their furrow oft the stubborn glebe has broke;[17]
How jocund did they drive their team[18] afield!

How bowed the woods beneath their sturdy stroke!

Let not Ambition[19] mock their useful toil,
Their homely joys, and destiny obscure;[20]
Nor Grandeur hear with a disdainful smile
The short and simple annals[21] of the poor.

【注释】
1. curfew：晚钟。中世纪遗留下来的习惯，晚八点敲钟宵禁。一天结束，晚钟好比是白昼的丧钟（knell）。
2. lowing：牛叫声。o'er：over；lea：草地。
3. all the air a solemn stillness holds：a solemn stillness holds all the air。
4. Save：except，除了，同第 9 行。wheels：（甲虫）旋转飞舞。
5. folds：羊栏。
6. ivy-mantled tower：爬满常青藤的教堂塔楼。
7. moping：忧郁的。
8. reign：（古）realm，领土。
9. rugged elms：树皮多皱的榆树。
10. turf：草皮。草皮的鼓起（heaves）说明这里是一个个墓地。
11. cell：墓穴。
12. rude：untaught，没有文化的。hamlet：村落，常指无教堂的小村庄。
13. incense-breathing：吐出芬芳；Morn：morning。
14. horn：猎人的号角。
15. rouse：初版作 wake；lowly bed：指坟墓。
16. For them…share：此节想象死者在生前得到妻子的精心照顾、孩子见到父亲回家高兴地迎上前去。这和诗人 James Thomson（1700 – 1748）的《四季诗》(*The Seasons*) 中"冬季"（Winter）一章的情节颇为相似。ply her evening care：忙着料理傍晚的家务。
17. oft：often。glebe：（诗）土地，田地。broke：broken；broke 的宾语是 glebe。主语 furrow 似乎可做犁解。
18. team：套在一起拉犁的牲畜。
19. Ambition：拟人化，同节中的 Grandeur 也与此相同。
20. destiny obscure：默默无闻的命运。
21. annals：编年史，此处指一生的历史。

Questions for discussion:
1. Whom does the poet show sympathy to? What does the poet glorify then?
2. Why do the words "Ambition" and "Grandeur" capitalize? Would you find more examples from the poems you have read?

7 The Tiger

William Blake

Tiger! Tiger! burning bright
In the forests of the night,[1]
What immortal hand or eye
Could frame thy fearful symmetry?[2]

In what distant deeps or skies
Burnt the fire of thine eyes?
On what wings dare he[3] aspire?
What the hand dare seize the fire?

And what shoulder & what art,[4]
Could twist the sinews of thy heart?[5]
And when thy heart began to beat,
What dread hand? & what dread feet?[6]

What the hammer? what the chain?
In what furnace was thy brain?
What the anvil? What dread grasp
Dare its deadly terrors clasp?[7]

When the stars threw down their spears,
And water'd heaven with their tears,[8]
Did he smile his work to see?
Did he who made the Lamb make thee?

Tiger! Tiger! burning bright
In the forests of the night,
What immortal hand or eye,
Dare[9] frame thy fearful symmetry?

【注释】

1. burning bright / In the forests of the night：老虎的皮色和炯炯目光象征着火，老虎栖居深山密林幽暗如夜。《旧约·耶利米书》21：12 - 14："Deliver him that is spoiled out of the hand of the oppressor, lest my fury go out like fire, and burn

that none can quench it, because of the evil of your doings ... But I will punish you according to the fruit of your doings, saith the lord; and I will kindle a fire in the forest there of, and it shall devour all things round about it. "

2. What immortal hand or eye / Could frame the fearful symmetry：谁的非凡的手或眼力能够制造或设计你这可怕的形体。此句形容老虎的创作者有神的力量和灵感。symmetry：体态匀称。注意描写老虎的创造过程由整体开始，以下逐个描绘其身体的各主要部位。

3. he：指老虎的创造者。第二节写创造老虎的眼睛。创造者鼓起怎样的翅膀能飞到极远的高天，以怎样的手抓住怒火，造就了你炯炯发光的双眼？

4. what shoulder, & what art：谁有如此大的力量，以及如此高超的技巧？

5. twist the sinews of thy heart：制造你强健的心脏。twist the sinews 指用力把筋或腱扭弯成一定的形状；sinews 常作"力量"解。

6. What dread hand? & what dread feet：此系省略句，意为你的心一旦开始跳动，谁能用可怕的手脚来控制你？dread：即 dreadful。

7. what dread grasp / Dare its deadly terrors clasp：谁能有巨大的力量控制住可怖的老虎？

8. When the stars threw down their spears, / and water'd heaven with their tears：有的注家认为此两行暗指天使撒旦一伙反抗上帝的败绩。上帝是否看到天庭之战的胜利而微笑，并且创造了比撒旦的骄傲更可怕的老虎？"羊和你是否皆他创造"一句，则进一步说明了此诗的寓意。羊历来是和平和基督精神的象征。《圣经》中曾把狮子和羊作为自然界中的对立面。老虎和狮子类同。本节意为上帝既制造暴力，又创造和平。

9. Dare：注意末节和首节仅一字之差。上节说上帝微笑着欣赏他的创造。此处又用"dare"一词。上帝压倒了撒旦的叛乱，竟然又"敢于"创造出更加可怕的破坏力量。

Questions for discussion：

1. What does the poem glorify, the tiger or the maker of the tiger?
2. How do you understand the symbolic meaning of tiger?
3. What's the significance of the refrain of the last stanza? How do you interpret the change of the word "dare" in the last stanza?

名言摘录

  To see a world in a grain of sand
  And a heaven in a wild flower
  Hold infinity in the palm of your hand
  And eternity in an hour

——*William Blake* (*1757 – 1827*)

8 A Red, Red Rose

Robert Burns

O, my luve[1] is like a red, red rose,
That's newly sprung in June.
O, my luve is like the melodie,[2]
That's sweetly play'd in tune.[3]

As fair art thou, my bonie lass,[4]
So deep in luve am I,
And I will luve you still,[5] my dear,
Till a' the seas gang[6] dry.

Till a' the seas gang dry, my dear,
And the rocks melt wi'[7] the sun!
And I will luve thee still, my dear,
While the sands o' life[8] shall run.

And fare thou weel,[9] my only luve!
And fare thou weel, a while!
And I will come again, my luve,
Tho' it were ten thousand mile!

【注释】

1. luve: love。
2. melodie: melody 曲调。
3. in tune: 和谐地。
4. art: care; bonie lass: pretty girl。
5. still: always, constantly。
6. a': all; gang: go。
7. wi': with, 作用如 by。
8. o': of; sands o' life: 古时用沙漏计时，故 sands 代表时间。
9. fare thee weel: 再见吧，别了; weel: well。

Questions for discussion:

1. How do you think of the language style in this poem?

2. How does the plain dialect work with the expression with the direct expression of passion?

3. Please point out main techniques used by the poet to create the sound effect.

9 I Wondered Lonely As a Cloud

William Wordsworth

I wondered lonely as a cloud
That floats on high o'er vales[1] and hills,
When all at once I saw a crowd,
A host, of golden daffodils;
Beside the lake, beneath the trees,
Fluttering and dancing in the breeze.

Continuous[2] as the stars that shine
And twinkle on the milky way,
They stretched in the never-ending line
Along the margin of a bay:[3]
Ten thousand saw I at a glance,[4]
Tossing their heads[5] in sprightly dance.

The waves beside them danced; but they
Outdid the sparkling waves in glee;[6]
A poet could not but[7] be gay,
In such a jocund company;
I gazed—and gazed——but little thought
What wealth the show to me had brought:[8]

For oft,[9] when on my couch I lie
In vacant or in pensive[10] mood,
They flash upon that inward eye
Which is the bliss of solitude;[11]
And then my heart with pleasure fills,
And dances with the daffodils.

【注释】
1. vale：（主要用于诗歌）溪谷，山谷。
2. continuous：连绵不断的。
3. the margin of a bay：在湖边上。

4. Ten thousand saw I at a glance：I saw ten thousand at a glance。
5. tossing their heads：原指突然抬头，此处指摇摆不定。
6. in glee：欢乐。
7. could not but：不能不。
8. but little thought/ What wealth the show to me had brought：但是几乎没有想到这种景象给我带来了怎样的财富。意为这使诗人产生了丰富的联想。
9. oft：often。
10. vacant：茫然若失的；pensive：忧郁的。
11. They flash upon that inward eye/ Which is the bliss of solitude：水仙花突然闯入诗人的心中（inward eye），使他在孤寂中得到一种幸福。

Questions for discussion：

1. What does the image of cloud suggest to you?
2. What has the poet meditated from what he has described? And the theme?
3. Pay attention to the tense used in the poem. What does it indicate?

名言摘录

All good poetry is the spontaneous overflow of powerful feelings.

Poetry takes its origin from emotion recollections in tranquility ... tranquil contemplation of an emotional experience matures the feeling and sensation, and makes possible the creation of good poetry like the mellow of old wine.

——*William Wordsworth（1770 – 1850）*

10 Ode to the West Wind

Percy Bysshe Shelley

I

O wild West Wind, thou breath of Autumn's being,[1]
Thou from whose unseen presence[2] the leaves dead
Are driven, like ghosts from an enchanter[3] fleeing,

Yellow, and black, and pale, and hectic red,[4]
Pestilence-stricken multitudes:[5] O thou,
Who chariotest[6] to their dark wintry bed

The winged seeds,[7] where they lie cold and low,
Each like a corpse within its grave, until
Thine azure sister of the Spring[8] shall blow

Her clarion o'er[9] the dreaming earth, and fill
(Driving sweet buds like flocks to feed in air)[10]
With living hues and odours plain and hill:

Wild Spirit, which art[11] moving everywhere:
Destroyer and preserver: hear, oh hear!

II

Thou on whose stream, mid the steep sky's commotion,[12]
Loose clouds like earth's decaying leaves are shed,
Shook from the tangled boughs of Heaven and Ocean.[13]

Angels[14] of rain and lightning: there are spread
On the blue surface of thine aëry surge,
Like the bright hair uplifted from the head

Of some fierce Maenad, even[15] from the dim verge
Of the horizon to the zenith's height,
The locks of the approaching storm.[16] Thou dirge

Of the dying year, to which this closing night
Will be the dome of a vast sepulchre,
Vaulted with all thy congregated might

Of vapours,[17] from whose solid atmosphere
Black rain, and fire, and hail will burst: oh hear!

III

Thou who didst[18] waken from his summer dreams
The blue Mediterranean, where he lay,
Lulled by the coil of his crystalline streams,[19]

Beside a pumice isle in Baiae's bay,[20]
And saw in sleep old palaces and towers
Quivering within the wave's intenser day,[21]

All overgrown with azure moss and flowers
So sweet, the sense faints picturing them![22] Thou
For whose path the Atlantic's level powers

Cleave themselves into chasms,[23] while far below
The sea-blooms and the oozy woods which wear
The sapless foliage of the ocean, know

Thy voice, and suddenly grow gray with fear,
And tremble and despoil themselves:[24] oh hear!

IV

If I were a dead leaf thou mightest bear;
If I were a swift cloud to fly with thee;
A wave to pant beneath thy power, and share

The impulse of thy strength, only less free
Than thou,[25] O uncontrollable! If even
I were as in my boyhood, and could be

The comrade of thy wanderings over Heaven,
As then, when to outstrip thy skiey speed
Scarce seemed a vision; I would ne'er have striven

As thus with thee in prayer in my sore need.[26]
Oh, lift me as a wave, a leaf, a cloud!
I fall upon the thorns of life! I bleed![27]

A heavy weight of hours has chained and bowed
One too like thee: tameless, and swift, and proud.[28]

V

Make me thy lyre,[29] even as the forest is:
What if[30] my leaves are falling like its own!
The tumult of thy mighty harmonies

Will take from both[31] a deep, autumnal tone,
Sweet though in sadness. Be thou, Spirit fierce,
My spirit! Be thou me, impetuous one![32]

Drive my dead thoughts over the universe
Like withered leaves to quicken a new birth!
And, by the incantation of this verse,[33]

Scatter, as from an unextinguished hearth
Ashes and sparks, my words among mankind!
Be through my lips to unawakened earth

The trumpet of a prophecy![34] O Wind,
If Winter comes, can Spring be far behind?

【注释】
1. thou breath of Autumn's being: 秋之生命的呼吸。thou: you; Autumn 大写，拟人化用法。being: existence, life。
2. unseen presence: 无形的存在。
3. enchanter: 魔法师。枯叶被秋风吹散，犹如鬼魂见了魔法师匆匆逃跑。
4. hectic red: 肺病患者面颊通红。指树叶的颜色。
5. Pestilence-stricken multitudes: 枯叶被西风吹散，好像是害怕瘟疫而逃离。multitudes: 成团的枯叶。
6. chariotest: 配合 thou 的谓语动词；在现代英语中应为 chariot。原为名词，意为"战车"解，此处作"驱车送往"解。
7. winged seed: 轻盈飘飞的种子如同长了翅膀。
8. Thine azure sister of the Spring: 春天吹的西风。Spring 大写，亦为拟人化

用法。Thine：此处不用 thy（your）是因为后面接以元音字母开首的词"azure"，与第 19 行 thine aëry surge 同。地中海的天空呈蔚蓝色，故说 azure。按：意大利所在的阿尔卑斯山以南终年刮西风，雪莱描写的是秋末冬初的西风，摧枯拉朽，并把种子送到冬眠的床上（如第 6 行），而春天的西风则将唤醒它们。所以把春季的秋风称作"你蔚蓝色的姐妹"。

9. clarion：号角，一种音调很高的喇叭。o'er：over。

10. Driving sweet buds like flocks to feed in air：春天的蓓蕾好比羊群。西风像牧羊人放羊吃草那样赶着蓓蕾呼吸新鲜空气。

11. Spirit：在希伯来语、拉丁语、希腊语和其他很多语言中，wind, breath, soul 和 inspiration 的意义都很相近。雪莱歌颂的西风乃是一种"精灵"，象征在秋季摧枯拉朽，在来年春天勃发新生的力量。下行 Destroyer and preserver 即是此意。art：are，和 thou 连用。

12. stream：气流。mid：amid；the steep sky's commotion：高空中一片混乱。

13. Loose clouds like earth's decaying leaves are shed, / Shook from the tangled boughs of Heaven and Ocean：零碎的云像枯死的树叶，被风从更大更高的云团上（boughs）吹散下来；tangled boughs of Heaven and Ocean：天与海交叉的枝桠，指海面上蒸腾起来的水汽和空中的云团凝在一起。shook：shaken。

14. Angels：（古）messengers, harbingers，使者，先行者。乱云是大雨和闪电的先行者。

15. Maenad ['mi:næd]：迈娜得，希腊神话中酒神巴克斯（Bacchus）的女祭司，举动疯狂。这几行诗形容乱云像狂女上冲的头发。even：just。

16. The locks of the approaching storm：即将来临的风暴的卷发；"卷发"指乱云像狂女的头发。Thou dirge：西风是残年的挽歌。

17. to which this closing night ... vapours：残年的最后之夜（closing night）像是巨大墓穴的拱顶，笼罩在密集的蒸汽之中。

18. didst：did。

19. the coil of his crystalline steams：地中海的水流常呈现出不同的颜色，所以能看出曲折的波漩（coil）。

20. pumice isle：白色浮石构成的岛；Baiae's bay：意大利拿不勒斯（Naples）西部的休假地，古代罗马国王在此建造了许多行宫。

21. quivering within the wave's intenser day：（地中海从夏梦中醒来，看到古宫殿和城堡的倒影）在水波中颤动，光彩浓烈。雪莱曾说，色彩经水折射后更加鲜艳和和谐。

22. the sense faints picturing them：香得连感官也醉倒了。

23. For whose path the Atlantic's level powers / Cleave themselves into chasms：大西洋的波涛被西风吹开，好像被劈成了巨壑。level powers：平流的波涛。

24. far below ... themselves：雪莱自注："The phenomenon alluded to at the conclusion of the third stanze is well known to naturalists. The vegetation at the bottom of the sea, of rivers, and of lakes, sympathizes with that of the land in the change of

seasons, and is consequently influenced by the winds which announce it." 海底的植物也受到西风威力的影响，战栗变色，纷纷落叶。

25. A wave to pant ... Than thou：像波浪那样在西风的巨大威力下喘息。虽然不像西风那样自由自在，但是也能与它猛烈地冲劲共鸣。

26. If even ... in my sore need：雪莱认为童年时代充满天真的幻想，能自由地随风遨游长空，那时要超过急速的风暴似乎并非幻想，而现在却只能向西风祈求了。

27. I fall upon the thorns of life! I bleed：诗人祈求西风把他高高吹起，但是，却跌落到人生的荆棘之上，鲜血淋漓。

28. A heavy weight of hours ... proud：岁月的重轭束缚了我，而我原来也像你一样狂放不羁，迅猛高傲。

29. lyre：Eolian. lyre. 风鸣琴；西风吹得树林飒飒作响，诗人愿作风鸣琴，在西方的吹动下演奏。

30. what if：即使……又何妨？

31. both：指树木和风声。

32. be thou, Spirit fierce, / My spirit! Be thou me, impetuous one!：诗人希望和西风合而为一。

33. by the incantation of this verse：凭借这首诗的法力；incantation：符咒。

34. the trumpet of a prophecy：呼应第 10 行的 clarion。《新约·启示录》(*Revelation*) xi. 15："And the seventh angel sounded; and there were great voices in heaven, saying, the kingdoms of this world are become the kingdoms of our Lord, and of his Christ; and he shall reign for ever and ever."

Questions for discussion：

1. In what way is the West Wind both a destroyer and a preserver?
2. As "the trumpet of prophecy", what does the West Wind predict in physical reality? How do you understand it symbolically?
3. What are the features of the stanza form in the poem? Shall we call it a sonnet?

名言摘录

Poets are the unacknowledged legislators of the world.
Poetry sows the seeds of social revolution. It creates anew the universe.

——*Percy Shelley* (1792 – 1822)

11 The Isles of Greece

George Gordon, Lord Byron

1

The isles of Greece, the isles of Greece!
Where burning Sappho loved and sung,[1]
Where grew the arts of war and peace,[2]
Where Delos rose, and Phœbus sprung![3]
Eternal summer gilds them yet,
But all, except their sun, is set.

2

The Scian and the Teian muse,[4]
The Hero's harp, the Lover's lute,[5]
Have found the fame your shores refuse:[6]
Their place of birth alone is mute
To sounds which echo further west
Than your sires' "Islands of the Blest."[7]

3

The mountains look on Marathon—[8]
And Marathon looks on the sea;
And musing there an hour alone,
I dream'd that Greece might still be free;
For standing on the Persians' grave,[9]
I could not deem myself a slave.

4

A king sate on the rocky brow[10]
Which looks o'er sea-born Salamis;[11]
And ships, by thousands, lay below,
And men in nations;[12]—all were his!
He counted them at break of day—
And when the Sun set where were they?[13]

5

And where are they? And where art thou,
My country?[14] On thy voiceless shore
The heroic lay[15] is tuneless now—
The heroic bosom beats no more!
And must thy lyre, so long divine,
Degenerate into hands like mine?[16]

6

'Tis something, in the dearth of fame,[17]
Though linked among a fetter'd race,[18]
To feel at least a patriot's shame,
Even as I sing, suffuse my face;
For what is left the poet here?
For Greeks a blush—for Greece a tear.[19]

7

Must we but weep o'er days more blest?
Must we but blush?—Our fathers bled.[20]
Earth! render back from out thy breast
A remnant of our Spartan dead!
Of the three hundred grant but three,
To make a new Thermopylæ![21]

8

What, silent still? and silent all?
Ah! no;—the voices of the dead
Sound like a distant torrent's fall,
And answer,[22] "Let one living head,
But one arise,—we come, we come!"
'Tis but the living who are dumb.

9

In vain—in vain: strike other chords;
Fill high the cup with Samian wine![23]
Leave battles to the Turkish hordes,
And shed the blood of Scio's vine![24]
Hark! rising to the ignoble call—[25]
How answers each bold Bacchanal![26]

10

You have the Pyrrhic dance[27] as yet,
Where is the Pyrrhic phalanx[28] gone?
Of two such lessons, why forget
The nobler and manlier one?
You have the letters Cadmus[29] gave—
Think ye he meant them for a slave?

11

Fill high the bowl with Samian wine!
We will not think of themes like these!
It made Anacreon's song divine:[30]
He served—but served Polycrates—[31]
A Tyrant,[32] but our masters then
Were still, at least, our countrymen.

12

The Tyrant of the Chersonese[33]
Was Freedom's best and bravest friend;
That tyrant was Miltiades![34]
Oh! that the present hour would lend
Another despot of the kind![35]
Such chains as his were sure to bind.[36]

13

Fill high the bowl with Samian wine!
On Suli's rock, and Parga's shore,[37]
Exists the remnant of a line
Such as the Doric mothers bore;[38]
And there, perhaps, some seed is sown,
The Heracleidan blood might own.[39]

14

Trust not for freedom to the Franks—[40]
They have a king who buys and sells;
In native swords, and native ranks,[41]
The only hope of courage dwells;
But Turkish force, and Latin fraud,
Would break your shield, however broad.

15

Fill high the bowl with Samian wine!
Our virgins dance beneath the shade—
I see their glorious black eyes shine;
But gazing on each glowing maid,
My own the burning tear-drop laves,[42]
To think such breasts must suckle slaves.

16

Place me on Sunium's marbled steep,[43]
Where nothing, save[44] the waves and I,
May hear our mutual murmurs sweep;
There, swan-like, let me sing and die;[45]
A land of slaves shall ne'er be mine—
Dash down yon[46] cup of Samian wine!

【注释】

1. Sappho：莎弗，公元前 7 世纪末至 6 世纪初古希腊杰出的女抒情诗人，其作品热情奔放，炽烈如火（burning）；sung：sang。

2. the arts of war and peace：文治武功；arts：技巧，本领。

3. Delos：爱琴海中的得洛斯岛；Phæbus：即太阳神阿波罗（Apollo），相传生在得洛斯岛。sprung：sprang。

4. the Scian and the Teian muse：the Scian Muse 指荷马，史诗《伊利亚特》（*Illiad*）和《奥德赛》（*Odyssey*）的作者；the Teian Muse 指古希腊诗人阿那克里昂（Anacreon，公元前 6 世纪）。Muse：缪斯，希腊神话中掌管文艺、音乐等的九位女神，转指诗神。

5. the hero's harp, the lover's lute：诗人以大型乐器竖琴喻写爱情诗的阿那克里昂。

6. Have found the fame your shores refuse：他们的名声却被希腊故土忘却了。

7. sires'：祖先的；Islands of the Blest：古希腊诗人以此称现代的佛得角群岛（Cape de Jerd）或加那利群岛（the Canaries）。此处意为古希腊诗人的名声已远远超越了他们同代人所知的地理范围。Blest：blessed；据说宙斯（Zeus）让他所宠爱的人住在大地边缘的忘忧之岛，无人生之苦，故曰 blest。

8. Marathon：马拉松，位于雅典的东北。公元前 490 年雅典人在此处击败入侵的波斯军。

9. Persians' grave：入侵的波斯军葬身于此。

10. A king sate on the rocky brow：据伊斯库罗斯（Aeschylus）在悲剧《波斯人》（*Persian*）中说，波斯王 Xerxes（公元前 519？—465）曾在公元前 480 年 9 月 9 日坐在山上观察 Salamis 岛旁的海战，原以为强大的波斯舰队必胜，不料被希腊海军一举全歼。sate: sat; rocky brow: 悬崖。实际上当时 Xerxes 坐在 Aegaleos 山上。

11. Salamis: 岛名，在雅典以西。

12. Men in nations: Xerxes 军中的士兵有的来自被他征服的亚非各国的队伍。

13. And when the sun set where were they: 日暮时波斯人全军覆没。

14. And where are they? and where art thou, / My country?: 诗人调转笔锋，从古代波斯人的败绩转到今日被奴役的希腊。拜伦假托一位希腊人在怀古讽今，故曰 my country。

15. The heroic lay: 英雄之歌。

16. And must thy lyre, so long divine, / Degenerate into hands like mine?: 古希腊出过多少杰出的诗人，难道竟沦落到要由我这样的人来歌咏她么? lyre: 七弦琴，古希腊人作为伴唱诗歌的乐器，此处转指诗歌。

17. 'Tis: it is; in the dearth of fame: 在这屈辱的时候。

18. link'd among a fetter'd race: 被锁在一个被奴役的民族之内。

19. For Greeks a blush—for Greece a tear: 希腊的不幸催人泪下，但希腊当为之羞愧。

20. Must we but blush—Our fathers bled: 拜伦仿古老的头韵体诗以 but, blush, bled 押头韵，诗行中略作停顿，造成强烈的效果。我们的祖先洒下热血，难道我们仅仅脸红?

21. Earth! ... a new Thermopylæ: 公元前 480 年，斯巴达王 Leonidas 率领三百名斯巴达勇士，在通往希腊东部的关隘 Thermopylæ 和 Xerxes 率领的波斯侵略军血战。后因一希腊奸细给波斯人示路，Leonidas 及部下腹背受敌，全部阵亡。斯巴达勇士的英勇业绩使诗人呼吁，只要有三名勇士能复活，我们就可以在 Thermopylæ 再来一次壮烈的战役。

22. And answer: 拜伦为鼓动希腊人奋起反抗，想象死难勇士的回答："只要有一个活人站起来，我们死者将立即响应。"

23. Samian wine: Samos 岛的产之酒。Samos 是希腊群岛中较大的一岛。

24. Leave battles to the Turkish hordes, / And shed the blood of Scio's vine: 打仗让土耳其人去管吧，我们且饮酒作乐。当时希腊人正遭受土耳其"蛮人"(hordes) 的奴役，但是希腊人不去战场流血，而只饮葡萄之血（即葡萄酒）。

25. the ignoble call: 号召大家饮酒作乐，而不是奋起反抗，故称 ignoble。

26. bold Bacchanal: 勇敢的酒徒，意含讽刺。Bacchanal 来源于 Bacchus（巴科斯），希腊神话中的酒神。

27. Pyrrhic dance: 古希腊战舞，源出于 Thessaly 南部 Doris，是斯巴达士兵的部分训练内容，武者身穿盔甲。后在希腊的节日里流行这种舞蹈，以急速的笛子伴奏，舞者作各种进攻和防守状。这种风俗一直流传至罗马时代的后期。

28. Pyrrhic phalanx: 步兵的方阵。据传说希腊西北部 Epirus 城邦的君主 Pyrrhus 曾在公元前 3 世纪以这种方阵多次击败罗马军队。

29. Cadmus: 古希腊 Agenor 之子，Phoenicia 国王。大约生在公元前 14 世

纪,据说他从腓尼基人学到字母,传入希腊。

30. It made Anacreon's song divine: it 指 Samian wine; 它使阿那克里昂的诗歌成为天上之曲。阿那克里昂歌颂醇酒和爱情,诗风壮丽,可谓神化所主,不似人间来者。

31. Polycrates: 公元前 6 世纪希腊 Samos 岛的君主。波斯人在公元前 510 年入侵小亚细亚 Teos 城(阿那克里昂诞生地)时,他逃到 Thrace 的 Abdera,又从那儿到 Samos 岛,投奔 Polycrates。

32. tyrant: 按古希腊原义,此词指拥有绝对权力的统治者,或者不是由宪法赋予权力的统治者(an absomte ruler, or one whose power has not been constitutionally arrived at),现往往作"暴君"解。Polycrates 建立起强大的海军,与波斯对抗,又重文艺,尊贤人,颇有美名。

33. the Chersonese: 即 Grallipoli, 位于 Dardanelles 海的北面。

34. Miltiades: 上文所述 Marathon 战役中希腊军的统帅之一。公元前 5 世纪初,Miltiades 成为 Thracian Chersonesus(今达达及亚半岛)的君主。他曾和波斯王大流士一起和 Scythians 作战,后脱离波斯人,逃到雅典。虽曾遭致专制罪指控,但获开释。公元前 480 年波斯人全国入侵 Attica 时,他被任命为十大元帅之一,率军抵抗侵略者。他鼓动希腊人奋起御敌,并在 Marathon 击败波斯侵略军。

35. Oh! that the present hour would lend/ Another despot of the kind: 意为但愿现在能有像 Miltiades 这样一位专制的君主,他能鼓动人们起来斗争。

36. Such chains 一词,说明 Miltiades 既是独裁者,又有团结人民的组织才干。

37. On Suli's rock, and Parga's shore: Suli 是地区名, Parga 是其中一城,在今阿尔巴尼亚南部。拜伦在 *Childe Harold's Pilgrimage* (Canto Ⅱ.42) 中说:"Morn downs: and with it stern Albania's hills, Dark Suli's rocks…" 现在当地的人民正在抗击土耳其侵略军,故他认为爱好自由的古希腊人的后代(a line)应当在那里战斗。

38. Such as the Doric mothers bore: 指斯巴达勇士。Doric mothers: 是古希腊最早的居民 Dorians 人,后进入 Eurotas 河谷,改称 Lacedaemonians,建立了斯巴达城。

39. The Heracleidan: blood, 即古希腊人的血统。Heracleidan 来自 Heraclidae,传说为希腊神话中大力神海克勒斯(Hercules)的后代。own: 承认。

40. Franks: 地中海东部诸国和岛屿(包括叙利亚、黎巴嫩等在内的自希腊至埃及的地区)的人们对西欧人的统称。拜伦认为希腊人要获得自由,只能依靠自己。三年后,他在《青铜世纪》(*The Age of Bronze*, 289-9)记:"Greeks should only free Greece, / Not the barbarian, with his masque of peace." 此处 the barbarian 不仅指西欧人,尤指俄国人和亚历山大一世。

41. In native swords, and native ranks: 只有依靠自己的武装,只有依靠自己的队伍。

42. laves: washes。

43. Sunium's marbled steep：指雅典保护神 Athena 之庙，建在 Sunium，即今天的 Cape Coloni。拜伦于 1809 年到此一游。

44. save：except。

45. swan-like, let me sing and die：传说天鹅将死时会唱起悲歌。又诗人被比作天鹅，如以 the Swan of Avon 喻莎士比亚。

46. yon：yonder。

Questions for discussion：

1. Allusions are frequently used in this poem. Try to interpret the function of allusions in the first stanza.

2. What's special effect in the line of "Must we but blush? —Our fathers bled"?

3. What are the main methods does the poet utilize to awaken contemporary Greeks? Do the methods work?

名言摘录

I awoke one morning and found myself famous.

——*George Gordon Byron* (*1788 - 1824*)

12　On First Looking into Chapman's Homer

John Keats

Much have I travell'd in the realms of gold,[1]
And many goodly states and kingdoms[2] seen;
Round many western islands have I been
Which bards in fealty to Apollo hold.[3]
Oft[4] of one wide expanse had I been told
That deep-brow'd Homer ruled as his demesne;[5]
Yet did I never breathe its pure serene[6]
Till I heard Chapman speak out loud and bold;
Then felt I like some watcher of the skies[7]
When a new planet swims into his ken;[8]
Or like stout Cortez when with eagle eyes[9]
He star'd at the Pacific—and all his men
Look'd at each other with a wild surmise[10]—
Silent, upon a peak in Darien.[11]

【注释】

1. Much have I travell'd in the realms of gold：济慈自喻为探险家，探索过充满黄金的宝地。the realms of gold：意为"充满黄金的领地"，喻伟大的文学作品。

2. goodly states and kingdoms：仍指伟大的文学作品。goodly：beautiful。

3. Round many western islands have I been / Which bards in fealty to Apollo hold："到过许多西方的岛屿"指济慈曾涉猎过许多希腊文学作品。古希腊的许多岛以及岛上的诗人都向诗神阿波罗效忠，漫游希腊群岛意即领略希腊文学。bards：诗人；in fealty：（臣仆对封建主的）效忠。

4. oft：often；one wide expanse：广袤的领域。

5. deep-brow'd Homer ruled as his demesne：浓眉的荷马作为他的领地统治着。demesne：（领主的）领地。

6. never breathe its pure serene：从未呼吸到这个领域里的沉静的空气。pure serene：喻荷马的诗风纯真深沉。

7. watcher of the skies：观星家，天文家。

8. ken：视野。

9. Cortez：即 Hernando Cortez（1485—1547）：西班牙探险家，墨西哥的发

现者。济慈误记，实际上第一个发现太平洋的西方人是另一位西班牙人 Vasco Nuñez de Balboa（1475—1517），他在达连湾（Darien）的山上第一次看到太平洋。eagle eyes：原稿为 wond'ring eyes；据济慈朋友 Leigh Hunt 在回忆录中说，济慈曾见过意大利文艺复兴时著名画家 Titian（1477—1576）绘的 Cortez 肖像，他的双眼似鹰目。

10. a wild surmise：奇怪的猜测。
11. Darien：加勒比海的达连湾，在巴拿马和哥伦比亚之间。

Questions for discussion:

1. What feelings does the poet convey his first looking into Chapman's Homer?
2. Who is Homer? What's the significance of Chapman's Homer to the readers in the 19th century?

名言摘录

I mean negative capability that is when a man is capable of being in uncertainties, mysteries, doubts, without any irritable reaching after fact and reason.

——*John Keats（1795 - 1821）*

13 The Eagle

Alfred, Lord Tennyson

He clasps[1] the crag[2] with crooked hands;
Close to the sun in lonely lands,
Ringed with the azure world[3], he stands.

The wrinkled sea beneath him crawls;
He watches from his mountain walls,
And like a thunderbolt he falls.

【注释】
1. clasp：紧紧抓住。
2. crag：峭壁。
3. ringed with the azure world：被蔚蓝色的世界所环绕。

Questions for discussion:

1. What characters of the eagle does the poem present? What's your understanding on the significance of the portrait of eagle?
2. Why is the word "crawls" employed to describe the sea?
3. The poem is filled with musical beauty. What main techniques does the poet use to create the effect?

名言摘录

'Tis better to have loved and lost
Than never to have loved at all.

——*Alfred, Lord Tennyson* (1809 - 1892)

14 My Last Duchess

Robert Browning

That's my last Duchess painted on the wall,
Looking as if she were alive. I call
That piece a wonder, now: Frà Pandolf's[1] hands
Worked busily a day, and there she stands.[2]
Will't please you sit and look[3] at her? I said
'Frà Pandolf' by design, for never read
Strangers like you that pictured countenance,[4]
The depth and passion of its earnest glance,[5]
But to myself they turned (since none puts by
The curtain I have drawn for you, but I)[6]
And seemed as they would ask me, if they durst,[7]
How such a glance came there; so, not the first
Are you to turn and ask thus. Sir, 'twas not
Her husband's presence only, called that spot
Of joy into the Duchess' cheek:[8] perhaps
Frà Pandolf chanced to say, 'Her mantle laps
Over my lady's wrist too much,'[9] or 'Paint
Must never hope to reproduce the faint
Half-flush that dies along her throat': such stuff
Was courtesy, she thought, and cause enough
For calling up that spot of joy.[10] She had
A heart—how shall I say?—too soon made glad,[11]
Too easily impressed; she liked whate'er
She looked on, and her looks went everywhere.[12]
Sir, 'twas all one! my favour at her breast,[13]
The dropping of the daylight in the West,
The bough of cherries some officious fool[14]
Broke in the orchard for her, the white mule
She rode with round the terrace—all and each
Would draw from her alike the approving speech,
Or blush, at least. She thanked men,—good![15] but thanked
Somehow—I know not how—as if she ranked

My gift of a nine-hundred-years-old name[16]
With anybody's gift. Who'd stoop to blame
This sort of trifling?[17] Even had you skill
In speech— (which I have not) —to make your will
Quite clear to such an one,[18] and say, 'Just this
Or that in you disgusts me; here you miss,
Or there exceed the mark'[19]—and if she let
Herself be lessoned so, nor plainly set
Her wits to yours, forsooth,[20] and made excuse,
—E'en then would be some stooping;[21] and I choose
Never to stoop. Oh sir, she smiled, no doubt,
Whene'er I passed her; but who passed without
Much the same smile? This grew; I gave commands;[22]
Then all smiles stopped together.[23] There she stands
As if alive. Will 't please you rise?[24] We'll meet
The company below, then. I repeat,
The Count your master's known munificence
Is ample warrant that no just pretence
Of mine for dowry will be disallowed;[25]
Though his fair daughter's self, as I avowed
At starting, is my object.[26] Nay, we'll go
Together down, sir. Notice Neptune, though,
Taming a sea-horse, thought a rarity,[27]
Which Claus of Innsbruck[28] cast in bronze for me!

【注释】

1. I call/That piece a wonder：我认为（公爵夫人的）这幅画像是杰作。Frà Pandolf：Brother Pandolf, an imaginery painter, 假想的画家。Frà 意为"教兄"，当时许多画家均为教士，故称。

2. there she stands：这幅画现在就挂在这里。

3. Will't：will it. sit and look：to sit and look。

4. by design：有意识地；意为知你必然要问画家是谁，故不等你发问，事先告诉你。read：主语是 strangers like you。read 意为观察，理解。pictured countenance：画像上的面容。

5. the depth and passion of its earnest glance：its 指 countenance, 面容上的目光所流露的那深沉的情意。

6. But to myself they turned：意为像你这样的客人总是不能理解画像的表情，而总是转过身来问我。since none puts by / The curtain I have drawn for you, but I：因为除我以外，无人可以为客人拉开遮盖画像的帷幕。暗示公爵爱护此画是因为它是一件艺术品而不是对夫人的怀念。

7. if they durst：如果他们有勇气（问我）。durst：dare 的过去式，主要在虚拟式中，现已不常用。

8. 'twas not …the Duchess' cheek：公爵夫人脸上之所以露出那片喜悦的红晕，不只是因为有丈夫在旁。'twas：it was。called：唤起，使露出，前面省略 that（关系代词）。

9. Her mantle laps /Over my lady's wrist too much：夫人的外套将她的手盖得太多了。Her 和 my lady 均指公爵夫人，用第三人称来称呼表示尊敬。

10. dies along her throat：（那片淡淡的红晕）沿着喉部逐渐消失。such stuff…that spot of joy：公爵夫人以为画家的那番话是礼貌的表示，因而值得为之（cause enough）感到高兴。此处讲夫人脸上红晕的来历，公爵认为她大可不必为这种恭维话而激动，似乎有失尊严。

11. how shall I say：我该怎么说才好；too soon made glad：要使她心里高兴十分容易。

12. she liked whate'er /She looked on, and her looks went everywhere：她什么都爱看，看到了什么都喜欢。

13. 'twas all one：指以下列举的一切在公爵夫人的眼中都是同等之物。My favour at her breast：我送给她的胸饰。favour: a thing given or worn as a token of favour。

14. some officious fool：某个多事的蠢才。

15. She thanked men,—good：她向人道谢——那好啊！语含讽刺。

16. a nine-hundred-years-old name：公爵家系有九百年的光荣历史。公爵不满意他夫人把普通人（anybody）的礼品和他名门望族的悠久历史的荣誉同等看待。

17. Who'd stoop to blame /This sort of trifling：谁能降低身份去指责这种鸡毛蒜皮的小事呢？

18. such an one：指公爵夫人。

19. here you miss, /Or there exceed the mark：这儿你做得不够，那儿你又太过分。mark 是 miss 和 exceed 的宾语。

20. be lessoned so：听从教训。plainly set /Her wits to yours：公然和你顶嘴；forsooth: in truth, certainly, "真是！"

21. —E'en then would be some stooping：即便如此，也有点屈尊降格。E'en: even。

22. This grew：这种情况变本加厉，愈来愈严重。I gave commands：我下了命令。

23. Then all smiles stopped together：一般认为这是暗示公爵下令将其妻杀掉。布朗宁在答 Corson 问时说："Yes, I meant that the commands were that she be put to death." 停了会又说："Or he might have had her shut up in a convent."

24. Will't pleast you rise：will it please you to rise?

25. The Count …disallowed：你主人伯爵大人素以慷慨闻名（munificence），这可以保证（ample warrant）他不会拒绝我对于嫁妆的正当要求（just pretence）。刚说完杀死前妻之事，立即对来客提出嫁妆的要求。

26. Though his fair daughter's self, as I avowed /At starting, is my object：虽然我一开始就已申明，我所追求的是他美丽的女儿本人。

27. Notice Neptune, though, /Taming a sea-horse, thought a rarity：不过，请你看看海神驯服海马的铜像，据说是绝世的杰作。thought：which is thought。

28. Claus of Innsbruck：Innsbruck 地方的 Claus，也是假想的雕刻家。Innsbruck 在今奥地利境内，为当时 Tyrol 邦的首府，以当雕刻家著称。

Questions for discussion：

1. Why does the Duke want to show his guest his art collection?

2. Why is the Duke dissatisfied with his last Duchess? What can you say about the Duchess' personality from the Duke's monologue?

3. How do you understand the line "I gave commands/ then all smiles stopped together"?

15 The Dover Beach

Matthew Arnold

The sea is calm to-night.
The tide is full, the moon lies fair
Upon the Straits;[1]—on the French coast, the light
Gleams, and is gone; the cliffs of England stand,
Glimmering and vast, out in the tranquil bay.
Come to the window, sweet is the night air!
Only, from the long line of spray,[2]

Where the ebb meets the moon-blanch'd sand,[3]
Listen! you hear the grating roar[4]
Of pebbles which the waves suck back, and fling,
At their return, up the high stand,
Begin, and cease, and then again begin,
With tremulous cadence slow, and bring
The eternal note of sadness in.

Sophocles[5] long ago
Heard it on the Ægæan,[6] and it brought
Into his mind the turbid ebb and flow
Of human misery; we
Find also in the sound a thought,
Hearing it by this distant northern sea.

The sea of faith
Was once, too, at the full, and round earth's shore
Lay like the folds of a bright girdle furl'd;[7]
But now I only hear
Its melancholy, long, withdrawing roar,
Retreating to the breath
Of the night-wind down the vast edges drear
And naked shingles[8] of the world.

Ah, love, let us be true
To one another! for the world, which seems
To lie before us like a land of dreams,
So various,⁹ so beautiful, so new,
Hath really neither joy, nor love, nor light,
Nor certitude, nor peace, nor help for pain;
And we are here as on a darkling plain
Swept with confused alarms of struggle and flight,
Where ignorant armies clash by night.¹⁰

【注释】

1. the moon lies fair /Upon the Straits：皎洁的月亮浮在多佛海峡上。the Straits：即 the Straits of Dover，是英吉利海峡的窄口，法国海岸上的灯光与英国海岸仅二十英里之遥。

2. the long line of spray：浪花飞溅的长长的海岸线。

3. the moon-blanch'd sand：披上银白色月光的沙滩。

4. the grating roar：猛烈的摩擦声响。

5. Sophocles：索福克勒斯（约公元前496—公元前406），古希腊悲剧诗人，与埃斯库罗斯（Aischulos）和欧里庇得斯（Euripides）齐名。主要作品有悲剧《埃阿斯》（约公元前442年）、《安提戈涅》（约公元前441年）和《奥狄浦斯王》（约公元前431年）等。

6. the Ægæan：the Ægæan Sea，爱琴海。关于索福克勒斯听到海潮涨落之声想到人类悲苦的事，见《安提戈涅》（Antigone）第583～591行，合唱队把奥狄浦斯一家的命运变迁比作大海的波浪。

7. Lay like the folds of a bright girdle furl'd：此行颇费解，大致可理解为在涨潮时，大海把陆地紧紧地包围住，就像收紧的闪光的腰带（a bright girdle furled）的褶子。

8. shingles：beaches covered with pebbles，铺满圆卵石的海滩。

9. various：千姿百态。

10. ignorant armies clash by night：也许指1848年革命，或许指法国军队在1849年包围罗马之战。

Questions for discussion：

1. Why is the poem entitled "The Dover Beach"? What does the poem meditate here?

2. What is special in the stanza form? And what is its significance?

名言摘录

My poems represent, on the whole, the main movement of mind of the last quarter of a century, and thus they will probably have their day as people become conscious to themselves of what that movement of mind is, and interested in the literary productions which reflect it. It might be fairly urged that I have less poetical sentiment than Tennyson and less intellectual vigor and abundance than Browning; yet because I have perhaps more of a fusion of the two than either of them, and have more regularly applied that fusion to the main line of modern development, I am likely enough to have my turn as they have had theirs.

——*Mathew Arnold (1822 – 1888)*

16 In the Station of Metro

Ezra Pound

The apparition[1] of these faces in a crowd;
Petals on a wet, black bough.

【注释】
1. Apparition: appearance like ghost; something that cannot be clearly observed.

Questions for discussion:
1. What feelings does the poet convey in the poem?
2. By what way does the poet capture and convey the feelings?

名言摘录

An image is that which presents an intellectual and emotional complex in an instant of time.

——*Ezra Pound* (1885 – 1972)

17 The Love Song of J. Alfred Prufrock

Thomas Stearns Eliot

Let us go then, you and I,
When the evening is spread out against the sky
Like a patient etherized upon a table;[1]
Let us go, through certain half-deserted streets,
The muttering retreats
Of restless nights in one-night cheap hotels
And sawdust restaurants with oyster-shells:
Streets that follow like a tedious argument
Of insidious intent
To lead you to an overwhelming question…[2]
Oh, do not ask, 'What is it?'
Let us go and make our visit.

In the room[3] the women come and go
Talking of Michelangelo.[4]

The yellow fog that rubs its back[5] upon the window-panes,
The yellow smoke that rubs its muzzle on the window-panes
Licked its tongue into the corners of the evening,
Lingered upon the pools that stand in drains,
Let fall upon its back the soot that falls from chimneys,
Slipped by the terrace, made a sudden leap,
And seeing that it was a soft October night,
Curled[6] once about the house, and fell asleep.

And indeed there will be time[7]
For the yellow smoke that slides along the street
Rubbing its back upon the window-panes;
There will be time, there will be time
To prepare a face to meet the faces that you meet;
There will be time to murder and create,
And time for all the works and days[8] of hands

That lift and drop a question on your plate;
Time for you and time for me,
And time yet for a hundred indecisions,
And for a hundred visions and revisions,[9]
Before the taking of a toast and tea.

In the room the women come and go
Talking of Michelangelo.

And indeed there will be time
To wonder, 'Do I dare?' and, 'Do I dare?'
Time to turn back and descend the stair,
With a bald spot in the middle of my hair—
(They will say: 'How his hair is growing thin!')
My morning coat, my collar mounting firmly to the chin,[10]
My necktie rich and modest, but asserted[11] by a simple pin—
(They will say: 'But how his arms and legs are thin!')
Do I dare
Disturb the universe?
In a minute there is time
For decisions and revisions which a minute will reverse.

For I have known them all already, known them all—
Have known the evenings, mornings, afternoons,
I have measured out my life with coffee spoons;[12]
I know the voices dying with a dying fall[13]
Beneath the music from a farther room.
So how should I presume?

And I have known the eyes already, known them all—
The eyes that fix you in a formulated phrase,[14]
And when I am formulated, sprawling on a pin,
When I am pinned and wriggling on the wall,
Then how should I begin
To spit out all the butt-ends of my days and ways?
And how should I presume?

And I have known the arms already, known them all—
Arms that are braceleted and white and bare

(But in the lamplight, downed with light brown hair!)
Is it perfume from a dress
That makes me so digress?
Arms that lie along a table, or wrap about a shawl.
And should I then presume?
And how should I begin?

Shall I say, I have gone at dusk through narrow streets
And watched the smoke that rises from the pipes
Of lonely men in shirt-sleeves, leaning out of windows? ...
……
I should have been a pair of ragged claws[15]
Scuttling across the floors of silent seas.
……

And the afternoon, the evening, sleeps so peacefully!
Smoothed by long fingers,
Asleep...tired...or it malingers,[16]
Stretched on the floor, here beside you and me.
Should I, after tea and cakes and ices,
Have the strength to force the moment to its crisis?
But though I have wept and fasted, wept and prayed,
Though I have been my head (grown slightly bald) brought in upon a platter,[17]
I am no prophet—and here's no great matter;
I have seen the moment of my greatness flicker,
And I have seen the eternal Footman hold my coat, and snicker,[18]
And in short, I was afraid.

And would it have been worth it, after all,[19]
After the cups, the marmalade, the tea,
Among the porcelain, among some talk of you and me,
Would it have been worth while,
To have bitten off the matter with a smile,
To have squeezed the universe into a ball[20]
To roll it toward some overwhelming question,
To say: 'I am Lazarus,[21] come from the dead,
Come back to tell you all, I shall tell you all' —
If one,[22] settling a pillow by her head,
Should say: 'That is not what I meant at all.

That is not it, at all.'

And would it have been worth it, after all,
Would it have been worth while,
After the sunsets and the dooryards and the sprinkled streets,
After the novels, after the teacups, after the skirts that trail along the floor—
And this, and so much more? —
It is impossible to say just what I mean!
But as if a magic lantern threw the nerves in patterns on a screen:
Would it have been worth while
If one, settling a pillow or throwing off a shawl,
And turning toward the window, should say:
'That is not it at all,
That is not what I meant, at all.'
……
No! I am not prince Hamlet,[23] nor was meant to be;
Am an attendant lord,[24] one that will do
To swell a progress,[25] start a scene of two,
Advise the prince; no doubt, an easy tool,
Deferential, glad to be of use,
Politic, cautious, and meticulous;
Full of high sentence, but a bit obtuse;
At times, indeed, almost ridiculous—
Almost, at times, the Fool.

I grow old... I grow old...
I shall wear the bottoms of my trousers rolled.[26]

Shall I part my hair behind? Do I dare to eat a peach?
I shall wear white flannel trousers, and walk upon the beach.
I have beard the mermaids[27] singing, each to each.

I do not think that they will sing to me.

I have seen them riding seaward on the waves
Combing the white hair of the waves blown back
When the wind blows the water white and black.

We have lingered in the chambers of the sea

By sea-girls wreathed with seaweed red and brown
Till human voices wake us, and we drown.

【注释】

1. Like a patient etherised upon a table：像一个病人被乙醚麻醉了，躺在手术台上。etherise：用乙醚麻醉。etherise 暗示 ether（太空）一词，自由的苍天和手术台上无知无觉的病体，造成强烈的对比效果。

2. an overwhelming question：使人不知所措的大难题。

3. in the room：也许是普洛佛洛克和一位女友谈话的房间。

4. Michelangelo（1475—1564）：米开朗基罗。意大利文艺复兴时期的著名画家、雕塑家、建筑师和诗人。

5. rubs its back：比较以下的 muzzle 和 tongue。把黄雾比作动物，如狗或猫。

6. curled：蜷缩。黄雾包围着屋子。

7. And indeed there will be time：比较马韦尔（Andrew Marvell）诗《致他娇羞的女友》(To His Coy Mistress)："Had we but world enough and time, /This coyness, Lady, were no crime."

8. works and days：这是公元前8世纪希腊诗人 Hesiod 描写农事一诗的题目。诗人以有益的农业劳动来对照毫无意义的社交姿态（That lift and drop a question on your plate）。

9. visions and revisions：脑子里出现的幻想和幻想的种种变化。

10. my collar mounting firmly to the chin：硬领子直挺挺地顶着下巴。

11. asserted：维护。此处指别针系住了领带。

12. measured out my life with coffee spoons：喝咖啡消磨时光。measure out：原指分派。

13. with a dying fall：比较莎士比亚的《第十二夜》(Twelfth Night) Ⅰ.ⅰ.："That strain again! It had a dying fall."

14. in a formulated phrase：用公式化的词语，喻为僵化固定的表情。

15. a pair of ragged claws：一对毛蓬蓬的爪子，指蟹的爪子。

16. malingers：托病逃差。

17. Though I have seen my head (grown slightly bald) brought in upon a platter：据《新约·马太福音》(Matthew 14：3—11) 和《新约·马可福音》(Mark 6：14—29)，施洗的约翰反对希律王娶其兄弟腓力的妻子希罗底，遭她怀恨。后来希罗底伺机指使女儿要求将施洗的约翰杀死，并把他的头放在盘子里送到她面前。施洗的约翰在艺术形象中蓄着胡须，长头发，但普洛佛洛克不忘自己的头是微秃的（grown slightly bald）。

18. the eternal Footman：可能指死亡或命运。snicker：snigger, 窃笑。

19. And would it have been worth it, after all：用虚拟式表示事情已经过去，情景转移。

20. To have squeezed the universe into a ball：比较马韦尔诗 To His Coy

Mistress: "Let us roll all strength and all /Our sweetness up into a ball, /And tear our pleasure with rough strife /Through the iron gates of life."

21. Lazarus: 拉撒路，他死了四天以后，耶稣使之复活。见《新约·约翰福音》(*John*, 11: 1—4)
22. One: 普鲁佛洛克去拜访的那个女人。
23. Prince Hamlet: 莎士比亚《哈姆雷特》(*Hamlet*) 一剧中的主人公。
24. attendant lord: 宫廷的侍从，指《哈姆雷特》一剧中的波罗纽斯。
25. progress: 帝王等的巡游 (royal journey)，前后由宫臣等簇拥。加入巡游队伍即为 swell a progress。
26. wear the bottoms of my trousers rolled: 把裤管边翻起来。
27. mermaids: 传说中的美人鱼。

Questions for discussion:

1. Please summarize the main characters of Prufrock in the poem. How do you comment on the characterization? Shall we call it a case of anti-hero?

2. What is objective correlative according to T. S. Eliot's definition? Please find out some examples and explain the emotion hidden behind the objective correlatives then.

3. Beside objective correlative, what else techniques used by the poet to present Prufrock's spiritual state?

名言摘录

The only way of expressing emotion in the form of art is by finding an "objective correlative"; in other words, a set of objects, a situation, a chain of events which shall be the formula of that particular emotion; such that when the external facts, which must terminate in sensory experience, are given, the emotion is immediately evoked.

——*T. S. Eliot (1888 – 1965)*

18 Church Going

Philip Larkin

Once I am sure there's nothing going on
I step inside, letting the door thud shut.
Another church: matting, seats, and stone,
And little books; sprawlings of flowers, cut[1]
For Sunday, brownish[2] now; some brass and stuff
Up at the holy end; the small neat organ;
And a tense, musty, unignorable silence,
Brewed God knows how long. Hatless, I take off
My cycle-clips[3] in awkward reverence,

Move forward, run my hand around the font.[4]
Form where I stand, the roof looks almost new—
Cleaned, or restored? Someone would know: I don't.
Mounting the lectern,[5] I peruse a few
Hectoring large scale verses, and pronounce
'Here endeth'[6] much more loudly than I'd meant.
The echoes snigger briefly. Back at the door
I sign the book, donate an Irish sixpence,
Reflect[7] the place was not worth stopping for.

Yet stop I did: in fact I often do,
And always end much at a loss like this,
Wondering what to look for; wondering, too,
When churches fall completely out of use
What we shall turn them into, if we shall keep
A few cathedrals chronically on show,
Their parchment, plate and pyx[8] in locked cases,
And let the rest rent-free to rain and sheep.[9]
Shall we avoid them as unlucky places?

Or, after dark, will dubious women come
To make their children touch a particular stone;[10]

Pick simples[11] for a cancer; or on some
Advised night[12] see walking a dead one?
Power of some sort or other will go on
In games, in riddles, seemingly at random;
But superstition, like belief, must die,
And what remains when disbelief has gone?
Grass, weedy pavement, brambles, buttress,[13] sky,

A shape less recognizable each week,
A purpose more obscure. I wonder who
Will be the last, the very last, to seek
This place for what it was; one of the crew
That tap and jot and know what rood-lofts[14] were?
Some ruin-bibber, randy[15] for antique,
Or Christmas-addict, counting on a whiff
Of gown-and-bands and organ-pipes and myrrh?[16]
Or will he be my representative,

Bored, uninformed, knowing the ghostly silt
Dispersed, yet tending to this cross of ground
Through suburb scrub[17] because it held unspilt
So long and equably what since is found
Only in separation—marriage, and birth,
And death, and thoughts of these—for whom was built
This special shell? For, though I've no idea
What this accoutred frowsty barn[18] is worth,
It pleases me to stand in silence here;

A serious house on serious earth it is,
In whose blent air all our compulsions meet,
Are recognised, and robed as destinies.
And that much never can be obsolete,
Since someone will forever be surprising
A hunger in himself to be more serious,
And gravitating with it to this ground,
Which, he once heard, was proper to grow wise in,
If only that so many dead lie round.[19]

【注释】

1. cut：（为星期日）摘的鲜花。这种摘下来的鲜花称为 cut flowers（插花）。
2. brownish：（花因干枯而变成）褐色的。
3. cycle-clips：骑车时用的裤管夹子。
4. font：圣水器，洗礼盘。
5. lectern：教堂里的读经台。
6. "Here endeth"：到此结束；endeth 是 ends 的古体。
7. reflect：consider。
8. parchment：羊皮纸，写在羊皮纸上的文稿。plate：餐具。pyx：圣体容器，放圣饼（wafers）的盆子。餐具和圣饼盆大多是精制的金器或银器，这些都是进行"圣餐"（Holy Communion）仪式时所用的器皿，一般视为神圣，凡人不得触动。
9. let the rest rent-free to rain and sheep：其他东西则任凭风吹雨淋，或让教区居民（sheep）随便动用。
10. a particular stone：一块墓碑。
11. simples：medicinal herbs，药草。
12. Advised night：经人告知的某一夜里。
13. brambles：荆棘。buttress：扶壁，支柱。
14. rood-lofts：a gallery over the rood screen，中世纪教堂中的楼座，位于合唱队席位和中殿（座位所在部分）之间的隔墙（rood-screen）之上。楼座用来放置十字架（rood），并在此诵读福音书。
15. ruin-bibber：古物古玩迷。randy：贪求的。
16. myrrh：没药。古人用来做焚香的香料。《新约·马太福音》（*Matthew* 2：11）："they presented unto him gifts, gold, and frankincense, and myrrh."
17. scrub：灌木丛。
18. this accoutred frowsty barn：这装备起来的发霉的大仓库，指教堂。
19. so many dead lie round：教堂旁边的墓地葬着很多死人。

Questions for discussion：

1. Why does the speaker call the church "a serious house"?
2. What are the connotations of "to seek" "This place for what it was"?
3. What ironies are employed in this poem?
4. What is the meaning of the first stanza of this poem?

名言摘录

I love the commonplace; I lead a very commonplace life. Everyday things are lovely to me.

I am not someone who's lost faith: I never had it.

I write poems to preserve things I have seen/ thought/ felt (if I may so indicate a composite and complex experience) both for myself and for others, though I feel that my prime responsibility is to the experience itself, which I am trying to keep from oblivion for its own sake.

——*Philip Larkin（1922 - 1985）*

19 Hawk Roosting

Ted Hughes

I sit in the top of the wood, my eyes closed.
Inaction, no falsifying dream
Between my hooked head and hooked feet:
Or in sleep rehearse perfect kills and eat.[1]

The convenience of the high trees!
The air's buoyancy and the sun's ray
Are of advantage to me;
And the earth's face upward for my inspection.[2]

My feet are locked upon[3] the rough bark,
It took the whole of Creation[4]
To produce my foot, my each feather:
Now I hold Creation in my foot[5]

Or fly up, and revolve it all slowly—
I kill where I please because it is all mine.
There is no sophistry[6] in my body:
My manners are tearing off heads—[7]

The allotment[8] of death.
For the one path of my flight is direct
Through the bones of the living.
No arguments assert my right:

The sun is behind me.
Nothing has changed since I began.
My eye has permitted no change,
I am going to keep things like this.

【注释】
1. rehearse perfect kills and eat：练习（把猎获物）杀死、吃个精光。

2. And the earth's face upward for my inspection：大地的脸面朝上，便于我观察。

3. locked upon：紧紧抓住。

4. Creation：指上帝创造万物。

5. I hold Creation in my foot：我把万物揪在爪中。

6. sophistry：谬论、诡辩。

7. My manners are tearing off heads：我的作风就是把猎获物的头掐断。按：鹰先把捕获物的头掐掉，再食其肉。

8. allotment：分配。

Questions for discussion：

1. What kind of image of hawk may you have after reading the poem?
2. What do you think of the line "I kill where I please because it is all mine"?

20 Clearances

Seamus Heaney

When all the others were away at Mass
I was all hers as we peeled potatoes.
They broke the silence, let fall one by one
Like solder weeping off the soldering iron[1];
Cold comforts set between us, things to share
Gleaming in a bucket of clean water
And again let fall. Little pleasant splashes
From each other's work would bring us to our senses.

So while the parish priest at her bedside
Went hammer and tongs at the prayers for the dying
And some were responding and some crying
I remembered her head bent towards my head
Her breath in mine, our fluent dipping knives—
Never closer the whole rest of our lives.

【注释】
1. solder, soldering iron：电焊加热焊接金属时发出的嘶嘶声。

Questions for discussion:

1. What kind of relationship is the persona to "she" in the poem? How do you interpret the cold comforts to describe the relationship?

2. Do you think this is an elegy? Why or why not?

3. Please comment on the structure of the two-part sonnet. Any significance in this kind of design?

诗 歌 术 语

1. **Aestheticism**: the doctrine that regards beauty as an end in itself, and attempts to preserve the arts from subordination to moral, didactic, or political purposes. The term is often used synonymously with the Aesthetic Movement, a literary and artistic tendency of the late 19th century which may be understood as a further phase of Romanticism in reaction against philistine bourgeois values of practical efficiency and morality. Oscar Wilde, and several poets of the 1890s under the slogan "art for art's sake" were sometimes known as aesthetes.

2. **Alliteration**, also known as "head rhyme" or "initial rhyme", refers to the repetition of the same sounds—usually initial consonants of words or of stressed syllables—in any sequence of neighboring words. Now an optional and incidental decorative effect in verse or prose, it was once a required element in the poetry of Germanic language (including Old English and Old Norse) and in Celtic verse (where alliterated sounds could regularly be placed in positions other than the beginning of a word or syllable). Such poetry, in which alliteration rather than "rhyme is the chief principle of repetition", is known as alliterative verse; its rules also allow a vowel sound to alliterate with any other vowel.

3. **Assonance**: the repetition of identical or similar vowel sounds in the stressed syllables (and sometimes in the following unstressed syllables of neighboring words). It is distinct from rhyme in that the consonants differ although the vowels or diphthongs match: *sweet dreams*, *hit or miss*. As a substitute for rhyme at the ends of verse lines, assonance (sometimes called vowel rhyme or vocalic rhyme) had a significant function in early Celtic Spanish, and French versification (notably in the *chansons de geste*). But in English it has been an optional poetic device used within and between lines of verse for emphasis or musical effect.

4. **Blank verse**: unrhymed lines of iambic pentameter. Blank verse is a very flexible English verse form which can attain rhetorical grandeur while echoing the natural rhythms of speech and allowing smooth enjambment. First used by Henry Howard, Earl of Surrey, it soon became both the standard meter for dramatic poetry and a widely used form for narrative and meditative poems. Much of the finest verse in English—by Shakespeare, Milton, Wordsworth, Tennyson, and Stevens—has been written in blank verse. In other languages, notably Italian (in hendecasyllables) and

German, blank verse has been an important medium for *people drama*. Blank verse should not be confused with free verse, which has no regular meter.

5. **Byronic**: belonging to or derived from Lord Byron or his works. The Byronic hero is a character type found in his celebrated narrative poem *Childe Harold's Pilgrimage*, his verse drama *Manfred* and other works: he is boldly defiant but bitterly self-tormenting outcast, proud contemptuous of social norms but suffering from some unnamed sin.

6. **Dramatic monologue**: a kind of poem in which a single fictional or historical character other than the poet speaks to a silent "audience" of one or more persons. Such poems reveal not the poet's own thoughts but the mind of the impersonated character, whose personality is revealed unwittingly; this distinguished a dramatic monologue from a lyric, while the implied presence of an auditor distinguishes it from a soliloquy.

7. **Elegy**: an elaborately formal lyric poem lamenting the death of a friend or public figure, or reflecting seriously on a solemn subject.

8. **Epic**: a long narrative poem celebrating the great deeds of one or more legendary heroes, in a grand ceremonious style, The hero. usually protected by or even descended from gods, performs superhuman exploits in battle or in marvelous voyages, often saving or founding a nation. The Anglo-Saxon poem *Beowulf* (8th century AD) is a primary epic, as is the oldest surviving epic poem. The action of epics takes place on a grand scale, and in this sense the term has sometimes been extended to long romances, to ambitious historical novels like Tolstoy's *War and Peace* (1883 – 9), and to some large-scale film productions on heroic or historical subjects.

9. **Heroic couplet**:, a rhymed pair of iambic pentameter lines. Named from its use by Dryden and others in the heroic drama of the late 17th century, the heroic couplet had been established much earlier by Chaucer as a major English verse-form for narrative and other kinds of non-dramatic poetry: it dominated English poetry of the 18th century, notably in the closed couplets of Pope, before declining in importance in the early 19th century.

10. **Iambic pentameter**:, a metrical verse line having five main stresses, traditionally described as a line of five "feet". In English poetry since Chaucer, the pentameter—almost always an iambic line normally of 10 syllables—has had a special status as the standard line in many important forms including blank verse, the heroic

couplet, ottava rima, rhyme royal, and the sonnet. In its pure iambic form, the pentameter shows a regular alternation of stressed and unstressed syllables.

There are, however, several permissible variations in the placing of stresses, which help to avoid the monotony of such regular alternation; and the pentameter may be lengthened from 10 syllables to 11 by a feminine ending. In classical Greek and Latin poetry, the second line of the elegiac distich, commonly but inaccurately referred to as a "pentameter" is in fact composed of two half-lines of two and a half feet each, with dactyls or spondees in the first half and dactyls in the second.

11. **Imagism**: the doctrine and poetic practice of a small but influential group of American and British poets calling themselves Imagist or Imagistes between 1912 and 1917. Led at first by Ezra Pound, and then—after his defection to Vorticism—by Amy Lowell, the group rejected most 19th-century poetry as cloudy verbiage, and aimed instead at a new clarity and exactness in the short lyric poem. Influenced by the Japanese haiku and partly by ancient Greek lyrics, the imagists cultivated concision and directness, building their short poems around single images; they also preferred looser cadences to traditional regular rhythms. Apart from Pound and Lowell, the group also included Richard Aldington, "H. D." (Hilda Doolittle), F. S. Flint and William Carlos Williams.

12. **Lake poets**: Lake poets refer to William Wordsworth, Samuel Coleridge and Robert Southey who lived in the Lake District in the northwestern part of England. They traversed the same path in politics and in poetry, beginning as radicals and ending up as conservatives.

13. **Lyric**: in the modern sense, any fairly short poem expressing the personal mood, feeling, or meditation of a single speaker (who may sometimes be an inverted character, not the poet). In ancient Greece, a lyric was a song for accompaniment on the lyre, and could be a choral lyric sung by a group (see chorus), such as a dirge or hymn. The modern sense, current since the Renaissance, often suggests a song-like quality in the poems to which it refers. Lyric poetry is the most extensive category of verse, especially after the decline—since the 19th century in the West—of the other principal kinds: narrative and dramatic verse. Lyrics may be composed in almost any metre and on almost every subject, although the most usual emotions presented are those of love and grief. Among the common lyric forms are the sonnets, ode, elegy, haiku, and the more personal kinds of hymn. Lyricism is the emotional or song-like quality, the lyrical property, of lyric poetry. A writer of lyric poems may be called a lyric poet, a lyricist, or a lyrist. In another sense, the lyrics of a popular song or other musical composition are the words as opposed to the music: these may not always be lyrical in

the poetic sense (e. g. in a narrative song like a ballad).

14. **Metaphysical poetry**: the name given to a diverse group of 17th-century English poets whose work is notable for its ingenious use of intellectual and theological concepts in surprising conceits, strange paradoxes, and far-fetched imagery. The leading metaphysical poet was John Donne, whose colloquial, argumentative abruptness of rhythm and tone distinguishes his style from the conventions of Elizabethan love-lyrics. Other poets to whom the label is applied include Andrew Marvell, Abraham Cowley, John Cleveland, and the predominantly religious poets George Herbert, Henry Vaughan, and Richard Crashaw. In the 20th century, T. S. Eliot and others revived their reputation, stressing their quality of wit, in the sense of intellectual strenuousness and flexibility rather than smart humor. The term metaphysical poetry usually refers to the works of these poets, but it can sometimes denote any poetry that discusses metaphysics, that is, the philosophy of knowledge and existence.

15. **Ode**: an elaborately formal lyric poem, often in the form of a lengthy ceremonious address to a person or abstract entity, always serious and elevated in tone. There are two different classical models: Pindar's Greek choral odes devoted to public praise of athletes (5th century BC), and Horace's more privately reflective odes in Latin. In English, these include the celebrated odes of John Keats, notably "Ode on a Grecian Urn" and "Ode to a Nightingale" (both 1820).

16. **Rhyme**: the identity of sound between syllables or paired groups of syllables, usually at the ends of verse lines; also a poem employing this device. Normally the last stressed vowel in the line and all sounds following it make up the rhyming element: this may be a monosyllable (love/ above—known as "masculine rhyme"), or two syllables (whether/together—known as "feminine rhyme" or "double rhyme"), or even three syllables (glamourous /amorous—known as "triple rhyme"). Where a rhyming element in a feminine or triple rhyme uses more than one word (famous /shame us), this is known as a "mosaic rhyme". The rhyming pairs illustrated so far are all examples of "full rhyme" (also called "perfect rhyme" or "true rhyme"). Departures from this norm take tree main forms: (i) rime riche, in which the consonants preceding the rhyming elements are also identical, even if the spellings and meanings of the words differ (made/maid); (ii) eye rhyme, in which the spellings of the rhyming elements match, but the sounds do not (love/prove); (iii) half-rhyme or "slant rhyme", where the vowel sounds do not match (love /have); or with rich consonance (love/leave). Half-rhyme is known by several other names: "imperfect rhyme", "near rhyme", "pararhyme", etc. Although rhyme is most often used at the ends of verse lines, internal rhyme between syllables within the same line is also found.

Rhyme is not essential to poetry: many languages rarely use it, and in English it finally replaced alliteration as the usual patterning device of verse only in the late 14th century.

17. **Rhythm**: the pattern of sounds perceived as the recurrence of equivalent "beats" at more or less equal intervals. In most English poetry, an underlying rhythm (commonly a sequence of four or five beats) is manifested in a metrical pattern—a sequence of measured beats and "off beats" arranged in verse lines and governing the alternation of stressed and unstressed syllables. While meter involves the recurrence of measured sound units, rhythm is a less clearly structured principle: one can refer to the unmeasured rhythm of everyday speech, or of prose, and to the rhythms or cadences of non-metrical verse (i.e. Free verse).

18. **Soliloquy**: a dramatic speech uttered by one character speaking aloud while alone on the stage (or while under the impression of being alone). The soliloquist thus reveals his or her inner thoughts and feelings to the audience, either in supposed self-communion or in a consciously direct address. Soliloquies often appear in plays from the age of Shakespeare, notably in his *Hamlet* and *Macbeth*. Soliloquy is a form of monologue, but a monologue is not a soliloquy if (as in the dramatic monologue) the speaker is not alone.

19. **Sonnet** (**Italian sonnet, English sonnet**): a lyric poem comprising 14 rhyming lines of equal length: iambic pentameters in English and hendeca syllables in Italian. Therefore sonnet has two types as Italian sonnet and English sonnet.

Originating in Italy, the sonnet was established by Petrarch in the 14th century as a major form of love poetry. The standard subject-matter of early sonnets was the torments of sexual love (usually within a courtly love convention). The Italian sonnet comprises an 8-line octave followed by a 6-line sestet. The transition from octave to sestet coincides with a turn in the argument or mood of the poem. The Italian pattern has remained the most widely used in English and other languages.

The English sonnet (also called the Shakespearean sonnet) comprises three quatrains and a final couplet, rhyming ababcdcdefefgg.

20. **Tone**: a very vague critical term usually designating the mood or atmosphere of a work, although in some more restricted uses it refers to the author's attitude to the reader (e.g. formal, intimate, pompous) or to the subject-matter (e.g. ironic, light, solemn, satiric, sentimental).

第二章　英国小说

导 言

在现代英语中，小说（novel）的定义是指以散文写成的长篇虚构作品，但小说所涵盖的文学形式是非常多的。

按照著名小说史家瓦特的理解，小说兴起于 18 世纪早期，而以笛福（Daniel Defoe，1660 - 1731）、理查逊（Samuel Richardson，1689 - 1761）和菲尔丁（Henry Fielding，1707 - 1754）为其肇始。他认为，界定小说特征的是"现实主义"，即力图描绘人类经历的每一个方面，而不仅限于那些适合某种特殊文学观的生活。小说的基本标准是个人经验的独特、真实、新鲜，而小说家的根本任务就是要传达对人类经验的精确印象。一种个人主义的、以个人经验取代集体传统的做法是鼓励独创性的，因此小说一词所指代的就是在特征或风格上显得新奇、新鲜的东西了。这也暗合小说（novel）一词的本意，即新颖、新奇。

实际上，早在古希腊、中世纪、17 世纪法国等历史时期和地域，也出现过不同类型的散文虚构故事。在乔叟（Geoffrey Chaucer，1343 - 1400）、斯宾塞（Edmund Spencer，1552 - 1599）、莎士比亚（William Shakespeare，1564 - 1616）和弥尔顿（John Milton，1608 - 1674）等英国作家的作品里，也可以说有大量的故事、情节或其他的小说要素，虽然个人主义的特殊性和特定性在先前的文学形式中不曾得到 18 世纪的那种强调。在先前的文学作品中常常找不到特定的时间，作家们常常运用无时间的故事来反映不变的道德真理；同样，地点也呈现出笼统含混的状态。只是从笛福开始，作家们才开始叙述实际存在的真实环境以及普通人的日常生活。

瓦特的著作在西方影响很大，学术界也倾向于把笛福的时代看作小说的发轫期。这样，我们也许可以把笛福以前的散文虚构故事，包括英国文学之父乔叟的《坎特伯雷故事集》（The Canterbury Tales）、西班牙作家塞万提斯的《堂吉诃德》、意大利作家薄伽丘的《十日谈》等比较接近于瓦特所谓的小说的散文虚构作品，都看作小说的前身。在此基础上，我们或可对英国小说的发展做一个综述。

古英语时期或盎格鲁—撒克逊时期（450 - 1066）以英国人民的英雄史诗《贝奥武夫》（Beowulf）成就最大。史诗叙事性明显，对后代小说影响甚大。

中古英语时期（1066 - 1500）的《玫瑰传奇》（Roman de la Rose）、《亚瑟王之死》（Morte d'Arthur）、《坎特伯雷故事集》、《农夫皮尔斯》（Piers Plowman）、《高文爵士和绿衣骑士》（Sir Gawain and the Green Knight）等名作都是叙事作品，对后来的小说产生了影响。

早期现代英语时期或英国文艺复兴时期（1500 – 1660）是英国文学的辉煌时代，出现了一些优秀的散文作家，而登峰造极的戏剧创作，特别是莎士比亚的剧作，以其优美的文笔和曲折的情节，深刻影响了历代小说家。

新古典主义时期（1600 – 1785）出版了班扬（John Bunyan, 1628 – 1688）的《天路历程》(*The Pilgrim's Progress*)、斯威夫特（Jonathan Swift）的《格列佛游记》(*Gulliver's Travels*) 这样的名家名作。他们的散文作品一些时候也被看作小说，是由分类标准不同所致。英国小说之父笛福就是在这一小说创作名家辈出的时代写小说，他的《鲁滨逊漂流记》(*Robinson Crusoe*) 成功地塑造了资产阶级开拓者和殖民者的形象，反映了那个时代进取和冒险的精神。理查逊的书信体小说《帕梅拉》(*Pamela*) 和《克拉丽莎》(*Clarissa*) 叙写了年轻女孩的内心世界，心理描写可谓细致入微。菲尔丁的《汤姆·琼斯》(*Tom Jones*) 也是现实主义小说的鸿篇巨制。斯特恩（Lawrence Sterne, 1713 – 1768）的《项狄传》(*The Life and Opinions of Tristram Shandy*) 则是一部怪书，在小说形式方面做了大量的实验。

浪漫主义时期（1785 – 1830）最有名的小说家包括奥斯汀（Jane Austen, 1775 – 1817）和司各特（Sir Walter Scott, 1771 – 1832）。奥斯汀的小说对时代风尚，特别是对中上层人士的生活刻画得生动幽默而又不乏含蓄蕴藉。脍炙人口的《傲慢与偏见》(*Pride and Prejudice*) 以达西的傲慢和伊丽莎白的偏见切入，而以有情人终成眷属结尾；有趣的是，有经济学家把奥斯汀的小说作为经济学教材，因为女主角对经济问题的考虑常常支配着她们对配偶的选择。司各特的《艾凡赫》(*Ivanhoe*) 是非常有名的历史小说，作者也因其写作的历史题材小说而被誉为西欧历史小说之父。

维多利亚时期（1832 – 1901）是英国小说史上群星灿烂的时期。夏洛特·勃朗特（Charlotte Brontë, 1816 – 1855）、艾米丽·勃朗特（Emily Brontë, 1818 – 1848）、狄更斯（Charles Dickens, 1812 – 1870）、萨克雷（William Makepeace Thackeray, 1811 – 1863）、艾略特（George Eliot, 1819 – 1880）、哈代（Thomas Hardy, 1840 – 1928）等中国读者耳熟能详的作家都是这一时期的重要小说家。狄更斯的小说代表着英国现实主义小说创作的高峰，其代表作《大卫·科波菲尔》(*David Copperfield*) 叙事绵密，格局谨严，被誉为饶有史家风范。

现代文学始于 1914 年"一战"。现代英国小说以乔伊斯（James Joyce, 1882 – 1941）、伍尔夫（Virginia Woolf, 1882 – 1941）、劳伦斯（D. H. Lawrence, 1885 – 1930）等小说家的创作为代表。乔伊斯的《都柏林人》(*Dubliners*) 以系列短篇小说描写都柏林各阶层人士的生活，反映他们"精神上的瘫痪"。较后的作品，特别是意识流小说《尤利西斯》(*Ulysses*) 在形式上做了大胆的实验，成为经典的现代主义作品。女作家伍尔夫在创作上反对维多利亚时期小说的因循守旧，主张文学反映人物的内心世界，其创作无论短篇还是长篇都有不俗的表现。例如，《墙上的斑点》（*The Mark of the Wall*）通过某人对墙上斑点的观察和相应联想为主题，大量展开意识流描写，让其同时代的读者感到耳目一新。长篇小说《达罗卫夫人》（*Ms. Dalloway*）以英国上流社会妇女达罗卫夫人在某一天的思绪为题材，主要叙述她在举办家庭晚会前后的活动和思想，同时穿插了她与前男友的故事，以及一个退伍军人由于精神失常而自杀的故事。其作品在某种意义上具有自传性质，特别是《达罗卫夫人》对退伍军人的精神状态的描写据说反映了作者本人经受的精神疾病折磨。劳伦斯的创作对两性之间灵与肉的结合多有描写，作品细腻耐读。其代表作《儿子与情人》（*Sons and Lovers*）具有自传性质。故事主人公具有恋母情结，影响到他与女友的交往。劳伦斯的创作正值弗洛伊德的精神分析理论盛行的时期，所以也明显受了这方面的影响。

1 Robinson Crusoe

Daniel Defoe

[Crusoe Visits the Wreck]

I was now landed, and safe on shore, and began to look up and thank God that my life was saved in a case wherein there was some minutes before scarce any room to hope.[1] I believe it is impossible to express to the life[2] what the ecstasies and transports of the soul are, when it is so saved, as I may say, out of the very grave; and I do not wonder now at that custom, viz., that when a malefactor who has the halter about his neck[3], is tied up, and just going to be turned off, and has a reprieve brought to him: I say, I do not wonder that they bring a surgeon with it, to let him blood[4] that very moment they tell him of it, that the surprise may not drive the animal spirits from the heart, and overwhelm him[5].

For sudden joys, like griefs, confound at first.

I walked about on the shore, lifting up my hands, and my whole being, as I may say, wrapt up in the contemplation of my deliverance[6], making a thousand gestures and motions which I cannot describe, reflecting upon all my comrades that were drowned, and that there should not be one soul saved but my self; for, as for them, I never saw them afterwards, or any sign of them, except three of their hats, one cap, and two shoes that were not fellows[7].

I cast my eyes to the stranded vessel[8], when the breach and froth of the sea being so big, I could hardly see it, it lay so far off, and considered, Lord! How was it possible I could get on shore?

After I had solaced my mind with the comfortable part of my condition, I began to look round me to see what kind of place I was in, and what was next to be done, and I soon found my comforts abate, and that in a word I had a dreadful deliverance: For I was wet, had no clothes to shift me, nor any thing either to eat or drink to comfort me, neither did I see any prospect before me, but that of perishing with hunger, or being devoured by wild beasts; and that which was particularly afflicting to me, was, that I had no weapon either to hunt and kill any creature for my sustenance[9], or to defend my self against any other creature that might desire to kill me for theirs: In a word, I had nothing about me but a knife, a tobacco-pipe, and a little tobacco in a box, this was all my provision, and this threw me into terrible agonies of mind, that for a while I run about like a mad-man; night coming upon me, I began with a heavy heart to consider what would be my lot if there were any ravenous beasts in that country, seeing at night they always come abroad[10] for their prey.

All the remedy that offered to my thoughts at that time, was, to get up into a thick bushy tree like a fir, but thorny, which grew near me, and where I resolved to set all night, and consider the next day what death I should dye, for as yet I saw no prospect of life; I walked about a furlong from the shore, to see if I could find any fresh water to drink, which I did, to my great joy; and having drank and put a little tobacco in my mouth to prevent hunger, I went to the tree, and getting up into it, endeavored to place my self so, as that if I should sleep I might not fall; and having cut me a short stick, like a truncheon, for my defence, I took up my lodging, and having been excessively fatigued, I fell fast asleep, and slept as comfortably as, I believe, few could have done in my condition, and found my self the cost refreshed with it, that I think I ever was on such an occasion.

When I waked it was broad day, the weather clear, and the storm abated, so that the sea did not rage and swell as before: but that which surprised me most, was, that the ship was lifted off in the night from the sand where she lay, by the swelling of the tide, and was driven up almost as far as the rock which I first mentioned, where I had been so bruised by the dashing me against it[11]; this being within about a mile from the shore where I was, and the ship seeming to stand upright still, I wished my self on board, that, at least, I might save some necessary things for my use.

When I came down from my apartment in the tree, I looked about me again, and the first thing I found was the boat, which lay as the wind and the sea had tossed her up upon the land, about two miles on my right hand. I walked as far as I could upon the shore to have got to her, but found a neck or inlet of water between me and the boat, which was about half a mile broad, so I came back for the present, being more intent upon getting at the ship, where I hoped to find something for my present subsistence.

A little after noon I found the sea very calm, and the tide ebbed so far out, that I could come within a quarter of a mile of the ship; and here I found a fresh renewing of my grief, for I saw evidently, that if we had kept on board, we had been all safe, that is to say, we had all got safe on shore, and I had not been so miserable as to be left entirely destitute of all comfort and company, as I now was; this forced tears from my eyes again, but as there was little relief in that, I resolved, if possible, to get to the ship, so I pulled off my clothes, for the weather was hot to extremity[12], and took the water, but when I came to the ship, my difficulty was still greater to know how to get on board, for as she lay a ground, and high out of the water, there was nothing within my reach to lay hold of; I swam round her twice, and the second time I spied a small piece of a rope, which I wondered I did not see at first, hang down by the fore-chains so low, as that with great difficulty I got hold of it, and by the help of that rope, got up into the forecastle of the ship; here I found that the ship was bulged, and had a great deal of water in her hold, but that she lay so on the side of a bank of hard sand, or rather earth, that her stern lay lifted up upon the bank, and her head low almost to the water; by this means all her quarter was free[13], and all that was in that part was dry; for you may be sure my first work was to search and to see what was spoiled and what was free; and first I found that all the ship's provisions were dry and untouched by the water, and being very well disposed to eat, I went to the bread-room and filled my pockets with biscuit, and eat it as I went about other things, for I had no time to lose; I also found some rum in the great cabin, of which I took a large dram, and which I had indeed need enough of to spirit me[14] for what was before me: now I wanted nothing but a boat to furnish my self with many things which I foresaw would be very necessary to me.

It was in vain to sit still and wish for what was not to be had, and this extremity roused my application[15]; we had several spare Yards, and two or three large spars of wood, and a spare top-mast or two in the ship; I resolved to fall to work[16] with these, and I flung as many of them over board as I could manage for their weight, tying every one with a rope that they might not drive away; when this was done I went down the ship's side, and pulling them to me, I tied four of them fast together at both ends as well as I could, in the form of a raft, and laying two or three short pieces of plank upon them cross-ways, I found I could walk upon it very well, but that it was not able to bear any great weight, the pieces being too light; so I went to work, and with the carpenter's saw I cut a spare top-mast into three lengths, and added them to my raft, with a great deal of labor and pains, but hope of furnishing my self with necessaries, encouraged me to go beyond what I should have been able to have done upon another occasion.

My raft was not strong enough to bear any reasonable weight; my next care was what to load it with, and how to preserve what I laid upon it from the surf of the sea; but I was not long considering this, I first laid all the plank or boards upon it that I could get, and having considered well what I most wanted, I first got three of the seamen's chests, which I had broken open and emptied, and lowered them down upon my raft; the first of these I filled with provision, viz., bread, rice, three Dutch cheeses, five pieces of dried goat's flesh, which we lived much upon, and a little remainder of European corn which had been laid by for some fowls which we brought to sea with us, but the fowls were killed; there had been some barley and wheat together, but, to my great disappointment, I found afterwards that the rats had eaten or spoiled it all; as for liquors, I found several cases of bottles belonging to our skipper[17], in which some cordial waters[18], and in all about five or six gallons of rack, these I stowed by themselves, there being no need to put them into the chest, nor no room for them. While I was doing this, I found the tide began to flow, tho' very calm, and I had the mortification to see my coat, shirt, and wast-coat which I had left on shore upon the sand, swim away; as for my breeches which were only linnen and open kneed, I swam on board in them and my stockings: however this put me upon rummaging for clothes, of which I found enough, but took no more than I wanted for present use, for I had other things which my eye was more upon, as first tools to work with on shore, and it was after long searching that I found out the carpenter's chest, which was indeed a very useful prize to me, and much more valuable than a ship loading of gold would have been at that time; I got it down to my raft, even whole as it was, without losing time to look into it, for I knew in general what it contained.

My next care was for some ammunition and arms; there were two very good fowling-pieces in the great cabin, and two pistols, these I secured first, with some powder-horns, and a small bag of shot, and two old rusty swords; I knew there were three barrels of powder in the ship, but knew not where our gunner had stowed them, but with much search I found them, two of them dry and good, the third had taken water, those two I got to my raft, with the arms, and now I thought my self pretty well freighted, and began to think how I should get to shore with them, having neither sail, oar, or rudder, and the least cap full of wind would have overset all my navigation[19].

I had three encouragements. 1. A smooth calm sea. 2. The tide rising and setting in to the shore. 3. What little wind there was blew me towards the land. And thus, having found two or three broken oars belonging to the boat, and besides the tools which were in the chest, I found two saws, an axe, and a hammer, and with this cargo I put to sea. For a mile, or thereabouts, my raft went very well, only that I found it drive a little distant from the place where I had landed before, by which I perceived that there was some indraft of the water, and consequently I hoped to find some creek or river there, which I might make use of as a port to get to land with my cargo.

As I imagined, so it was, there appeared before me a little opening of the land, and I found a strong current of the tide set into it, so I guided my raft as well as I could to keep in the middle of the stream: but here I had like to have suffered a second shipwreck[20], which, if I had, I think verily would have broke my heart, for knowing nothing of the coast, my raft run a-ground at one end of it upon a shoal, and not being a-ground at the other end, it wanted but a little that all my cargo had slipped off towards that end that was a-float, and so fallen into the water: I did my utmost by setting my back against the chests, to keep them in their places, but could not thrust off the raft with all my strength, neither durst I stir from the posture I was in, but holding up the chests with all my might, stood in that manner near half an hour, in which time the rising of the water brought me a little more upon a level, and a little after, the water still rising, my raft floated again, and I thrust her off with the oar I had, into the channel, and then driving up higher, I at length found my self in the mouth of a little river, with land on both sides, and a strong current or tide running up, I looked on both sides for a proper place to get to shore, for I was not willing to be driven too high up the river, hoping in time to see some ship at sea, and therefore resolved to place my self as near the coast as I could.

At length I spied a little cove on the right shore of the creek, to which with great pain and difficulty I guided my raft, and at last got so near, as that, reaching ground with my oar, I could thrust her directly in, but here I had like to have dipt all my cargo in the sea again; for that shore lying pretty steep, that is to say sloping, there was no place to land, but where one end of my float, if it run on shore, would lie so high, and the other sink lower as before, that it would endanger my cargo again: all that I could do, was to wait 'till the tide was at highest, keeping the raft with my oar like an anchor to hold the side of it fast to the shore, near a flat piece of ground, which I expected the water would flow over; and so it did: as soon as I found water enough, for my raft drew about a foot of water, I thrust her on upon that flat piece of ground, and there fastened or moored her by sticking my two broken oars into the ground; one on one side near one end, and one on the other side near the other end; and thus I lay 'till the water ebbed away, and left my raft and all my cargo safe on shore.

My next work was to view the country, and seek a proper place for my habitation, and where to stow my goods to secure them from whatever might happen; where I was I yet knew not, whether on the continent or on an island, whether inhabited or not inhabited, whether in danger of wild beasts or not: there was a hill not above a mile from me, which rose up very steep and high, and which seemed to over-top some other hills which lay as in a ridge from it northward; I took out one of the fowling pieces, and one of the pistols, and an horn of powder, and thus armed I travelled for discovery up to the top of that hill, where after I had with great labor and difficulty got to the top, I saw my Fate to my great affliction, (viz.) that I was in an island environed every way with the sea, no land to be seen, except some rocks which lay a great way off, and two small islands less than this, which lay about three leagues to the west. I found also that the island I was in was barren, and, as I saw good reason to believe, un-inhabited, except by wild beasts, of whom however I saw none, yet I saw abundance of fowls, but knew not their kinds, neither when I killed them could I tell what was fit for food, and what not; at my coming back, I shot at a great bird which I saw sitting upon a tree on the side of a great wood, I believe it was the first gun that had been fired there since the creation of the world; I had no sooner fired, but from all the parts of the wood there arose an innumerable number of fowls of many sorts, making a confused screaming, and crying every one according to his usual note; but not one of them of any kind that I knew: as for the creature I killed, I took it to be a kind of a hawk, its color and beak resembling it, but had no talons or claws more than common, its flesh was carrion, and fit for nothing.

Contented with this discovery, I came back to my raft, and fell to work to bring my cargo on shore, which took me up the rest of that day, and what to do with my self at night I knew not, nor indeed where to rest; for I was afraid to lie down on the ground, not knowing but some wild beast might devour me, tho', as I afterwards found, there was really no need for those fears. However, as well as I could, I barricaded my self round with the chests and boards that I had brought on shore, and me a kind of a hut for that night's lodging; as for food, I yet saw not which way to supply my self, except that I had seen two or three creatures like hares run out of the wood where I shot the fowl.

I now began to consider, that I might yet get a great many things out of the ship, which would be useful to me, and particularly some of the rigging, and sails, and such other things as might come to land, and I resolved to make another voyage on board the vessel, if possible; and as I knew that the first storm that blew must necessarily break her all in pieces, I resolved to set all other things apart, 'till I got every thing out of the ship that I could get; then I called a council, that is to say, in my thoughts, whether I should take back the raft, but this appeared impracticable; so I resolved to go as before, when the tide was down, and I did so, only that I stripped before I went from my hut, having nothing on but a chequered shirt, and a pair of linnen drawers, and a pair of pumps on my feet.

I got on board the ship, as before, and prepared a second raft, and having had experience of the first, I neither made this so unwieldy, nor loaded it so hard, but yet I brought away several things very useful to me; as first, in the carpenter's stores I found two or three bags full of nails and spikes, a great screw-jack[21], a dozen or two of hatchets, and above all, that most useful thing called a grindstone; all these I secured together, with several things belonging to the gunner, particularly two or three iron crows, and two barrels of musquet bullets, seven musquets, and another fowling piece, with some small quantity of powder more; a large bag full of small shot, and a great roll of sheet lead; but this last was so heavy, I could not hoise it up to get it over the ship's side. Besides these things, I took all the men's clothes that I could find, and a spare fore-top-sail, a hammock, and some bedding; and with this I loaded my second raft, and brought them all safe on shore to my very great comfort.

I was under some apprehensions[22] during my absence from the land, that at least my provisions might be devoured on shore; but when I came back, I found no sign of any visitor, only there sat a creature like a wild cat upon one of the chests, which when I came towards it, ran away a little distance, and then stood still; she sat very composed, and unconcerned, and looked full in my Face, as if she had a mind to be acquainted with me, I presented my gun at her, but as she did not understand it, she was perfectly unconcerned at it, nor did she offer to stir away; upon which I tossed her a bit of biscuit, tho' by the way I was not very free of it, for my store was not great. However, I spared her a bit, I say, and she went to it, smelled of it, and ate it, and looked (as pleased) for more, but I thanked her, and could spare no more; so she marched off.

Having got my second cargo on shore, though I was fain to[23] open the barrels of powder, and bring them by parcels, for they were too heavy, being large casks, I went to work to make me a little tent with the sail and some poles which I cut for that purpose, and into this tent I brought every thing that I knew would spoil, either with rain or sun, and I piled all the empty chests and casks up in a circle round the tent, to fortify it from any sudden attempt, either from man or beast.

When I had done this I blocked up the door of the tent with some boards within, and an empty chest set up an end without, and spreading one of the beds upon the ground, laying my two pistols just at my head, and my gun at length by me, I went to bed for the first time, and slept very quietly all night, for I was very weary and heavy, for the night before I had slept little, and had labored very hard all day, as well to fetch all those things from the ship, as to get them on shore.

【注释】

1. there was some minutes before scarce any room to hope：几分钟前几乎没有希望（存活）。

2. to express to the life：生动逼真地表达。

3. has the halter about his neck：即将被绞死。halter：缰绳，绞索。

4. to let him blood：to bleed him, a method formerly employed by a surgeon to cure some of his patients：放血治病。

5. that the surprise may not drive the animal spirits from the heart, and overwhelm him：that the surprise may not make him faint away；lose his natural vigor and be overpowered. overwhelm：（强烈地影响而）使不知所措。

6. my whole being wrapt up in the contemplation of my deliverance：我全神贯注地思考如何解救自己。

7. two shoes that were not fellows：两只不成双的鞋子。

8. the stranded vessel：指失事搁浅的船。stranded：搁浅的。

9. sustenance：食物。

10. come abroad：在户外出没。

11. by the dashing me against it：由于我撞到（石头）上面。

12. hot to extremity：极其炎热。

13. all her quarter was free：船的后半部分没有进水。

14. to spirit me：鼓舞我。

15. this extremity roused my application：这极端的困境促使我勤奋。

16. to fall to work：开始工作。

17. skipper：船长。

18. cordial waters：alcoholic solutions to give strength and vigor, medical drinks：药酒。

19. overset all my navigation：搅乱我的航行。

20. I had like to have suffered a second shipwreck：我可能遭遇第二次失事。I had like：archaic it was likely for me.

21. screw-jack：= jack-screw, 螺旋。

22. I was under some apprehensions: 我有些恐惧。
23. was fain to: was forced to. fain: 强迫的，不得不的。

Questions for discussion:

1. If you are going to live on an uninhabited island, what would you choose to bring with you and why?

2. Give an analysis of Robinson Crusoe's character from both positive and negative sides.

3. Why is the novel labeled as a realistic novel? What are the features of realistic novels in terms of plot, setting, characterization, and point of view?

名言摘录

So long as I also can delimit the water, I am not willing to be drown to death, so long as I also can stand, I am not willing to drop down.

——*Daniel Defoe*

2 Gulliver's Travels

Jonathan Swift

Part IV. A Voyage to the Country of the Houyhnhnms[1]
CHAPTER 3

[The author studies to learn the language. The Houyhnhnm, his master, assists in teaching him. The language described. Several Houyhnhnms of quality come out of curiosity to see the author. He gives his master a short account of his voyage.]

My principal endeavour was to learn the language, which my master (for so I shall henceforth call him), and his children, and every servant of his house, were desirous to teach me; for they looked upon it as a prodigy, that a brute animal should discover such marks of a rational creature. I pointed to every thing, and inquired the name of it, which I wrote down in my journal-book when I was alone, and corrected my bad accent by desiring those of the family to pronounce it often. In this employment, a sorrel nag,[2] one of the under-servants, was very ready to assist me. In speaking, they pronounced through the nose and throat, and their language approaches nearest to the High-Dutch, or German, of any I know in Europe; but is much more graceful and significant. The emperor Charles V made almost the same observation, when he said "that if he were to speak to his horse, it should be in High-Dutch."

The curiosity and impatience of my master were so great, that he spent many hours of his leisure to instruct me. He was convinced (as he afterwards told me) that I must be a YAHOO;[3] but my teachableness, civility, and cleanliness, astonished him; which were qualities altogether opposite to those animals. He was most perplexed about my clothes, reasoning sometimes with himself, whether they were a part of my body: for I never pulled them off till the family were asleep, and got them on before they waked in the morning. My master was eager to learn "whence I came; how I acquired those appearances of reason, which I discovered in all my actions; and to know my story from my own mouth, which he hoped he should soon do by the great proficiency I made in learning and pronouncing their words and sentences." To help my memory, I formed all I learned into the English alphabet and writ the words down, with the translations. This last, after some time, I ventured to do in my master's presence. It cost me much trouble to explain to him what I was doing; for the inhabitants have not the least idea of books or literature.

In about ten weeks' time, I was able to understand most of his questions; and in three months, could give him some tolerable answers. He was extremely curious to know "from what part of the country I came, and how I was taught to imitate a rational creature; because the YAHOOS (whom he saw I exactly resembled in my head, hands, and face, that were only visible), with some appearance of cunning, and the strongest disposition to mischief,[4] were observed to be the most unteachable of all brutes." I answered, "that I came over the sea, from a far place, with many others of my own kind, in a great hollow vessel made of the bodies of trees:[5] that my companions forced me to land on this coast, and then left me to shift for myself." It was with some difficulty, and by the help of many signs, that I brought him to understand me. He replied, "that I must needs be mistaken, or that I said the thing which was not;" for they have no word in their language to express lying or falsehood. "He knew it was impossible that there could be a country beyond the sea, or that a parcel of brutes could move a wooden vessel whither they pleased upon water. He was sure no HOUYHNHNM alive could make such a vessel, nor would trust YAHOOS to manage it."

The word HOUYHNHNM, in their tongue, signifies a HORSE, and, in its etymology, the PERFECTION OF NATURE.[6] I told my master, "that I was at a loss for expression, but would improve as fast as I could; and hoped, in a short time, I should be able to tell him wonders." He was pleased to direct his own mare, his colt, and foal, and the servants of the family, to take all opportunities of instructing me;[7] and every day, for two or three hours, he was at the same pains himself. Several horses and mares of quality in the neighbourhood came often to our house, upon the report spread of "a wonderful YAHOO that could speak like a HOUYHNHNM, and seemed, in his words and actions, to discover some glimmerings of reason." These delighted to converse with me:[8] they put many questions, and received such answers as I was able to return. By all these advantages I made so great a progress, that, in five months from my arrival I understood whatever was spoken, and could express myself tolerably well.

The HOUYHNHNMS, who came to visit my master out of a design of seeing and talking with me, could hardly believe me to be a right YAHOO, because my body had a different covering from others of my kind. They were astonished to observe me without the usual hair or skin, except on my head, face, and hands; but I discovered that secret to my master upon an accident which happened about a fortnight[9] before.

I have already told the reader, that every night, when the family were gone to bed, it was my custom to strip, and cover myself with my clothes. It happened, one morning early, that my master sent for me by the sorrel nag, who was his valet. When he came I was fast asleep, my clothes fallen off on one side, and my shirt above my waist. I awaked at the noise he made, and observed him to deliver his message in some disorder; after which he went to my master, and in a great fright gave him a very confused account of what he had seen. This I presently discovered, for, going as soon as I was dressed to pay my attendance upon his honour,[10] he asked me "the meaning of what his servant had reported, that I was not the same thing when I slept, as I appeared to be at other times; that his vale assured him, some part of me was white, some yellow, at least not so white, and some brown."

I had hitherto concealed the secret of my dress, in order to distinguish myself, as much as possible, from that cursed race of YAHOOS; but now I found it in vain to do so any longer. Besides, I considered that my clothes and shoes would soon wear out, which already were in a declining condition, and must be supplied by some contrivance from the hides of YAHOOS, or other brutes; whereby the whole secret would be known. I therefore told my master, "that in the country whence I came, those of my kind always covered their bodies with the hairs of certain animals prepared by art, as well for decency as to avoid the inclemencies of air, both hot and cold;[11] of which, as to my own person, I would give him immediate conviction, if he pleased to command me: only desiring his excuse, if I did not expose those parts that nature taught us to conceal." He said, "my discourse was all very strange, but especially the last part; for he could not understand, why nature should teach us to conceal what nature had given; that neither himself nor family were ashamed of any parts of their bodies; but, however, I might do as I pleased." Whereupon I first unbuttoned my coat, and pulled it off. I did the same with my waistcoat. I drew off my shoes, stockings, and breeches.[12] I let my shirt down to my waist, and drew up the bottom; fastening it like a girdle about my middle, to hide my nakedness.

My master observed the whole performance with great signs of curiosity and admiration. He took up all my clothes in his pastern,[13] one piece after another, and examined them diligently; he then stroked my body very gently, and looked round me several times; after which, he said, it was plain I must be a perfect YAHOO; but that I differed very much from the rest of my species in the softness, whiteness, and smoothness of my skin; my want of hair in several parts of my body; the shape and shortness of my claws behind and before; and my affectation of walking continually on my two hinder feet. He desired to see no more; and gave me leave to put on my clothes again, for I was shuddering with cold.[14]

I expressed my uneasiness at his giving me so often the appellation of YAHOO, an odious animal, for which I had so utter a hatred and contempt: I begged he would forbear applying that word to me,[15] and make the same order in his family and among his friends whom he suffered to see me. I requested likewise, "that the secret of my having a false covering to my body, might be known to none but himself, at least as long as my present clothing should last; for as to what the sorrel nag, his valet, had observed, his honour might command him to conceal it."

All this my master very graciously consented to; and thus the secret was kept till my clothes began to wear out, which I was forced to supply by several contrivances that shall hereafter be mentioned. In the meantime, he desired "I would go on with my utmost diligence to learn their language, because he was more astonished at my capacity for speech and reason, than at the figure of my body, whether it were covered or not;" adding, "that he waited with some impatience to hear the wonders which I promised to tell him."

Thenceforward he doubled the pains he had been at to instruct me: he brought me into all company, and made them treat me with civility; "because," as he told them, privately, "this would put me into good humour, and make me more diverting."[16]

Every day, when I waited on him, beside the trouble he was at in teaching, he would ask me several questions concerning myself, which I answered as well as I could, and by these means he had already received some general ideas, though very imperfect. It would be tedious to relate the several steps by which I advanced to a more regular conversation; but the first account I gave of myself in any order and length was to this purpose:

"That I came from a very far country, as I already had attempted to tell him, with about fifty more of my own species; that we travelled upon the seas in a great hollow vessel made of wood, and larger than his honour's house. I described the ship to him in the best terms I could, and explained, by the help of my handkerchief displayed, how it was driven forward by the wind. That upon a quarrel among us, I was set on shore on this coast, where I walked forward, without knowing whither, till he delivered me from the persecution of those execrable YAHOOS."[17] He asked me, "who made the ship, and how it was possible that the HOUYHNHNMS of my country would leave it to the management of brutes?" My answer was, "that I durst proceed no further in my relation, unless he would give me his word and honour that he would not be offended, and then I would tell him the wonders I had so often promised." He agreed; and I went on by assuring him, that the ship was made by creatures like myself; who, in all the countries I had travelled, as well as in my own, were the only governing rational animals; and that upon my arrival hither, I was as much astonished to see the HOUYHNHNMS act like rational beings, as he, or his friends, could be, in finding some marks of reason in a creature he was pleased to call a YAHOO; to which I owned my resemblance in every part, but could not account for their degenerate and brutal nature.[18] I said farther, "that if good fortune ever restored me to my native country, to relate my travels hither, as I resolved to do, everybody would believe, that I said the thing that was not, that I invented the story out of my own head; and (with all possible respect to himself, his family, and friends, and under his promise of not being offended) our countrymen would hardly think it probable that a HOUYHNHNM should be the presiding creature of a nation, and a YAHOO the brute."

【注释】

1. 格列佛最后航行到一个叫慧骃国的地方,那里的主人是马,是具有高度的智慧、自制力、礼节的马。在那个世界里,没有贪婪,没有欺骗,没有战争,没有陷害,就像生存在幻境中似的。

2. A sorrel nag：一匹栗色的驽马。

3. 慧骃圈养一种叫做"耶胡"的人形怪物，让他们为自己劳作。

4. strongest disposition to mischief：最强的恶作剧禀赋。

5. a great hollow vessel made of the bodies of trees：意即把大树的树身挖空，做成航海的大船。

6. The word HOUYHNHNM, in their tongue, signifies a HORSE, and, in its etymology, the PERFECTION OF NATURE：以"慧骃"族的语言来讲，慧骃一词的意思是"马"，而且这个词就其词源来说表示的是"自然完美"。

7. He was pleased to direct his own mare, his colt, and foal, and the servants of the family, to take all opportunities of instructing me：他感到愉快，因此让他家里的母马、小雄马、马驹以及家里的仆人都抓住各种机会来指导我。

8. These delighted to converse with me：这些（慧骃）很乐意与我交谈。

9. fortnight：两星期；十四天。

10. pay my attendance upon his honour：与尊贵的主人会面。

11. to avoid the inclemencies of air, both hot and cold：躲避严寒酷暑。

12. I drew off my shoes, stockings, and breeches：我脱掉了鞋、长袜和马裤。

13. He took up all my clothes in his pastern：他用自己的趾关节抓起我的衣服。

14. He desired to see no more; and gave me leave to put on my clothes again, for I was shuddering with cold：他不想再看了；他允许我穿上衣服，因为我正冷得发抖。

15. I begged he would forbear applying that word to me：我恳求他不要把那个词用到我身上。

16. this would put me into good humour, and make me more diverting：这会让我心情好，变得更快乐。

17. those execrable YAHOOS：那些可恶的耶胡。

18. their degenerate and brutal nature：他们的堕落而残忍的天性。

Questions for discussion：

1. As a kind of fantastic literature, *Gulliver's Travels* has many imaginative descriptions. Could you give an account of the imaginative genius of the author?

2. In this selection, the narrator is trying to learn the language of the horses. Do you think this is comparable to the kind of second language acquisition that we discuss in theoretical linguistics?

名言摘录

And truly, as they say a man is known by his company, so it should seem that a man's company may be known by his means of expressing himself, either in public assemblies or private conversations.

——*Jonathan Swift*

3 Pride and Prejudice

Jane Austen

CHAPTER 34

When they were gone, Elizabeth, as if intending to exasperate[1] herself as much as possible against Mr. Darcy, chose for her employment the examination of all the letters which Jane had written to her since her being in Kent[2]. They contained no actual complaint, nor was there any revival of past occurrences, or any communication of present suffering. But in all, and in almost every line of each, there was a want of that cheerfulness which had been used to characterize her style, and which, proceeding from the serenity[3] of a mind at ease with itself, and kindly disposed towards every one, had been scarcely ever clouded. Elizabeth noticed every sentence conveying the idea of uneasiness with an attention which it had hardly received on the first perusal[4]. Mr. Darcy's shameful boast of what misery he had been able to inflict gave her a keener sense of her sister's sufferings. It was some consolation to think that his visit to Rosings[5] was to end on the day after the next, and a still greater that in less than a fortnight she should herself be with Jane again, and enabled to contribute to the recovery of her spirits by all that affection could do.

She could not think of Darcy's leaving Kent without remembering that his cousin was to go with him; but Colonel Fitzwilliam had made it clear that he had no intentions at all, and agreeable as he was, she did not mean to be unhappy about him.

While settling this point, she was suddenly roused by the sound of the door bell, and her spirits were a little fluttered by the idea of its being Colonel Fitzwilliam himself, who had once before called late in the evening, and might now come to enquire particularly after her. But this idea was soon banished, and her spirits were very differently affected, when, to her utter amazement, she saw Mr. Darcy walk into the room. In a hurried manner he immediately began an enquiry after her health, imputing his visit to a wish of hearing that she were better. She answered him with cold civility. He sat down for a few moments, and then getting up, walked about the room. Elizabeth was surprised, but said not a word. After a silence of several minutes, he came towards her in an agitated[6] manner, and thus began,

"In vain have I struggled. It will not do. My feelings will not be repressed. You must allow me to tell you how ardently I admire and love you."

Elizabeth's astonishment was beyond expression. She stared, coloured, doubted, and was silent. This he considered sufficient encouragement, and the avowal of all that he felt and had long felt for her immediately followed. He spoke well, but there were feelings besides those of the heart to be detailed, and he was not more eloquent on the subject of tenderness than of pride[7]. His sense of her inferiority—of its being a degradation—of the family obstacles which judgment had always opposed to inclination, were dwelt on with a warmth which seemed due to the consequence he was wounding, but was very unlikely to recommend his suit.

In spite of her deeply-rooted[8] dislike, she could not be insensible to the compliment of such a man's affection, and though her intentions did not vary for an instant, she was at first sorry for the pain he was to receive; till, roused to resentment by his subsequent language, she lost all compassion in anger. She tried, however, to compose herself to answer him with patience, when he should have done. He concluded with representing to her the strength of that attachment which, in spite of all his endeavours, he had found impossible to conquer; and with expressing his hope that it would now be rewarded by her acceptance of his hand. As he said this, she could easily see that he had no doubt of a favourable answer. He spoke of apprehension[9] and anxiety, but his countenance expressed real security. Such a circumstance could only exasperate farther, and when he ceased, the colour rose into her cheeks, and she said, —

"In such cases as this, it is, I believe, the established mode to express a sense of obligation for the sentiments avowed, however unequally they may be returned. It is natural that obligation should be felt, and if I could feel gratitude, I would now thank you. But I cannot. I have never desired your good opinion, and you have certainly bestowed it most unwillingly. I am sorry to have occasioned pain to any one. It has been most unconsciously done, however, and I hope will be of short duration. The feelings which, you tell me, have long prevented the acknowledgment of your regard, can have little difficulty in overcoming it after this explanation."

Mr. Darcy, who was leaning against the mantelpiece[10] with his eyes fixed on her face, seemed to catch her words with no less resentment than surprise. His complexion became pale with anger, and the disturbance of his mind was visible in every feature. He was struggling for the appearance of composure[11], and would not open his lips, till he believed himself to have attained it. The pause was to Elizabeth's feelings dreadful. At length, in a voice of forced calmness, he said, —

"And this is all the reply which I am to have the honour of expecting! I might, perhaps, wish to be informed why, with so little endeavour at civility, I am thus rejected. But it is of small importance."

"I might as well enquire," replied she, "why, with so evident a design of offending and insulting me, you chose to tell me that you liked me against your will, against your reason, and even against your character? Was not this some excuse for incivility, if I was uncivil? But I have other provocations. You know I have. Had not my own feelings decided against you, had they been indifferent, or had they even been favourable, do you think that any consideration would tempt me to accept the man, who has been the means of ruining, perhaps for ever, the happiness of a most beloved sister?"

As she pronounced these words, Mr. Darcy changed colour; but the emotion was short, and he listened without attempting to interrupt her while she continued, —

"I have every reason in the world to think ill of you. No motive can excuse the unjust and ungenerous part you acted there. You dare not, you cannot deny that you have been the principal, if not the only means of dividing them from each other, of exposing one to the censure of the world for caprice and instability, the other to its derision for disappointed hopes, and involving them both in misery of the acutest kind."

She paused, and saw with no slight indignation that he was listening with an air which proved him wholly unmoved by any feeling of remorse[12]. He even looked at her with a smile of affected incredulity[13].

"Can you deny that you have done it?" she repeated.

With assumed tranquillity[14] he then replied, "I have no wish of denying that I did every thing in my power to separate my friend from your sister, or that I rejoice in my success. Towards him I have been kinder than towards myself."

Elizabeth disdained the appearance of noticing this civil reflection, but its meaning did not escape, nor was it likely to conciliate, her.

"But it is not merely this affair," she continued, "on which my dislike is founded. Long before it had taken place, my opinion of you was decided. Your character was unfolded in the recital which I received many months ago from Mr. Wickham. On this subject, what can you have to say? In what imaginary act of friendship can you here defend yourself? Or under what misrepresentation, can you here impose upon others?"

"You take an eager interest in that gentleman's concerns," said Darcy in a less tranquil tone, and with a heightened colour.

"Who that knows what his misfortunes have been, can help feeling an interest in him?"

"His misfortunes!" repeated Darcy contemptuously; "yes, his misfortunes have been great indeed."

"And of your infliction," cried Elizabeth with energy. "You have reduced him to his present state of poverty, comparative poverty. You have withheld the advantages, which you must know to have been designed for him. You have deprived the best years of his life, of that independence which was no less his due than his desert. You have done all this! And yet you can treat the mention of his misfortunes with contempt and ridicule."

"And this," cried Darcy, as he walked with quick steps across the room, "is your opinion of me! This is the estimation in which you hold me! I thank you for explaining it so fully. My faults, according to this calculation, are heavy indeed! But perhaps," added he, stopping in his walk, and turning towards her, "these offences might have been overlooked, had not your pride been hurt by my honest confession of the scruples that had long prevented my forming any serious design. These bitter accusations might have been suppressed, had I with greater policy concealed my struggles, and flattered you into the belief of my being impelled by unqualified, unalloyed inclination—by reason, by reflection, by every thing. But disguise of every sort is my abhorrence. Nor am I ashamed of the feelings I related. They were natural and just. Could you expect me to rejoice in the inferiority of your connections? —to congratulate myself on the hope of relations, whose condition in life is so decidedly beneath my own?"

Elizabeth felt herself growing more angry every moment; yet she tried to the utmost to speak with composure when she said, —

"You are mistaken, Mr. Darcy, if you suppose that the mode of your declaration affected me in any other way, than as it spared me the concern which I might have felt in refusing you, had you behaved in a more gentleman-like manner."

She saw him start at this, but he said nothing, and she continued, —

"You could not have made me the offer of your hand[15] in any possible way that would have tempted me to accept it."

Again his astonishment was obvious; and he looked at her with an expression of mingled incredulity and mortification. She went on.

"From the very beginning, from the first moment I may almost say, of my acquaintance with you, your manners, impressing me with the fullest belief of your arrogance, your conceit, and your selfish disdain of the feelings of others, were such as to form that ground-work of disapprobation, on which succeeding events have built so immoveable a dislike; and I had not known you a month before I felt that you were the last man in the world whom I could ever be prevailed on to marry."

"You have said quite enough, madam. I perfectly comprehend your feelings, and have now only to be ashamed of what my own have been. Forgive me for having taken up so much of your time, and accept my best wishes for your health and happiness."

And with these words he hastily left the room, and Elizabeth heard him the next moment open the front door and quit the house. The tumult[16] of her mind was now painfully great. She knew not how to support herself, and from actual weakness sat down and cried for half an hour. Her astonishment, as she reflected on what had passed, was increased by every review of it. That she should receive an offer of marriage from Mr. Darcy, that he should have been in love with her for so many months! —so much in love as to wish to marry her in spite of all the objections which had made him prevent his friend's marrying her sister, and which must appear at least with equal force in his own case, was almost incredible! It was gratifying to have inspired unconsciously so strong an affection. But his pride, his abominable pride, his shameless avowal of what he had done with respect to Jane, his unpardonable[17] assurance in acknowledging, though he could not justify it, and the unfeeling manner in which he had mentioned Mr. Wickham, his cruelty towards whom he had not attempted to deny, soon overcame the pity which the consideration of his attachment had for a moment excited.

She continued in very agitating reflections till the sound of Lady Catherine's carriage made her feel how unequal she was to encounter Charlotte's observation, and hurried her away to her room.

【注释】

1. exasperate：使恼怒，激怒。
2. Kent：肯特，英国东南部州名。
3. serenity：宁静，平静。
4. perusal：精读，熟读。
5. Rosings：罗新斯庄园，指达西先生的姨妈凯瑟琳·德·鲍尔夫人的罗新斯庄园。
6. agitated：激动的，焦虑的。
7. he was not more eloquent on the subject of tenderness than of pride：他一方面滔滔不绝地表示深情密意，但是另外一方面却又说了许多傲慢无礼的话。
8. deeply-rooted：根深蒂固的。
9. apprehension：不安，忧虑，忧惧；理解（力），领悟。
10. mantelpiece：壁炉架。
11. composure：冷静，镇静。
12. remorse：懊悔，悔恨，自责。
13. incredulity：怀疑。
14. tranquillity：心神稳定，平静。
15. made me the offer of your hand：打动我心。
16. tumult：吵闹，骚动。
17. unpardonable：不可原谅的。

Questions for discussion：

1. How does the novelist present the proud character of Darcy and the prejudicial character of Elizabeth?
2. Could you use evidence within the text to illustrate the misunderstanding between Darcy and Elizabeth?
3. Why did Elizabeth refuse Darcy's proposal?

名言摘录

It is a truth universally acknowledged that a single man in possession of a good fortune must be in want of a wife.

——*Jane Austen*

4 David Copperfield

Charles Dickens

Chapter 11

I know enough of the world now, to have almost lost the capacity of being much surprised by anything; but it is matter of some surprise to me, even now, that I can have been so easily thrown away at such an age. A child of excellent abilities, and with strong powers of observation, quick, eager, delicate, and soon hurt bodily or mentally, it seems wonderful to me that nobody should have made any sign in my behalf.[1] But none was made; and I became, at ten years old, a little labouring hind in the service of Murdstone and Grinby.

Murdstone and Grinby's warehouse was at the waterside. It was down in Blackfriars. Modern improvements have altered the place; but it was the last house at the bottom of a narrow street, curving down hill to the river, with some stairs at the end, where people took boat. It was a crazy old house with a wharf[2] of its own, abutting on the water when the tide was in,[3] and on the mud when the tide was out, and literally overrun with rats.[4] Its panelled rooms, discoloured with the dirt and smoke of a hundred years, I dare say; its decaying floors and staircase; the squeaking and scuffling of the old grey rats down in the cellars; and the dirt and rottenness of the place; are things, not of many years ago, in my mind, but of the present instant. They are all before me, just as they were in the evil hour when I went among them for the first time, with my trembling hand in Mr. Quinion's.

Murdstone and Grinby's trade was among a good many kinds of people, but an important branch of it was the supply of wines and spirits to certain packet ships. I forget now where they chiefly went, but I think there were some among them that made voyages both to the East and West Indies. I know that a great many empty bottles were one of the consequences of this traffic, and that certain men and boys were employed to examine them against the light, and reject those that were flawed,[5] and to rinse[6] and wash them. When the empty bottles ran short,[7] there were labels to be pasted on full ones, or corks[8] to be fitted to them, or seals to be put upon the corks, or finished bottles to be packed in casks. All this work was my work, and of the boys employed upon it I was one.

There were three or four of us, counting me. My working place was established in a corner of the warehouse, where Mr. Quinion could see me, when he chose to stand up on the bottom rail of his stool in the counting-house, and look at me through a window above the desk. Hither, on the first morning of my so auspiciously[9] beginning life on my own account, the oldest of the regular boys was summoned to show me my business. His name was Mick Walker, and he wore a ragged apron and a paper cap. He informed me that his father was a bargeman, and walked, in a black velvet head-dress, in the Lord Mayor's Show. He also informed me that our principal associate would be another boy whom he introduced by the—to me—extraordinary name of Mealy Potatoes. I discovered, however, that this youth had not been christened[10] by that name, but that it had been bestowed upon him in the warehouse, on account of[11] his complexion, which was pale or mealy. Mealy's father was a waterman, who had the additional distinction of being a fireman, and was engaged as such at one of the large theatres; where some young relation of Mealy's—I think his little sister—did Imps in the Pantomimes.[12]

No words can express the secret agony of my soul as I sunk into this companionship; compared these henceforth everyday associates with those of my happier childhood—not to say with Steerforth, Traddles, and the rest of those boys; and felt my hopes of growing up to be a learned and distinguished man, crushed in my bosom. The deep remembrance of the sense I had, of being utterly without hope now; of the shame I felt in my position; of the misery it was to my young heart to believe that day by day what I had learned, and thought, and delighted in, and raised my fancy and my emulation[13] up by, would pass away from me, little by little, never to be brought back any more; cannot be written. As often as Mick Walker went away in the course of that forenoon, I mingled my tears with the water[14] in which I was washing the bottles; and sobbed as if there were a flaw in my own breast, and it were in danger of bursting.

The counting-house clock was at half past twelve, and there was general preparation for going to dinner, when Mr. Quinion tapped at the counting-house window, and beckoned to me to go in. I went in, and found there a stoutish, middle-aged person, in a brown surtout and black tights and shoes, with no more hair upon his head (which was a large one, and very shining) than there is upon an egg,[15] and with a very extensive face, which he turned full upon me. His clothes were shabby, but he had an imposing shirt-collar on. He carried a jaunty[16] sort of a stick, with a large pair of rusty tassels to it; and a quizzing-glass hung outside his coat, —for ornament, I afterwards found, as he very seldom looked through it, and couldn't see anything when he did.

"This," said Mr. Quinion, in allusion to[17] myself, "is 0068e."

"This," said the stranger, with a certain condescending roll in his voice, and a certain indescribable air of doing something genteel, which impressed me very much, "is Master Copperfield. I hope I see you well, sir?"

I said I was very well, and hoped he was. I was sufficiently ill at ease, Heaven knows; but it was not in my nature to complain much at that time of my life, so I said I was very well, and hoped he was.

"I am," said the stranger, "thank Heaven, quite well. I have received a letter from Mr. Murdstone, in which he mentions that he would desire me to receive into an apartment in the rear of my house, which is at present unoccupied—and is, in short, to be let as a—in short," said the stranger, with a smile and in a burst of confidence, "as a bedroom—the young beginner whom I have now the pleasure to—" and the stranger waved his hand, and settled his chin in his shirt-collar.

"This is Mr. Micawber," said Mr. Qunion to me.

"Ahem!" said the stranger, "that is my name."

"Mr. Micawber," said Mr. Quinion, "is known to Mr. Murdstone. He takes orders for us on commission, when he can get any. He has been written to by Mr. Murdstone, on the subject of your lodgings, and he will receive you as a lodger."

"My address," said Mr. Micawber, "is Windsor Terrace, City Road. I—in short," said Mr. Micawber, with the same genteel air, and in another burst of confidence— "I live there."

I made him a bow.

"Under the impression," said Mr. Micawber, "that your peregrinations[18] in this metropolis have not as yet been extensive, and that you might have some difficulty in penetrating the arcana[19] of the Modern Babylon in the direction of the City Road, —in short," said Mr. Micawber, in another burst of confidence, "that you might lose yourself—I shall be happy to call this evening, and install you in the knowledge of the nearest way."

I thanked him with all my heart, for it was friendly in him to offer to take that trouble.

"At what hour," said Mr. Micawber, "shall I—"

"At about eight," said Mr. Quinion.

"At about eight," said Mr. Micawber. "I beg to wish you good day, Mr. Quinion. I will intrude no longer."

So he put on his hat, and went out with his cane under his arm: very upright, and humming a tune when he was clear of the counting-house.

Mr. Quinion then formally engaged me to be as useful as I could in the warehouse of Murdstone and Grinby, at a salary, I think, of six shillings a week. I am not clear whether it was six or seven. I am inclined to believe, from my uncertainty on this head, that it was six at first and seven afterwards. He paid me a week down (from his own pocket, I believe), and I gave Mealy sixpence out of it to get my trunk carried to Windsor Terrace that night: it being too heavy for my strength, small as it was. I paid sixpence more for my dinner, which was a meat pie and a turn at a neighbouring pump; and passed the hour which was allowed for that meal, in walking about the streets.

At the appointed time in the evening, Mr. Micawber reappeared. I washed my hands and face, to do the greater honour to his gentility, and we walked to our house, as I suppose I must now call it, together; Mr. Micawber impressing the name of streets, and the shapes of corner houses upon me, as we went along, that I might find my way back, easily, in the morning.

Arrived at this house in Windsor Terrace (which I noticed was shabby like himself, but also, like himself, made all the show it could), he presented me to Mrs. Micawber, a thin and faded lady, not at all young, who was sitting in the parlour (the first floor was altogether unfurnished, and the blinds were kept down to delude the neighbours), with a baby at her breast. This baby was one of twins; and I may remark here that I hardly ever, in all my experience of the family, saw both the twins detached from Mrs. Micawber at the same time. One of them was always taking refreshment.

There were two other children; Master Micawber, aged about four, and Miss Micawber, aged about three. These, and a dark-complexioned young woman, with a habit of snorting, who was servant to the family, and informed me, before half an hour had expired, that she was "a Orfling", and came from St. Luke's workhouse, in the neighbourhood, completed the establishment. My room was at the top of the house, at the back: a close chamber; stencilled[20] all over with an ornament which my young imagination represented as a blue muffin; and very scantily furnished.

"I never thought," said Mrs. Micawber, when she came up, twin and all, to show me the apartment, and sat down to take breath, "before I was married, when I lived with papa and mama, that I should ever find it necessary to take a lodger. But Mr. Micawber being in difficulties, all considerations of private feeling must give way."

I said: "Yes, ma'am."

"Mr. Micawber's difficulties are almost overwhelming just at present,"[21] said Mrs. Micawber; "and whether it is possible to bring him through them, I don't know. When I lived at home with papa and mama, I really should have hardly understood what the word meant, in the sense in which I now employ it, but experiential[22] does it, —as papa used to say."

I cannot satisfy myself whether she told me that Mr. Micawber had been an officer in the Marines, or whether I have imagined it. I only know that I believe to this hour that he WAS in the Marines once upon a time, without knowing why. He was a sort of town traveller for a number of miscellaneous[23] houses, now; but made little or nothing of it, I am afraid.

"If Mr. Micawber's creditors will not give him time, "said Mrs. Micawber," they must take the consequences;[24] and the sooner they bring it to an issue the better. Blood cannot be obtained from a stone, neither can anything on account be obtained at present (not to mention law expenses) from Mr. Micawber."

I never can quite understand whether my precocious[25] self-dependence confused Mrs. Micawber in reference to my age, or whether she was so full of the subject that she would have talked about it to the very twins if there had been nobody else to communicate with, but this was the strain in which she began, and she went on accordingly all the time I knew her.

Poor Mrs. Micawber! She said she had tried to exert herself,[26] and so, I have no doubt, she had. The centre of the street door was perfectly covered with a great brass-plate, on which was engraved "Mrs. Micawber's Boarding Establishment for Young Ladies": but I never found that any young lady had ever been to school there; or that any young lady ever came, or proposed to come; or that the least preparation was ever made to receive any young lady. The only visitors I ever saw, or heard of, were creditors. THEY used to come at all hours,[27] and some of them were quite ferocious.[28] One dirty-faced man, I think he was a boot-maker, used to edge himself into the passage as early as seven o'clock in the morning, and call up the stairs to Mr. Micawber— "Come! You ain't out yet, you know. Pay us, will you? Don't hide, you know; that's mean. I wouldn't be mean if I was you. Pay us, will you? You just pay us, d'ye hear? Come!" Receiving no answer to these taunts, he would mount in his wrath to the words "swindlers" and "robbers"; and these being ineffectual too, would sometimes go to the extremity of crossing the street, and roaring up at the windows of the second floor, where he knew Mr. Micawber was. At these times, Mr. Micawber would be transported with grief and mortification, even to the length (as I was once made aware by a scream from his wife) of making motions at himself with a razor; but within half-an-hour afterwards, he would polish up his shoes with extraordinary pains, and go out, humming a tune with a greater air of gentility than ever. Mrs. Micawber was quite as elastic. I have known her to be thrown into fainting fits by the king's taxes at three o'clock, and to eat lamb chops, breaded, and drink warm ale (paid for with two tea-spoons that had gone to the pawnbroker's) at four. On one occasion, when an execution had just been put in, coming home through some chance as early as six o'clock, I saw her lying (of course with a twin) under the grate in a swoon, with her hair all torn about her face; but I never knew her more cheerful than she was, that very same night, over a veal cutlet before the kitchen fire, telling me stories about her papa and mama, and the company they used to keep.

In this house, and with this family, I passed my leisure time. My own exclusive breakfast of a penny loaf and a pennyworth of milk, I provided myself. I kept another small loaf, and a modicum of cheese, on a particular shelf of a particular cupboard, to make my supper on when I came back at night. This made a hole in the six or seven shillings, I know well; and I was out at the warehouse all day, and had to support myself on that money all the week. From Monday morning until Saturday night, I had no advice, no counsel, no encouragement, no consolation, no assistance, no support, of any kind, from anyone, that I can call to mind, as I hope to go to heaven!

I was so young and childish, and so little qualified—how could I be otherwise?

—to undertake the whole charge of my own existence, that often, in going to Murdstone and Grinby's, of a morning, I could not resist the stale pastry put out for sale at half-price at the pastrycooks' doors, and spent in that the money I should have kept for my dinner. Then, I went without my dinner, or bought a roll or a slice of pudding. I remember two pudding shops, between which I was divided, according to my finances. One was in a court close to St. Martin's Church—at the back of the church, —which is now removed altogether. The pudding at that shop was made of currants, and was rather a special pudding, but was dear, two pennyworth not being larger than a pennyworth of more ordinary pudding. A good shop for the latter was in the Strand—somewhere in that part which has been rebuilt since. It was a stout pale pudding, heavy and flabby, and with great flat raisins in it, stuck in whole at wide distances apart. It came up hot at about my time every day, and many a day did I dine off it. When I dined regularly and handsomely, I had a saveloy and a penny loaf, or a fourpenny plate of red beef from a cook's shop; or a plate of bread and cheese and a glass of beer, from a miserable old public-house opposite our place of business, called the Lion, or the Lion and something else that I have forgotten. Once, I remember carrying my own bread (which I had brought from home in the morning) under my arm, wrapped in a piece of paper, like a book, and going to a famous alamode[29] beef-house near Drury Lane, and ordering a "small plate" of that delicacy to eat with it. What the waiter thought of such a strange little apparition coming in all alone, I don't know; but I can see him now, staring at me as I ate my dinner, and bringing up the other waiter to look. I gave him a halfpenny for himself, and I wish he hadn't taken it.

We had half-an-hour, I think, for tea. When I had money enough, I used to get half-a-pint of ready-made coffee and a slice of bread and butter.[30] When I had none, I used to look at a venison shop in Fleet Street; or I have strolled, at such a time, as far as Covent Garden Market, and stared at the pineapples. I was fond of wandering about the Adelphi, because it was a mysterious place, with those dark arches. I see myself emerging one evening from some of these arches, on a little public-house close to the river, with an open space before it, where some coal-heavers were dancing; to look at whom I sat down upon a bench. I wonder what they thought of me!

I was such a child, and so little, that frequently when I went into the bar of a strange public-house for a glass of ale or porter, to moisten what I had had for dinner, they were afraid to give it me. I remember one hot evening I went into the bar of a public-house, and said to the landlord: "What is your best—your very best—ale a glass?" For it was a special occasion. I don't know what. It may have been my birthday.

"Two pence-halfpenny," says the landlord, "is the price of the Genuine Stunning ale."

"Then," says I, producing the money, "just draw me a glass of the Genuine

Stunning, if you please, with a good head to it."

The landlord looked at me in return over the bar, from head to foot, with a strange smile on his face; and instead of drawing the beer, looked round the screen and said something to his wife. She came out from behind it, with her work in her hand, and joined him in surveying me. Here we stand, all three, before me now. The landlord in his shirt-sleeves, leaning against the bar window-frame; his wife looking over the little half-door; and I, in some confusion, looking up at them from outside the partition. They asked me a good many questions; as, what my name was, how old I was, where I lived, how I was employed, and how I came there. To all of which, that I might commit nobody, I invented, I am afraid, appropriate answers. They served me with the ale, though I suspect it was not the Genuine Stunning; and the landlord's wife, opening the little half-door of the bar, and bending down, gave me my money back, and gave me a kiss that was half admiring and half compassionate, but all womanly and good, I am sure.

I know I do not exaggerate, unconsciously and unintentionally, the scantiness of my resources or the difficulties of my life. I know that if a shilling were given me by Mr. Quinion at any time, I spent it in a dinner or a tea. I know that I worked, from morning until night, with common men and boys, a shabby child. I know that I lounged about the streets, insufficiently and unsatisfactorily fed. I know that, but for the mercy of God, I might easily have been, for any care that was taken of me, a little robber or a little vagabond.

Yet I held some station at Murdstone and Grinby's too. Besides that Mr. Quinion did what a careless man so occupied, and dealing with a thing so anomalous,[31] could, to treat me as one upon a different footing from the rest, I never said, to man or boy, how it was that I came to be there, or gave the least indication of being sorry that I was there. That I suffered in secret, and that I suffered exquisitely, no one ever knew but I. How much I suffered, it is, as I have said already, utterly beyond my power to tell. But I kept my own counsel, and I did my work. I knew from the first, that, if I could not do my work as well as any of the rest, I could not hold myself above slight and contempt. I soon became at least as expeditious and as skilful as either of the other boys. Though perfectly familiar with them, my conduct and manner were different enough from theirs to place a space between us. They and the men generally spoke of me as "the little gent", or "the young Suffolker." A certain man named Gregory, who was foreman of the packers, and another named Tipp, who was the carman, and wore a red jacket, used to address me sometimes as "David": but I think it was mostly when we were very confidential, and when I had made some efforts to entertain them, over our work, with some results of the old readings; which were fast perishing out of my remembrance. Mealy Potatoes uprose once, and rebelled against my being so distinguished; but Mick Walker settled him in no time.

My rescue from this kind of existence I considered quite hopeless, and abandoned, as such, altogether. I am solemnly convinced that I never for one hour was reconciled to it, or was otherwise than miserably unhappy; but I bore it; and even to Peggotty, partly for the love of her and partly for shame, never in any letter (though many passed between us) revealed the truth.

Mr. Micawber's difficulties were an addition to the distressed state of my mind. In my forlorn state I became quite attached to the family, and used to walk about, busy with Mrs. Micawber's calculations of ways and means, and heavy with the weight of Mr. Micawber's debts. On a Saturday night, which was my grand treat, —partly because it was a great thing to walk home with six or seven shillings in my pocket, looking into the shops and thinking what such a sum would buy, and partly because I went home early, —Mrs. Micawber would make the most heart-rending confidences to me; also on a Sunday morning, when I mixed the portion of tea or coffee I had bought over-night, in a little shaving-pot, and sat late at my breakfast. It was nothing at all unusual for Mr. Micawber to sob violently at the beginning of one of these Saturday night conversations, and sing about jack's delight being his lovely Nan, towards the end of it. I have known him come home to supper with a flood of tears, and a declaration that nothing was now left but a jail; and go to bed making a calculation of the expense of putting bow-windows to the house, "in case anything turned up", which was his favourite expression. And Mrs. Micawber was just the same.

A curious equality of friendship, originating, I suppose, in our respective circumstances, sprung up between me and these people, notwithstanding[32] the ludicrous disparity in our years. But I never allowed myself to be prevailed upon to accept any invitation to eat and drink with them out of their stock (knowing that they got on badly with the butcher and baker, and had often not too much for themselves), until Mrs. Micawber took me into her entire confidence. This she did one evening as follows:

"Master Copperfield," said Mrs. Micawber, "I make no stranger of you, and therefore do not hesitate to say that Mr. Micawber's difficulties are coming to a crisis."

It made me very miserable to hear it, and I looked at Mrs. Micawber's red eyes with the utmost sympathy.

"With the exception of the heel of a Dutch cheese—which is not adapted to the wants of a young family," —said Mrs. Micawber, "here is really not a scrap of anything in the larder. I was accustomed to speak of the larder when I lived with papa and mama, and I use the word almost unconsciously. What I mean to express is, that there is nothing to eat in the house."

"Dear me!" I said, in great concern.

I had two or three shillings of my week's money in my pocket—from which I presume that it must have been on a Wednesday night when we held this conversation—and I hastily produced them, and with heartfelt emotion begged Mrs. Micawber to accept of them as a loan. But that lady, kissing me, and making me put them back in my pocket, replied that she couldn't think of it.

"No, my dear Master Copperfield," said she, "far be it from my thoughts! But you have a discretion beyond your years, and can render me another kind of service, if you will; and a service I will thankfully accept of."

I begged Mrs. Micawber to name it.

"I have parted with the plate myself," said Mrs. Micawber. "Six tea, two salt, and a pair of sugars, I have at different times borrowed money on, in secret, with my own hands. But the twins are a great tie; and to me, with my recollections, of papa and mama, these transactions are very painful. There are still a few trifles that we could part with. Mr. Micawber's feelings would never allow him to dispose of them; and Clickett"—this was the girl from the workhouse— "being of a vulgar mind, would take painful liberties if so much confidence was reposed in her. Master Copperfield, if I might ask you—"

I understood Mrs. Micawber now, and begged her to make use of me to any extent. I began to dispose of the more portable articles of property that very evening; and went out on a similar expedition almost every morning, before I went to Murdstone and Grinby's.

Mr. Micawber had a few books on a little chiffonier, which he called the library; and those went first. I carried them, one after another, to a bookstall in the City Road—one part of which, near our house, was almost all bookstalls and bird shops then—and sold them for whatever they would bring. The keeper of this bookstall, who lived in a little house behind it, used to get tipsy every night, and to be violently scolded by his wife every morning. More than once, when I went there early, I had audience of him in a turn-up bedstead, with a cut in his forehead or a black eye, bearing witness to his excesses over-night (I am afraid he was quarrelsome in his drink), and he, with a shaking hand, endeavouring to find the needful shillings in one or other of the pockets of his clothes, which lay upon the floor, while his wife, with a baby in her arms and her shoes down at heel, never left off rating him. Sometimes he had lost his money, and then he would ask me to call again; but his wife had always got some—had taken his, I dare say, while he was drunk—and secretly completed the bargain on the stairs, as we went down together. At the pawnbroker's shop, too, I began to be very well known. The principal gentleman who officiated behind the counter, took a good deal of notice of me; and often got me, I recollect, to decline a Latin noun or adjective, or to conjugate a Latin verb, in his ear, while he transacted my business. After all these occasions Mrs. Micawber made a little treat, which was generally a supper; and there was a peculiar relish in these meals which I well remember.

At last Mr. Micawber's difficulties came to a crisis, and he was arrested early one morning, and carried over to the King's Bench Prison in the Borough. He told me, as he went out of the house, that the God of day had now gone down upon him—and I really thought his heart was broken and mine too. But I heard, afterwards, that he was seen to play a lively game at skittles, before noon.

On the first Sunday after he was taken there, I was to go and see him, and have dinner with him. I was to ask my way to such a place, and just short of that place I should see such another place, and just short of that I should see a yard, which I was to cross, and keep straight on until I saw a turnkey. All this I did; and when at last I did see a turnkey (poor little fellow that I was!), and thought how, when Roderick Random was in a debtors' prison, there was a man there with nothing on him but an old rug, the turnkey swam before my dimmed eyes and my beating heart.

Mr. Micawber was waiting for me within the gate, and we went up to his room (top story but one), and cried very much. He solemnly conjured me, I remember, to take warning by his fate; and to observe that if a man had twenty pounds a-year for his income, and spent nineteen pounds nineteen shillings and sixpence, he would be happy, but that if he spent twenty pounds one he would be miserable. After which he borrowed a shilling of me for porter, gave me a written order on Mrs. Micawber for the amount, and put away his pocket-handkerchief, and cheered up.

We sat before a little fire, with two bricks put within the rusted grate, one on each side, to prevent its burning too many coals; until another debtor, who shared the room with Mr. Micawber, came in from the bakehouse with the loin of mutton which was our joint-stock repast. Then I was sent up to "Captain Hopkins" in the room overhead, with Mr. Micawber's compliments, and I was his young friend, and would Captain Hopkins lend me a knife and fork.

Captain Hopkins lent me the knife and fork, with his compliments to Mr. Micawber. There was a very dirty lady in his little room, and two wan girls, his daughters, with shock heads of hair. I thought it was better to borrow Captain Hopkins's knife and fork, than Captain Hopkins's comb. The Captain himself was in the last extremity of shabbiness, with large whiskers, and an old, old brown great-coat with no other coat below it. I saw his bed rolled up in a corner; and what plates and dishes and pots he had, on a shelf; and I divined (God knows how) that though the two girls with the shock heads of hair were Captain Hopkins's children, the dirty lady was not married to Captain Hopkins. My timid station on his threshold was not occupied more than a couple of minutes at most; but I came down again with all this in my knowledge, as surely as the knife and fork were in my hand.

There was something gipsy-like and agreeable in the dinner, after all. I took back Captain Hopkins's knife and fork early in the afternoon, and went home to comfort Mrs. Micawber with an account of my visit. She fainted when she saw me return, and made a little jug of egg-hot afterwards to console us while we talked it over.

I don't know how the household furniture came to be sold for the family benefit, or who sold it, except that I did not. Sold it was, however, and carried away in a van; except the bed, a few chairs, and the kitchen table. With these possessions we encamped, as it were, in the two parlours of the emptied house in Windsor Terrace; Mrs. Micawber, the children, the Orfling, and myself; and lived in those rooms night and day. I have no idea for how long, though it seems to me for a long time. At last Mrs. Micawber resolved[33] to move into the prison, where Mr. Micawber had now secured a room to himself. So I took the key of the house to the landlord, who was very glad to get it; and the beds were sent over to the King's Bench, except mine, for which a little room was hired outside the walls in the neighbourhood of that Institution, very much to my satisfaction, since the Micawbers and I had become too used to one another, in our troubles, to part. The Orfling was likewise accommodated with an inexpensive lodging in the same neighbourhood. Mine was a quiet back-garret with a sloping roof, commanding a pleasant prospect of a timberyard; and when I took possession of it, with the reflection that Mr. Micawber's troubles had come to a crisis at last, I thought it quite a paradise.

All this time I was working at Murdstone and Grinby's in the same common way, and with the same common companions, and with the same sense of unmerited degradation as at first. But I never, happily for me no doubt, made a single acquaintance, or spoke to any of the many boys whom I saw daily in going to the warehouse, in coming from it, and in prowling[34] about the streets at meal-times. I led the same secretly unhappy life; but I led it in the same lonely, self-reliant manner. The only changes I am conscious of are, firstly, that I had grown more shabby, and secondly, that I was now relieved of much of the weight of Mr. and Mrs. Micawber's cares; for some relatives or friends had engaged to help them at their present pass, and they lived more comfortably in the prison than they had lived for a long while out of it. I used to breakfast with them now, in virtue of[35] some arrangement, of which I have forgotten the details. I forget, too, at what hour the gates were opened in the morning, admitting of my going in; but I know that I was often up at six o'clock, and that my favourite lounging-place in the interval was old London Bridge, where I was want to sit in one of the stone recesses, watching the people going by, or to look over the balustrades at the sun shining in the water, and lighting up the golden flame on the top of the Monument. The Orfling met me here sometimes, to be told some astonishing fictions respecting the wharves and the Tower; of which I can say no more than that I hope I believed them myself. In the evening I used to go back to the prison, and walk up and down the parade with Mr. Micawber; or play casino with Mrs. Micawber, and hear reminiscences of her papa and mama. Whether Mr. Murdstone knew where I was, I am unable to say. I never told them at Murdstone and Grinby's.

Mr. Micawber's affairs, although past their crisis, were very much involved by reason of a certain "Deed", of which I used to hear a great deal, and which I suppose, now, to have been some former composition with his creditors, though I was so far from being clear about it then, that I am conscious of having confounded it with those demoniacal parchments which are held to have, once upon a time, obtained to a great extent in Germany. At last this document appeared to be got out of the way, somehow; at all events it ceased to be the rock-ahead it had been; and Mrs. Micawber informed me that "her family" had decided that Mr. Micawber should apply for his release under the Insolvent Debtors Act, which would set him free, she expected, in about six weeks.

"And then," said Mr. Micawber, who was present, "I have no doubt I shall, please Heaven, begin to be beforehand with the world, and to live in a perfectly new manner, if—in short, if anything turns up."

By way of going in for anything that might be on the cards, I call to mind that Mr. Micawber, about this time, composed a petition to the House of Commons, praying for an alteration in the law of imprisonment for debt. I set down this remembrance here, because it is an instance to myself of the manner in which I fitted my old books to my altered life, and made stories for myself, out of the streets, and out of men and women; and how some main points in the character I shall unconsciously develop, I suppose, in writing my life, were gradually forming all this while.

There was a club in the prison, in which Mr. Micawber, as a gentleman, was a great authority. Mr. Micawber had stated his idea of this petition to the club, and the club had strongly approved of the same. Wherefore Mr. Micawber (who was a thoroughly good-natured man, and as active a creature about everything but his own affairs as ever existed, and never so happy as when he was busy about something that could never be of any profit to him) set to work at the petition, invented it, engrossed it on an immense sheet of paper, spread it out on a table, and appointed a time for all the club, and all within the walls if they chose, to come up to his room and sign it.

When I heard of this approaching ceremony, I was so anxious to see them all come in, one after another, though I knew the greater part of them already, and they me, that I got an hour's leave of absence from Murdstone and Grinby's, and established myself in a corner for that purpose. As many of the principal members of the club as could be got into the small room without filling it, supported Mr. Micawber in front of the petition, while my old friend Captain Hopkins (who had washed himself, to do honour to so solemn an occasion) stationed himself close to it, to read it to all who were unacquainted with its contents. The door was then thrown open, and the general population began to come in, in a long file: several waiting outside, while one entered, affixed his signature, and went out. To everybody in succession, Captain Hopkins said: "Have you read it?" — "No." — "Would you like to hear it read?" If he weakly showed the least disposition to hear it, Captain Hopkins, in a loud sonorous voice, gave him every word of it. The Captain would have read it twenty thousand times, if twenty thousand people would have heard him, one by one. I remember a certain luscious roll he gave to such phrases as "The people's representatives in Parliament assembled," "Your petitioners therefore humbly approach your honourable house," "His gracious Majesty's unfortunate subjects," as if the words were something real in his mouth, and delicious to taste; Mr. Micawber, meanwhile, listening with a little of an author's vanity, and contemplating (not severely) the spikes on the opposite wall.

As I walked to and fro daily between Southwark and Blackfriars, and lounged about at meal-times in obscure streets, the stones of which may, for anything I know, be worn at this moment by my childish feet, I wonder how many of these people were wanting in the crowd that used to come filing before me in review again, to the echo of Captain Hopkins's voice! When my thoughts go back, now, to that slow agony of my youth, I wonder how much of the histories I invented for such people hangs like a mist of fancy over well-remembered facts! When I tread the old ground, I do not wonder that I seem to see and pity, going on before me, an innocent romantic boy, making his imaginative world out of such strange experiences and sordid things!

【注释】
1. in my behalf: 代表我。
2. wharf: 码头。
3. abut: 毗邻，邻接；此处描述码头的状态。
4. literally overrun with rats: 这里简直老鼠成灾。
5. flaw: 此处意为破裂的，有裂纹的。
6. rinse: 冲洗。
7. run short: 用完，不足。
8. cork: 软木塞。
9. auspicious: 吉利的，幸运的；auspicious day: 好日子，良辰吉日。
10. christen: 为……命名，为……施洗礼。
11. on account of: 由于……的缘故。
12. Pantomimes: （古罗马或现代的）哑剧；舞剧。
13. emulation: 竞争。
14. mingle A with B: A 和 B 混合。
15. 这句话形象地描述了麦考比先生头发之少。
16. jaunty: 快活的，活泼的。
17. in allusion to: 暗指，针对……而言。
18. peregrination: 旅行，旅程。
19. arcana: 奥秘的知识。
20. stencil: *v.* 用蜡纸或模板印刷；*n.* 模板。
21. overwhelming: 压倒性的，势不可挡的。
22. experiential: 经验的。

23. miscellaneous：混杂的，各种各样的。
24. take the consequences：承担责任。
25. precocious：早熟的。
26. exert oneself：尽力，努力。
27. at all hours：在任何时候，随时。
28. ferocious：残忍的，凶狠的。
29. alamode：流行的，时髦的。
30. 此处的 bread and butter 应理解为"加了黄油的面包"。
31. anomalous：异常的。
32. notwithstanding：虽然，尽管。
33. resolve to do sth.：决定做某事。
34. prowl：徘徊。
35. in virtue of：由于，凭借。

Questions for discussion：

1. What can we learn from the life experience of David Copperfield and Mr. Micawber?

2. This novel by Dickens has been praised by critics for its dense descriptions of minute events. Could you say something about this by citing evidence from the text itself?

名言摘录

Procrastination is the thief of time.

——*Charles Dickens*

5 Jane Eyre

Charlotte Brontë

"I grieve to leave Thornfield: I love Thornfield: —I love it, because I have lived in it a full and delightful life, —momentarily at least. I have not been trampled[1] on. I have not been petrified[2]. I have not been buried with inferior minds, and excluded from every glimpse of communion with what is bright and energetic and high. I have talked, face to face, with what I reverence[3], with what I delight in, —with an original, a vigorous, an expanded mind. I have known you, Mr. Rochester; and it strikes me with terror and anguish to feel I absolutely must be torn from you for ever. I see the necessity of departure; and it is like looking on the necessity of death."

"Where do you see the necessity?" he asked suddenly.

"Where? You, sir, have placed it before me."

"In what shape?"

"In the shape of Miss Ingram; a noble and beautiful woman, —your bride."

"My bride! What bride? I have no bride!"

"But you will have."

"Yes; —I will! —I will!" He set his teeth.

"Then I must go: —you have said it yourself."

"No: you must stay! I swear it—and the oath shall be kept."

"I tell you I must go!" I retorted, roused to something like passion. "Do you think I can stay to become nothing to you? Do you think I am an automaton[4]? —a machine without feelings? and can bear to have my morsel of bread snatched from my lips, and my drop of living water dashed from my cup? Do you think, because I am poor, obscure, plain, and little, I am soulless and heartless? You think wrong! —I have as much soul as you, —and full as much heart! And if God had gifted me with some beauty and much wealth, I should have made it as hard for you to leave me, as it is now for me to leave you. I am not talking to you now through the medium of custom, conventionalities, nor even of mortal flesh; —it is my spirit that addresses your spirit; just as if both had passed through the grave, and we stood at God's feet, equal, —as we are!"

"As we are!" repeated Mr. Rochester— "so," he added, enclosing me in his arms. Gathering me to his breast, pressing his lips on my lips: "so, Jane!"

"Yes, so, sir," I rejoined: "and yet not so; for you are a married man—or as good as a married man, and wed to one inferior to you—to one with whom you have no sympathy—whom I do not believe you truly love; for I have seen and heard you sneer at her. I would scorn such a union: therefore I am better than you—let me go!"

"Where, Jane? To Ireland?"

"Yes—to Ireland. I have spoken my mind, and can go anywhere now."

"Jane, be still; don't struggle so, like a wild frantic bird that is rending its own plumage in its desperation."

"I am no bird; and no net ensnares[5] me; I am a free human being with an independent will, which I now exert to leave you."

Another effort set me at liberty, and I stood erect before him.

"And your will shall decide your destiny," he said: "I offer you my hand, my heart, and a share of all my possessions."

"You play a farce, which I merely laugh at."

"I ask you to pass through life at my side—to be my second self, and best earthly companion."

"For that fate you have already made your choice, and must abide by it."

"Jane, be still a few moments: you are over-excited: I will be still too."

A waft of wind came sweeping down the laurel-walk, and trembled through the boughs of the chestnut: it wandered away—away—to an indefinite distance—it died. The nightingale's song was then the only voice of the hour: in listening to it, I again wept. Mr. Rochester sat quiet, looking at me gently and seriously. Some time passed before he spoke; he at last said—

"Come to my side, Jane, and let us explain and understand one another."

"I will never again come to your side: I am torn away now, and cannot return."

"But, Jane, I summon you as my wife: it is you only I intend to marry."

I was silent: I thought he mocked me.

"Come, Jane—come hither."

"Your bride stands between us."

He rose, and with a stride reached me.

"My bride is here," he said, again drawing me to him, "because my equal is here, and my likeness. Jane, will you marry me?"

Still I did not answer, and still I writhed myself from his grasp: for I was still incredulous.

"Do you doubt me, Jane?"

"Entirely."

"You have no faith in me?"

"Not a whit."

"Am I a liar in your eyes?" he asked passionately. "Little sceptic[6], you shall be convinced. What love have I for Miss Ingram? None: and that you know. What love has she for me? None: as I have taken pains to prove: I caused a rumour to reach her that my fortune was not a third of what was supposed, and after that I presented myself to see the result; it was coldness both from her and her mother. I would not—I could not—marry Miss Ingram. You—you strange, you almost unearthly thing! —I love as my own flesh. You—poor and obscure, and small and plain as you are—I entreat to accept me as a husband."

"What, me!" I ejaculated[7], beginning in his earnestness—and especially in his incivility—to credit his sincerity: "me who have not a friend in the world but you—if you are my friend: not a shilling but what you have given me?"

"You, Jane, I must have you for my own—entirely my own. Will you be mine? Say yes, quickly."

"Mr. Rochester, let me look at your face: turn to the moonlight."

"Why?"

"Because I want to read your countenance—turn!"

"There! you will find it scarcely more legible than a crumpled, scratched page. Read on: only make haste, for I suffer."

His face was very much agitated and very much flushed, and there were strong workings in the features, and strange gleams in the eyes.

"Oh, Jane, you torture me!" he exclaimed. "With that searching and yet faithful and generous look, you torture me!"

"How can I do that? If you are true, and your offer real, my only feelings to you must be gratitude and devotion—they cannot torture."

"Gratitude!" he ejaculated; and added wildly— "Jane accept me quickly. Say, Edward—give me my name—Edward—I will marry you."

"Are you in earnest? Do you truly love me? Do you sincerely wish me to be your wife?"

"I do; and if an oath is necessary to satisfy you, I swear it."

"Then, sir, I will marry you."

"Edward—my little wife!"

"Dear Edward!"

"Come to me—come to me entirely now," said he; and added, in his deepest tone, speaking in my ear as his cheek was laid on mine, "Make my happiness—I will make yours."

"God pardon me!" he subjoined ere long; "and man meddle[8] not with me: I have her, and will hold her."

"There is no one to meddle, sir. I have no kindred to interfere."

"No—that is the best of it," he said. And if I had loved him less I should have thought his accent and look of exultation savage; but, sitting by him, roused from the nightmare of parting—called to the paradise of union—I thought only of the bliss given me to drink in so abundant a flow. Again and again he said, "Are you happy, Jane?"

And again and again I answered, "Yes." After which he murmured, "It will atone—it will atone. Have I not found her friendless, and cold, and comfortless? Will I not guard, and cherish, and solace her? Is there not love in my heart, and constancy in my resolves? It will expiate at God's tribunal. I know my Maker sanctions what I do. For the world's judgment—I wash my hands thereof. For man's opinion—I defy it."

But what had befallen the night? The moon was not yet set, and we were all in shadow: I could scarcely see my master's face, near as I was. And what ailed the chestnut tree? it writhed and groaned: while wind roared in the laurel walk, and came sweeping over us.

"We must go in," said Mr. Rochester: "the weather changes. I could have sat with thee till morning, Jane."

"And so," thought I, "could I with you." I should have said so, perhaps, but a livid, vivid spark leapt out of a cloud at which I was looking, and there was a crack, a crash, and a close rattling peal; and I thought only of hiding my dazzled eyes against Mr. Rochester's shoulder.

The rain rushed down. He hurried me up the walk, through the grounds, and into the house; but we were quite wet before we could pass the threshold. He was taking off my shawl in the hall, and shaking the water out of my loosened hair, when Mrs. Fairfax emerged from her room. I did not observe her at first, nor did Mr. Rochester. The lamp was lit. The clock was on the stroke of twelve.

"Hasten to take off your wet things," said he; "and before you go, good-night—good-night, my darling!"

He kissed me repeatedly. When I looked up, on leaving his arms, there stood the widow, pale, grave, and amazed. I only smiled at her, and ran upstairs. "Explanation will do for another time," thought I. Still, when I reached my chamber, I felt a pang at the idea she should even temporarily misconstrue what she had seen. But joy soon effaced every other feeling; and loud as the wind blew, near and deep as the thunder crashed, fierce and frequent as the lightning gleamed, cataract-like as the rain fell during a storm of two hours' duration, I experienced no fear and little awe. Mr. Rochester came thrice to my door in the course of it, to ask if I was safe and tranquil: and that was comfort, that was strength for anything.

Before I left my bed in the morning, little Adèle came running in to tell me that the great horse-chestnut at the bottom of the orchard had been struck by lightning in the night, and half of it split away.

【注释】

1. trample：践踏；无视；侵犯。
2. petrified：非常害怕的；吓呆的。
3. reverence：尊敬；敬畏。

4. automaton：自动机，机器人。If you say that someone is an automaton, you are critical of them because they behave as if they are so tired or bored that they do things without thinking.

5. ensnare：诱捕，使入陷阱，使入圈套。

6. sceptic：多疑者；怀疑宗教的人；无神论者；怀疑论者。

7. ejaculate：突然说出。

8. meddle：干涉，插手。

Questions for discussion：

1. What are the characteristics of Jane reflected in this paragraph?
2. What do you think of the "equal" in love?
3. If you were Jane, would you believe Mr. Rochester and accept his love? Please share your ideas.

名言摘录

(Charloote says of her sister Emily) My sister's disposition was not naturally gregarious; circumstances favoured and fostered her tendency to seclusion; except to go to church or take a walk on the hills, she rarely crossed the threshold of home. Though her feeling for the people round was benevolent, intercourse with them she never sought; nor, with very few exceptions, ever experienced. And yet she knew them: knew their ways, their language, their family histories; she could hear of them with interest, and talk of them with detail, minute, graphic, and accurate; but with them, she rarely exchanged a word.

——*Charlotte Brontë*

6 Wuthering Heights

Emily Brontë

CHAPTER 15

Heathcliff had given me a letter for Catherine, but I decided not to show it to her until Mr Edgar was out of the house. My chance came four days after my visit to Wuthering Heights. As it was a Sunday, Mr Edgar and all the servants went to church, leaving me alone to look after Catherine.

She was sitting downstairs, by an open window, enjoying the spring sunshine. Her appearance[1] had changed since her illness, but there was a strange beauty in her pale face, She did not read or sew any more, but used to sit there silently, staring into the distance. Her eyes seemed fixed[2] on something far away, something beyond normal sight.

I showed her the letter, but she looked confused and could not seem to understand it, so I had to explain. "It's from Mr Heathcliff," I said gently. "He's in the garden, and wants to see you. What shall I tell him?"

She said nothing, but bent[3] forward in her chair to listen. We both heard someone coming through the hall. Heathcliff had realized the house was almost empty, and had found an open door. Catherine looked eagerly towards the entrance to the room. He appeared, and in two steps was by her side. For five whole minutes he held her in his arms and kissed her again and again, it gave him great pain to look at her face. He could see, as I could, that she would never recover, that she was certain to die.

"Oh, Catherine! Oh, my life! How can I bear[4] it!" he cried. "You and Edgar have broken my heart," said Catherine. "And you both want me to pity you! How strong you are, Heathcliff! You'll live for years after my death! Will you forget me, and be happy with others, when I'm in my grave?" "It's wicked[5] of you to say that, Catherine. You know your words will burn for ever in my memory after you've left me. You know I could never forget you!"

"I don't want you to suffer[6] more than I do, Heathcliff. I only want us to be together, always."

Heathcliff turned away, his shoulders shaking. "That isn't my Heathcliff," Catherine said to me. "I'll always love my Heathcliff, and take him with me. He's in my soul, you see. Oh, Ellen, I do want to escape from this prison. There's a beautiful world waiting for me out there. You feel sorry for me now because I'm ill. Well, very soon I'll feel sorry for you, because I'll be beyond[7] you all!"

Heathcliff turned towards her, his fierce eyes wet. For a moment they looked at each other, and then they were in each other's arms again. No one could have separated them.

"How cruel you've been to me, Catherine!" he cried wildly. "You loved me, so why did you marry Edgar Linton? It's all your fault! I haven't broken your heart, you've broken it! And you've broken mine too! Do you think I want to live after you are dead?" "If I've done wrong, I'm dying for it!" sobbed Catherine. "It's your fault too, Heathcliff! You left me, remember? But I forgive you. Now forgive me!"

"It's hard to forgive, when I look at your sad eyes, and feel your thin hands. Kiss me again, Catherine! I forgive you for making me suffer, but how can I forgive you for dying?"

Catherine sobbed quietly, hiding her face in his shoulder, and tears rolled down Heathcliff's dark face.

Suddenly I noticed, through the window, the servants coming back from church. I was afraid Mr Edgar would find Heathcliff with Catherine.

"My master will be here in a moment," I warned them. "I must go, Catherine," said Heathcliff. "No, no!" she screamed. "Don't go! It's the last time! Edgar won't hurt us! Heathcliff, I'll die if you go!" "All right, my darling, I'll stay. If he shot me in your arms, I'd die happy."

At that moment my master appeared at the door. When he saw Heathcliff holding his wife, he went pale with anger.

"Here, take care of her first," said Heathcliff, putting Catherine in her husband's arms, "then speak to me later if you wish." He walked out of the house.

Catherine seemed to be unconscious, and Mr Edgar was so worried about her that he forgot about Heathcliff for the moment. She recovered a little, but did not recognize any of us, and was clearly very ill. We put her to bed immediately, and at twelve o'clock that night her daughter, Cathy, was born, two months early. That's the young lady you saw at Wuthering Heights, Mr Lockwood. Two hours later, Catherine died, without calling for Heathcliff, or recognizing Edgar. My poor master was in the depths[8] of despair. I thought it was very unfortunate that Catherine had only given him a daughter, not a son. Now the Linton fortune would pass to Isabella and her husband after Mr Edgar's death.

Catherine's dead body lay peacefully on her bed. In death she looked more beautiful that in life. I wondered if she was now beyond us all, as she had said, and hoped that her soul had found a home with God.

In the morning I went to look for Heathcliff. I found him in the Grange garden, where he had been waiting for news all night. "She's dead, I know!" he caned to me as I came closer.

"Don't cry, she doesn't need your tears! Tell me—tell me, how did—?" He tried to say her name, but could not manage it. "How did she die?" he said at last, staring fiercely[9] at me. "Don't be sorry for me, I don't want your pity!" "Poor creature!" I thought. "You have a heart just like other men, but you are too proud to show it!"

Aloud I said, "She died quietly, in her sleep. Her life finished in a gentle dream. I hope she wakes as calmly in the other world!" "Where are you, Catherine?" he cried in despair. "Don't leave me here, where I can't find you! I pray that you will never rest while I'm alive. You said I killed you—haunt[10] me then! Murdered people do haunt their murderers, I believe. Come back as a ghost—drive me mad—I don't care! Oh, God! I can't bear it! I cannot live without you, my soul!"

He howled like a wild animal, and hit his forehead several times against a tree, until the wood was covered in blood. I knew I could no longer help him, so I left him.

Catherine was buried the following Friday. Her brother Hindley, although invited, did not come, and Isabella was not invited, so it was only Mr Edgar and the servants who attended the ceremony. To our surprise, she was not buried in the church with the Lintons, nor with the Earnshaws. She lies in an open corner of the churchyard, where she can breathe the air from the moors. Her husband's grave is next to hers.

【注释】

1. appearance：外貌，外观。
2. fix：固定；安装。
3. bent：bend 的过去式。bend：使弯曲、使倾斜；弯腰、俯身。
4. bear：作名词时，意思是"熊"；作动词时，意思是"承受、忍受"。
5. wicked：邪恶的；缺德的。
6. suffer：遭受、忍受、经历（不好的事情）。
7. beyond：超过；越过；那一边；在……较远的一边。
8. depths：深（depth 的名词复数）；深处；深厚；浓度。
9. fiercely：凶猛地；残酷地；猛烈地；激烈地。
10. haunt：时常萦绕心头，使困窘；常去；以鬼魂形式出现；时常出现在，弥漫。

Questions for discussion：

1. What do you think of the love between Heathcliff and Catherine?
2. Please point out Catherine's mood when she was dying.
3. Could you understand Heathcliff's love to Catherine? Please share your ideas.

名言摘录

Love is like the wild rose-briar, Friendship like the holly-tree.

——*Emily Brontë*

7 Tess of the D'Urbervilles

Thomas Hardy

Chapter 35 (excerpt)

Her narrative ended; even its re-assertions and secondary explanations were done. Tess's voice throughout had hardly risen higher than its opening tone; there had been no exculpatory phrase of any kind, and she had not wept.

But the complexion even of external things seemed to suffer transmutation as her announcement progressed. The fire in the grate looked impish—demoniacally funny, as if it did not care in the least about her strait. The fender grinned idly, as if it too did not care. The light from the water-bottle was merely engaged in a chromatic problem. All material objects around announced their irresponsibility with terrible iteration. And yet nothing had changed since the moments when he had been kissing her; or rather, nothing in the substance of things. But the essence of things had changed.

When she ceased the auricular impressions from their previous endearments seemed to hustle away into the corners of their brains, repeating themselves as echoes from a time of supremely purblind foolishness.

Clare performed the irrelevant act of stirring the fire; the intelligence had not even yet got to the bottom of him. After stirring the embers[1] he rose to his feet; all the force of her disclosure had imparted itself now. His face had withered. In the strenuousness[2] of his concentration he treadled[3] fitfully[4] on the floor. He could not, by any contrivance[5], think closely enough; that was the meaning of his vague movement. When he spoke it was in the most inadequate, commonplace voice of the many varied tones she had heard from him.

"Tess!"

"Yes, dearest."

"Am I to believe this? From your manner I am to take it as true. O you cannot be out of your mind! You ought to be! Yet you are not... My wife, my Tess—nothing in you warrants[6] such a supposition as that?"

"I am not out of my mind," she said.

"And yet—" He looked vacantly at her, to resume with dazed[7] senses: "Why didn't you tell me before? Ah, yes, you would have told me, in a way—but I hindered you, I remember!"

These and other of his words were nothing but the perfunctory[8] babble of the surface while the depths remained paralyzed. He turned away, and bent over a chair.

Tess followed him to the middle of the room where he was, and stood there staring at him with eyes that did not weep. Presently she slid down upon her knees beside his foot, and from this position she crouched[9] in a heap.

"In the name of our love, forgive me!" she whispered with a dry mouth. "I have forgiven you for the same!"

And, as he did not answer, she said again—

"Forgive me as you are forgiven! I forgive you, Angel."

"You—yes, you do."

"But you do not forgive me?"

"O Tess, forgiveness does not apply to the case! You were one person; now you are another. My God—how can forgiveness meet such a grotesque[10]—prestidigitation[11] as that!"

He paused, contemplating this definition; then suddenly broke into horrible laughter—as unnatural and ghastly[12] as a laugh in hell.

"Don't—don't! It kills me quite, that!" she shrieked[13]. "O have mercy upon me—have mercy!"

He did not answer; and, sickly white, she jumped up.

"Angel, Angel! What do you mean by that laugh?" she cried out.

"Do you know what this is to me?"

He shook his head.

"I have been hoping, longing, praying, to make you happy! I have thought what joy it will be to do it, what an unworthy wife I shall be if I do not! That's what I have felt, Angel!"

"I know that." "I thought, Angel, that you loved me—me, my very self! If it is I you do love, O how can it be that you look and speak so? It frightens me! Having begun to love you, I love you for ever—in all changes, in all disgraces, because you are yourself. I ask no more. Then how can you, O my own husband, stop loving me?"

"I repeat, the woman I have been loving is not you."

"But who?"

"Another woman in your shape."

【注释】

1. ember：灰烬；余烬。
2. strenuousness：费力；吃力。
3. treadle：踩；踏。
4. fitfully：断断续续地；一阵阵地。
5. contrivance：发明；发明物；想出的办法。
6. warrant：证明；正当的理由。
7. dazed：头昏的；茫然的。

8. perfunctory：敷衍的；马虎的；得过且过的。
9. crouch：蹲伏，蜷伏；卑躬屈膝。
10. grotesque：怪异的东西。
11. prestidigitation：变戏法。
12. ghastly：恐怖地；惨白地。
13. shriek：尖声发出；尖叫。

Questions for discussion：

1. What's the character of Tess?
2. What's the theme of this novel?
3. What're the features of Hardy's novels?

名言摘录

New love is brightest, and long love is greatest; but revived love is the tenderest thing known upon earth.

——*Thomas Hardy*

8 Araby

James Joyce

North Richmond Street, being blind, was a quiet street except at the hour when the Christian Brothers' School set the boys free. An uninhabited[1] house of two storeys stood at the blind end, detached from its neighbours in a square ground. The other houses of the street, conscious of decent lives within them, gazed at one another with brown imperturbable[2] faces.

The former tenant of our house, a priest, had died in the back drawing-room. Air, musty[3] from having been long enclosed, hung in all the rooms, and the waste room behind the kitchen was littered with old useless papers. Among these I found a few paper-covered books, the pages of which were curled and damp: *The Abbot*, by Walter Scott, *The Devout Communicant*, and The *Memoirs of Vidocq*. I liked the last best because its leaves were yellow. The wild garden behind the house contained a central apple-tree and a few straggling bushes, under one of which I found the late tenant's rusty bicycle-pump. He had been a very charitable[4] priest; in his will he had left all his money to institutions and the furniture of his house to his sister.

When the short days of winter came, dusk fell before we had well eaten our dinners. When we met in the street the houses had grown sombre[5]. The space of sky above us was the colour of ever-changing violet and towards it the lamps of the street lifted their feeble[6] lanterns. The cold air stung us and we played till our bodies glowed[7]. Our shouts echoed in the silent street. The career of our play brought us through the dark muddy lanes behind the houses, where we ran the gauntlet[8] of the rough tribes from the cottages, to the back doors of the dark dripping gardens where odours arose from the ashpits[9], to the dark odorous stables[10] where a coachman smoothed and combed[11] the horse or shook music from the buckled harness[12]. When we returned to the street, light from the kitchen windows had filled the areas. If my uncle was seen turning the corner, we hid in the shadow until we had seen him safely housed. Or if Mangan's sister came out on the doorstep to call her brother in to his tea, we watched her from our shadow peer up and down the street. We waited to see whether she would remain or go in and, if she remained, we left our shadow and walked up to Mangan's steps resignedly. She was waiting for us, her figure defined by the light from the half-opened door. Her brother always teased her before he obeyed, and I stood by the railings looking at her. Her dress swung as she moved her body, and the soft rope of her hair tossed from side to side.

Every morning I lay on the floor in the front parlour[13] watching her door. The blind was pulled down to within an inch of the sash[14] so that I could not be seen. When she came out on the doorstep my heart leaped. I ran to the hall, seized my books and followed her. I kept her brown figure always in my eye and, when we came near the point at which our ways diverged, I quickened my pace and passed her. This happened morning after morning. I had never spoken to her, except for a few casual words, and yet her name was like a summons to all my foolish blood.

Her image accompanied me even in places the most hostile to romance. On Saturday evenings when my aunt went marketing I had to go to carry some of the parcels. We walked through the flaring streets, jostled by drunken men and bargaining women, amid the curses of labourers, the shrill litanies of shop-boys who stood on guard by the barrels of pigs' cheeks, the nasal chanting of street-singers, who sang a come-all-you about O'Donovan Rossa, or a ballad about the troubles in our native land. These noises converged in a single sensation of life for me: I imagined that I bore my chalice safely through a throng of foes. Her name sprang to my lips at moments in strange prayers and praises which I myself did not understand. My eyes were often full of tears (I could not tell why) and at times a flood from my heart seemed to pour itself out into my bosom. I thought little of the future. I did not know whether I would ever speak to her or not or, if I spoke to her, how I could tell her of my confused adoration. But my body was like a harp and her words and gestures were like fingers running upon the wires.

One evening I went into the back drawing-room in which the priest had died. It was a dark rainy evening and there was no sound in the house. Through one of the broken panes I heard the rain impinge upon the earth, the fine incessant needles of water playing in the sodden beds. Some distant lamp or lighted window gleamed below me. I was thankful that I could see so little. All my senses seemed to desire to veil themselves and, feeling that I was about to slip from them, I pressed the palms of my hands together until they trembled, murmuring: "O love! O love!" many times.

At last she spoke to me. When she addressed the first words to me I was so confused that I did not know what to answer. She asked me was I going to Araby. I forgot whether I answered yes or no. It would be a splendid bazaar; she said she would love to go.

"And why can't you?" I asked.

While she spoke she turned a silver bracelet round and round her wrist. She could not go, she said, because there would be a retreat that week in her convent. Her brother and two other boys were fighting for their caps, and I was alone at the railings. She held one of the spikes, bowing her head towards me. The light from the lamp opposite our door caught the white curve of her neck, lit up her hair that rested there and, falling, lit up the hand upon the railing. At fell over one side of her dress and caught the white border of a petticoat, just visible as she stood at ease.

"It's well for you," she said.

"If I go," I said, "I will bring you something."

What innumerable follies laid waste my waking and sleeping thoughts after that evening! I wished to annihilate the tedious intervening days. I chafed against the work of school. At night in my bedroom and by day in the classroom her image came between me and the page I strove to read. The syllables of the word Araby were called to me through the silence in which my soul luxuriated and cast an Eastern enchantment over me. I asked for leave to go to the bazaar on Saturday night. My aunt was surprised, and hoped it was not some Freemason affair. I answered few questions in class. I watched my master's face pass from amiability to sternness; he hoped I was not beginning to idle. I could not call my wandering thoughts together. I had hardly any patience with the serious work of life which, now that it stood between me and my desire, seemed to me child's play, ugly monotonous child's play.

On Saturday morning I reminded my uncle that I wished to go to the bazaar in the evening. He was fussing at the hallstand, looking for the hat-brush, and answered me curtly:

"Yes, boy, I know."

As he was in the hall I could not go into the front parlour and lie at the window. I felt the house in bad humour and walked slowly towards the school. The air was pitilessly raw and already my heart misgave me.

When I came home to dinner my uncle had not yet been home. Still it was early. I sat staring at the clock for some time and, when its ticking began to irritate me, I left the room. I mounted the staircase and gained the upper part of the house. The high, cold, empty, gloomy rooms liberated me and I went from room to room singing. From the front window I saw my companions playing below in the street. Their cries reached me weakened and indistinct and, leaning my forehead against the cool glass, I looked over at the dark house where she lived. I may have stood there for an hour, seeing nothing but the brown-clad figure cast by my imagination, touched discreetly by the lamplight at the curved neck, at the hand upon the railings and at the border below the dress.

When I came downstairs again I found Mrs Mercer sitting at the fire. She was an old, garrulous woman, a pawnbroker's widow, who collected used stamps for some pious purpose. I had to endure the gossip of the tea-table. The meal was prolonged beyond an hour and still my uncle did not come. Mrs Mercer stood up to go: she was sorry she couldn't wait any longer, but it was after eight o'clock and she did not like to be out late, as the night air was bad for her. When she had gone I began to walk up and down the room, clenching my fists. My aunt said:

"I'm afraid you may put off your bazaar for this night of Our Lord."

At nine o'clock I heard my uncle's latchkey in the hall door. I heard him talking to himself and heard the hallstand rocking when it had received the weight of his overcoat. I could interpret these signs. When he was midway through his dinner I asked him to give me the money to go to the bazaar. He had forgotten.

"The people are in bed and after their first sleep now," he said.

I did not smile. My aunt said to him energetically:

"Can't you give him the money and let him go? You've kept him late enough as it is."

My uncle said he was very sorry he had forgotten. He said he believed in the old saying: "All work and no play makes Jack a dull boy." He asked me where I was going and, when I told him a second time, he asked me did I know The Arab's Farewell to his Steed. When I left the kitchen he was about to recite the opening lines of the piece to my aunt.

I held a florin tightly in my hand as I strode down Buckingham Street towards the station. The sight of the streets thronged with buyers and glaring with gas recalled to me the purpose of my journey. I took my seat in a third-class carriage of a deserted train. After an intolerable delay the train moved out of the station slowly. It crept onward among ruinous houses and over the twinkling river. At Westland Row Station a crowd of people pressed to the carriage doors; but the porters moved them back, saying that it was a special train for the bazaar. I remained alone in the bare carriage. In a few minutes the train drew up beside an improvised wooden platform. I passed out on to the road and saw by the lighted dial of a clock that it was ten minutes to ten. In front of me was a large building which displayed the magical name.

I could not find any sixpenny entrance and, fearing that the bazaar would be closed, I passed in quickly through a turnstile, handing a shilling to a weary-looking man. I found myself in a big hall girded at half its height by a gallery. Nearly all the stalls were closed and the greater part of the hall was in darkness. I recognized a silence like that which pervades a church after a service. I walked into the centre of the bazaar timidly. A few people were gathered about the stalls which were still open. Before a curtain, over which the words Café Chantant were written in coloured lamps, two men were counting money on a salver. I listened to the fall of the coins.

Remembering with difficulty why I had come, I went over to one of the stalls and examined porcelain vases and flowered tea-sets. At the door of the stall a young lady was talking and laughing with two young gentlemen. I remarked their English accents and listened vaguely to their conversation.

"O, I never said such a thing!"

"O, but you did!"

"O, but I didn't!"

"Didn't she say that?"

"Yes. I heard her."

"O, there's a... fib!" Observing me, the young lady came over and asked me did I wish to buy anything. The tone of her voice was not encouraging; she seemed to have spoken to me out of a sense of duty. I looked humbly at the great jars that stood like eastern guards at either side of the dark entrance to the stall and murmured:

"No, thank you."

The young lady changed the position of one of the vases and went back to the two young men. They began to talk of the same subject. Once or twice the young lady glanced at me over her shoulder.

I lingered before her stall, though I knew my stay was useless, to make my interest in her wares seem the more real. Then I turned away slowly and walked down the middle of the bazaar. I allowed the two pennies to fall against the sixpence in my pocket. I heard a voice call from one end of the gallery that the light was out. The upper part of the hall was now completely dark.

Gazing up into the darkness I saw myself as a creature driven and derided by vanity; and my eyes burned with anguish and anger.

【注释】

1. uninhabited：无人居住的；杳无人迹的。
2. imperturbable：冷静的；泰然自若的。
3. musty：发霉的。
4. charitable：慷慨的；仁慈的。
5. sombre：阴沉的；忧郁的；昏暗的。
6. feeble：微弱的，无力的。
7. glow：发热；洋溢；绚丽夺目。
8. gauntlet：长手套；严酷考验。
9. ashpit：火炉的灰坑。
10. stable：马厩；牛棚。
11. comb：梳理；梳头。
12. harness：马具。
13. parlour：客厅；会客室。
14. sash：窗格。

Questions for discussion:

1. How would you characterize elements of setting in the novel? How effectively do the adjectives help to create an atmosphere?
2. How might the bazaar, Araby, be considered symbolically in the story?
3. What does Araby symbolize for the protagonist before he gets there?

名言摘录

Mistakes are the portals of discovery.

——*James Joyce*

9 Mrs. Dalloway

Virginia Woolf

Mrs. Dalloway said she would buy the flowers herself.

For Lucy had her work cut out for her. The doors would be taken off their hinges; Rumpelmayer's men were coming. And then, thought Clarissa Dalloway, what a morning—fresh as if issued to children on a beach.

What a lark! What a plunge! For so it had always seemed to her, when, with a little squeak of the hinges, which she could hear now, she had burst open the French windows and plunged at Bourton into the open air. How fresh, how calm, stiller than this of course, the air was in the early morning; like the flap of a wave; the kiss of a wave; chill and sharp and yet (for a girl of eighteen as she then was) solemn, feeling as she did, standing there at the open window, that something awful was about to happen; looking at the flowers, at the trees with the smoke winding off them and the rooks rising, falling; standing and looking until Peter Walsh said, "Musing among the vegetables?" —was that it? — "I prefer men to cauliflowers" —was that it? He must have said it at breakfast one morning when she had gone out on to the terrace—Peter Walsh. He would be back from India one of these days, June or July, she forgot which, for his letters were awfully dull; it was his sayings one remembered; his eyes, his pocket-knife, his smile, his grumpiness and, when millions of things had utterly vanished—how strange it was! —a few sayings like this about cabbages.

She stiffened a little on the kerb[1], waiting for Durtnall's van to pass. A charming woman, Scrope Purvis thought her (knowing her as one does know people who live next door to one in Westminster); a touch of the bird about her, of the jay, blue-green, light, vivacious, though she was over fifty, and grown very white since her illness. There she perched, never seeing him, waiting to cross, very upright.

For having lived in Westminster—how many years now? Over twenty—one feels even in the midst of the traffic, or waking at night, Clarissa was positive, a particular hush, or solemnity; an indescribable pause; a suspense (but that might be her heart, affected, they said, by influenza) before Big Ben strikes. There! Out it boomed. First a warning, musical; then the hour, irrevocable. The leaden circles dissolved in the air. Such fools we are, she thought, crossing Victoria Street. For Heaven only knows why one loves it so, how one sees it so, making it up, building it round one, tumbling it, creating it every moment afresh; but the veriest frumps, the most dejected of miseries sitting on doorsteps (drink their downfall) do the same; can't be dealt with, she felt positive, by Acts of Parliament for that very reason: they love life². In people's eyes, in the swing, tramp, and trudge; in the bellow and the uproar; the carriages, motor cars, omnibuses, vans, sandwich men shuffling and swinging; brass bands; barrel organs; in the triumph and the jingle and the strange high singing of some aeroplane overhead was what she loved; life; London; this moment of June.

For it was the middle of June. The War was over, except for some one like Mrs. Foxcroft at the Embassy last night eating her heart out because that nice boy was killed and now the old Manor House must go to a cousin; or Lady Bexborough who opened a bazaar, they said, with the telegram in her hand, John, her favourite, killed; but it was over; thank Heaven—over. It was June. The King and Queen were at the Palace. And everywhere, though it was still so early, there was a beating, a stirring of galloping ponies, tapping of cricket bats; Lords, Ascot, Ranelagh and all the rest of it; wrapped in the soft mesh of the grey-blue morning air, which, as the day wore on, would unwind them, and set down on their lawns and pitches the bouncing ponies, whose forefeet just struck the ground and up they sprung, the whirling young men, and laughing girls in their transparent muslins who, even now, after dancing all night, were taking their absurd woolly dogs for a run; and even now, at this hour, discreet old dowagers were shooting out in their motor cars on errands of mystery; and the shopkeepers were fidgeting in their windows with their paste and diamonds, their lovely old sea-green brooches in eighteenth-century settings to tempt Americans (but one must economise, not buy things rashly for Elizabeth), and she, too, loving it as she did with an absurd and faithful passion, being part of it, since her people were courtiers once in the time of the Georges, she, too, was going that very night to kindle and illuminate; to give her party. But how strange, on entering the Park³, the silence; the mist; the hum; the slow-swimming happy ducks; the pouched birds waddling; and who should be coming along with his back against the Government buildings, most appropriately, carrying a despatch⁴ box stamped with the Royal Arms, who but Hugh Whitbread; her old friend Hugh—the admirable Hugh!

"Good-morning to you, Clarissa!" said Hugh, rather extravagantly, for they had known each other as children. "Where are you off to?"

"I love walking in London," said Mrs. Dalloway. "Really it's better than walking in the country."

They had just come up—unfortunately—to see doctors. Other people came to see pictures; go to the opera; take their daughters out; the Whitbreads came "to see doctors." Times without number Clarissa had visited Evelyn Whitbread in a nursing home. Was Evelyn ill again? Evelyn was a good deal out of sorts⁵, said Hugh, intimating by a kind of pout or swell of his very well-covered, manly, extremely handsome, perfectly upholstered body (he was almost too well dressed always, but presumably had to be, with his little job at Court) that his wife had some internal ailment, nothing serious, which, as an old friend, Clarissa Dalloway would quite understand without requiring him to specify. Ah yes, she did of course; what a nuisance; and felt very sisterly and oddly conscious at the same time of her hat. Not the right hat for the early morning, was that it? For Hugh always made her feel, as he bustled on, raising his hat rather extravagantly and assuring her that she might be a girl of eighteen, and of course he was coming to her party to-night, Evelyn absolutely insisted, only a little late he might be after the party at the Palace to which he had to take one of Jim's boys—she always felt a little skimpy beside Hugh; schoolgirlish; but attached to him, partly from having known him always, but she did think him a good sort in his own way, though Richard was nearly driven mad by him, and as for Peter Walsh, he had never to this day forgiven her for liking him.

She could remember scene after scene at Bourton—Peter furious; Hugh not, of course, his match in any way, but still not a positive imbecile as Peter made out; not a mere barber's block. When his old mother wanted him to give up shooting or to take her to Bath he did it, without a word; he was really unselfish, and as for saying, as Peter did, that he had no heart, no brain, nothing but the manners and breeding of an English gentleman, that was only her dear Peter at his worst; and he could be intolerable; he could be impossible; but adorable to walk with on a morning like this.

(June had drawn out every leaf on the trees. The mothers of Pimlico[6] gave suck to their young. Messages were passing from the Fleet[7] to the Admiralty. Arlington Street and Piccadilly seemed to chafe the very air in the Park and lift its leaves hotly, brilliantly, on waves of that divine vitality which Clarissa loved. To dance, to ride, she had adored all that.)

For they might be parted for hundreds of years, she and Peter; she never wrote a letter and his were dry sticks; but suddenly it would come over her, If he were with me now what would he say? —some days, some sights bringing him back to her calmly, without the old bitterness; which perhaps was the reward of having cared for people; they came back in the middle of St. James's Park on a fine morning—indeed they did. But Peter—however beautiful the day might be, and the trees and the grass, and the little girl in pink—Peter never saw a thing of all that. He would put on his spectacles, if she told him to; he would look. It was the state of the world that interested him; Wagner[8], Pope's[9] poetry, people's characters eternally, and the defects of her own soul. How he scolded her! How they argued! She would marry a Prime Minister and stand at the top of a staircase[10]; the perfect hostess he called her (she had cried over it in her bedroom), she had the makings of the perfect hostess, he said.

So she would still find herself arguing in St. James's Park, still making out that she had been right—and she had too—not to marry him. For in marriage a little licence, a little independence there must be between people living together day in day out in the same house; which Richard gave her, and she him. (Where was he this morning for instance? Some committee, she never asked what.) But with Peter everything had to be shared; everything gone into. And it was intolerable, and when it came to that scene in the little garden by the fountain, she had to break with him or they would have been destroyed, both of them ruined, she was convinced; though she had borne about with her for years like an arrow sticking in her heart the grief, the anguish; and then the horror of the moment when some one told her at a concert that he had married a woman met on the boat going to India! Never should she forget all that! Cold, heartless, a prude, he called her. Never could she understand how he cared. But those Indian women did presumably—silly, pretty, flimsy nincompoops. And she wasted her pity. For he was quite happy, he assured her—perfectly happy, though he had never done a thing that they talked of; his whole life had been a failure. It made her angry still.

She had reached the Park gates. She stood for a moment, looking at the omnibuses in Piccadilly.

She would not say of any one in the world now that they were this or were that. She felt very young; at the same time unspeakably aged. She sliced like a knife through everything; at the same time was outside, looking on. She had a perpetual sense, as she watched the taxi cabs, of being out, out, far out to sea and alone; she always had the feeling that it was very, very dangerous to live even one day. Not that she thought herself clever, or much out of the ordinary. How she had got through life on the few twigs of knowledge Fraulein Daniels gave them she could not think. She knew nothing; no language, no history; she scarcely read a book now, except memoirs in bed; and yet to her it was absolutely absorbing; all this; the cabs passing; and she would not say of Peter, she would not say of herself, I am this, I am that.

Her only gift was knowing people almost by instinct, she thought, walking on. If you put her in a room with some one, up went her back like a cat's; or she purred[11]. Devonshire House, Bath House, the house with the china cockatoo, she had seen them all lit up once; and remembered Sylvia, Fred, Sally Seton—such hosts of people; and dancing all night; and the waggons plodding past to market; and driving home across the Park. She remembered once throwing a shilling into the Serpentine[12]. But every one remembered; what she loved was this, here, now, in front of her; the fat lady in the cab. Did it matter then, she asked herself, walking towards Bond Street, did it matter that she must inevitably cease completely; all this must go on without her; did she resent it; or did it not become consoling to believe that death ended absolutely but that somehow in the streets of London, on the ebb and flow of things, here, there, she survived, Peter survived, lived in each other, she being part, she was positive, of the trees at home; of the house there, ugly, rambling all to bits and pieces as it was; part of people she had never met; being laid out like a mist between the people she knew best, who lifted her on their branches as she had seen the trees lift the mist, but it spread ever so far, her life, herself. But what was she dreaming as she looked into

Hatchards' shop window? What was she trying to recover? What image of white dawn in the country, as she read in the book spread open:

Fear no more the heat o' the sun
Nor the furious winter's rages[13].

This late age of the world's experience had bred in them all, all men and women, a well of tears. Tears and sorrows; courage and endurance; a perfectly upright and stoical bearing. Think, for example, of the woman she admired most, Lady Bexborough, opening the bazaar.

There were Jorrocks' *Jaunts and Jollities*; there were *Soapy Sponge* and Mrs. Asquith's *Memoirs* and *Big Game Shooting in Nigeria*[14], all spread open. Ever so many books there were; but none that seemed exactly right to take to Evelyn Whitbread in her nursing home. Nothing that would serve to amuse her and make that indescribably dried-up little woman look, as Clarissa came in, just for a moment cordial; before they settled down for the usual interminable talk of women's ailments. How much she wanted it—that people should look pleased as she came in, Clarissa thought and turned and walked back towards Bond Street, annoyed, because it was silly to have other reasons for doing things. Much rather would she have been one of those people like Richard who did things for themselves, whereas, she thought, waiting to cross, half the time she did things not simply, not for themselves; but to make people think this or that; perfect idiocy she knew (and now the policeman held up his hand) for no one was ever for a second taken in. Oh if she could have had her life over again! she thought, stepping on to the pavement, could have looked even differently!

She would have been, in the first place, dark like Lady Bexborough, with a skin of crumpled leather and beautiful eyes. She would have been, like Lady Bexborough, slow and stately; rather large; interested in politics like a man; with a country house; very dignified, very sincere. Instead of which she had a narrow pea-stick figure[15]; a ridiculous little face, beaked like a bird's. That she held herself well was true; and had nice hands and feet; and dressed well, considering that she spent little. But often now this body she wore (she stopped to look at a Dutch picture), this body, with all its capacities, seemed nothing—nothing at all. She had the oddest sense of being herself invisible; unseen; unknown; there being no more marrying, no more having of children now, but only this astonishing and rather solemn progress with the rest of them, up Bond Street, this being Mrs. Dalloway; not even Clarissa any more; this being Mrs. Richard Dalloway.

Bond Street fascinated her; Bond Street early in the morning in the season; its flags flying; its shops; no splash; no glitter; one roll of tweed in the shop where her father had bought his suits for fifty years; a few pearls; salmon on an iceblock. "That is all," she said, looking at the fishmonger's.

"That is all," she repeated, pausing for a moment at the window of a glove shop where, before the War, you could buy almost perfect gloves. And her old Uncle William used to say a lady is known by her shoes and her gloves. He had turned on his bed one morning in the middle of the War. He had said, "I have had enough." Gloves and shoes; she had a passion for gloves; but her own daughter, her Elizabeth, cared not a straw for either of them.

Not a straw, she thought, going on up Bond Street to a shop where they kept flowers for her when she gave a party. Elizabeth really cared for her dog most of all. The whole house this morning smelt of tar. Still, better poor Grizzle than Miss Kilman; better distemper and tar and all the rest of it than sitting mewed in a stuffy bedroom with a prayer book! Better anything, she was inclined to say. But it might be only a phase, as Richard said, such as all girls go through. It might be falling in love. But why with Miss Kilman? who had been badly treated of course; one must make allowances for that, and Richard said she was very able, had a really historical mind. Anyhow they were inseparable, and Elizabeth, her own daughter, went to Communion; and how she dressed, how she treated people who came to lunch she did not care a bit, it being her experience that the religious ecstasy made people callous (so did causes); dulled their feelings, for Miss Kilman would do anything for the Russians, starved herself for the Austrians, but in private inflicted positive torture, so insensitive was she, dressed in a green mackintosh coat. Year in year out she wore that coat; she perspired; she was never in the room five minutes without making you feel her superiority, your inferiority; how poor she was; how rich you were; how she lived in a slum without a cushion or a bed or a rug or whatever it might be, all her soul rusted with that grievance sticking in it, her dismissal from school during the War—poor embittered unfortunate creature! For it was not her one hated but the idea of her, which undoubtedly had gathered in to itself a great deal that was not Miss Kilman; had become one of those spectres with which one battles in the night; one of those spectres who stand astride us and suck up half our life-blood, dominators and tyrants; for no doubt with another throw of the dice, had the black been uppermost and not the white, she would have loved Miss Kilman! But not in this world. No.

It rasped her, though, to have stirring about in her this brutal monster! to hear twigs cracking and feel hooves planted down in the depths of that leaf-encumbered forest[16], the soul; never to be content quite, or quite secure, for at any moment the brute would be stirring, this hatred, which, especially since her illness, had power to make her feel scraped, hurt in her spine; gave her physical pain, and made all pleasure in beauty, in friendship, in being well, in being loved and making her home delightful rock, quiver, and bend as if indeed there were a monster grubbing at the roots, as if the whole panoply of content were nothing but self love! this hatred!

Nonsense, nonsense! She cried to herself, pushing through the swing doors of Mulberry's the florists.

She advanced, light, tall, very upright, to be greeted at once by buttonfaced Miss Pym, whose hands were always bright red, as if they had been stood in cold water with the flowers.

There were flowers: delphiniums[17], sweet peas, bunches of lilac; and carnations, masses of carnations. There were roses; there were irises. Ah yes—so she breathed in the earthy garden sweet smell as she stood talking to Miss Pym who owed her help, and thought her kind, for kind she had been years ago; very kind, but she looked older, this year, turning her head from side to side among the irises and roses and nodding tufts of lilac with her eyes half closed, snuffing in, after the street uproar, the delicious scent, the exquisite coolness. And then, opening her eyes, how fresh like frilled linen clean from a laundry laid in wicker trays the roses looked; and dark and prim the red carnations, holding their heads up; and all the sweet peas spreading in their bowls, tinged violet, snow white, pale—as if it were the evening and girls in muslin frocks came out to pick sweet peas and roses after the superb summer's day, with its almost blue-black sky, its delphiniums, its carnations, its arum lilies was over; and it was the moment between six and seven when every flower—roses, carnations, irises, lilac—glows; white, violet, red, deep orange; every flower seems to burn by itself, softly, purely in the misty beds; and how she loved the grey-white moths spinning in and out, over the cherry pie, over the evening primroses!

And as she began to go with Miss Pym from jar to jar, choosing, nonsense, nonsense, she said to herself, more and more gently, as if this beauty, this scent, this colour, and Miss Pym liking her, trusting her, were a wave which she let flow over her and surmount that hatred, that monster, surmount it all; and it lifted her up and up when—oh! a pistol shot in the street outside!

"Dear, those motor cars," said Miss Pym, going to the window to look, and coming back and smiling apologetically with her hands full of sweet peas, as if those motor cars, those tyres of motor cars, were all her fault.

【注释】

1. kerb = curb,马路两边镶石人行道。
2. For Heaven only knows…they love life:这句的大意是:只有老天知道为什么人们如此热爱生活,要这样看待生活,装点它,在自己周围建起空中楼阁,再推翻它,使生活每时每刻都充满新意;即使那些衣衫褴褛的老古董,那些最低落的坐在台阶上为穷困潦倒而喝得烂醉的人也这么做。她确信,人们要热爱生活,就连议会法令也无能为力。
3. the Park:指海德公园(Hyde Park)。
4. despatch = dispatch。
5. out of sorts:身体不适。
6. Pimlico:伦敦东南部地区。

7. the Fleet：舰队街，伦敦新闻界和报馆集中的地方。

8. Wagner：理查德·瓦格纳（Richard Wagner），德国作曲家，歌剧的革新者，首创"乐剧"形式，对当时的西方音乐有着决定性的影响。

9. Pope = Alexander Pope（1688 – 1744），英国新古典派诗人。

10. stand at the top of a staircase：指站在楼梯顶上迎接宾客。

11. If you put her…or she purred：大意是：如果你把她和另一个人放在一间屋子里，直觉会使她生气或让她满意。这句话用猫的形象来比拟黛洛维夫人。猫生气时会弓起背，开心时会叫唤。

12. the Serpentine：海德公园里的一个湖。

13. Fear no more…furious winter's rages：这两句诗出自莎士比亚的《辛白林》(*Cymbeline*)。

14. Jaunfs and Jollities…Big Game Shooting in Nigeria：均为 20 世纪 20 年代的流行读物。

15. pea-stick figure：像豆架棍似的身材。

16. leaf-encumbered forest：枝叶繁茂的森林。

17. delphinium：飞燕草属的植物，具有掌状叶形，和色彩各异的花蕾。

Questions for discussion：

1. "Fear no more the heat o' the sun / Nor the furious winter's rages" is a quote from Shakespeare's play Cymbeline. The words are repeated or alluded to many times throughout *Mrs. Dalloway*, by both Clarissa and Septimus. What do the words mean, and why do Clarissa and Septimus repeat them?

2. Woolf created Septimus Warren Smith as a double for Clarissa. In what ways are Clarissa and Septimus different? In what ways are they the same?

3. Conversion is seen as a constant threat in the novel. Which characters wish to convert others, and what are they trying to convert others to? Are some characters more susceptible to conversion than others?

名言摘录

Reading is not merely sympathizing and understanding; it is also criticizing and judging.

——*Virginia Woolf*

10 Sons and Lovers

D. H. Lawrence

CHPTER 9   Defeat of Miriam

Paul was dissatisfied with himself and with everything. The deepest of his love belonged to his mother. When he felt he had hurt her, or wounded his love for her, he could not bear it. Now it was spring, and there was battle between him and Miriam. This year he had a good deal against her. She was vaguely aware of it. The old feeling that she was to be a sacrifice to this love, which she had had when she prayed, was mingled in all her emotions. She did not at the bottom believe she ever would have him. She did not believe in herself primarily: doubted whether she could ever be what he would demand of her. Certainly she never saw herself living happily through a lifetime with him. She saw tragedy, sorrow, and sacrifice ahead. And in sacrifice she was proud, in renunciation[1] she was strong, for she did not trust herself to support everyday life. She was prepared for the big things and the deep things, like tragedy. It was the sufficiency of the small day-life she could not trust.

The Easter[2] holidays began happily. Paul was his own frank self. Yet she felt it would go wrong. On the Sunday afternoon she stood at her bedroom window, looking across at the oak-trees of the wood, in whose branches a twilight was tangled, below the bright sky of the afternoon. Grey-green rosettes of honeysuckle leaves hung before the window, some already, she fancied, showing bud. It was spring, which she loved and dreaded.

Hearing the clack of the gate she stood in suspense.[3] It was a bright grey day. Paul came into the yard with his bicycle, which glittered as he walked. Usually he rang his bell and laughed towards the house. To-day he walked with shut lips and cold, cruel bearing, that had something of a slouch and a sneer in it.[4] She knew him well by now, and could tell from that keen-looking, aloof young body of his what was happening inside him. There was a cold correctness in the way he put his bicycle in its place, that made her heart sink.

She came downstairs nervously. She was wearing a new net blouse that she thought became her. It had a high collar with a tiny ruff, reminding her of Mary, Queen of Scots,[5] and making her, she thought, look wonderfully a woman, and dignified. At twenty she was full-breasted and luxuriously formed. Her face was still like a soft rich mask, unchangeable. But her eyes, once lifted, were wonderful. She was afraid of him. He would notice her new blouse.

He, being in a hard, ironical mood, was entertaining the family to a description of a service given in the Primitive Methodist Chapel,[6] conducted by one of the well-known preachers of the sect. He sat at the head of the table, his mobile face, with the eyes that could be so beautiful, shining with tenderness or dancing with laughter, now taking on one expression and then another, in imitation of various people he was mocking. His mockery always hurt her; it was too near the reality. He was too clever and cruel. She felt that when his eyes were like this, hard with mocking hate, he would spare neither himself nor anybody else. But Mrs. Leivers[7] was wiping her eyes with laughter, and Mr. Leivers, just awake from his Sunday nap, was rubbing his head in amusement. The three brothers sat with ruffled, sleepy appearance in their shirt-sleeves, giving a guffaw from time to time. The whole family loved a "take-off"[8] more than anything.

He took no notice of Miriam. Later, she saw him remark her new blouse, saw that the artist approved, but it won from him not a spark of warmth.[9] She was nervous, could hardly reach the teacups from the shelves.

When the men went out to milk, she ventured to address him personally.

"You were late," she said.

"Was I?" he answered.

There was silence for a while.

"Was it rough riding?" she asked.

"I didn't notice it." She continued quickly to lay the table. When she had finished—

"Tea won't be for a few minutes. Will you come and look at the daffodils?"[10] she said.

He rose without answering. They went out into the back garden under the budding damson-trees.[11] The hills and the sky were clean and cold. Everything looked washed, rather hard. Miriam glanced at Paul. He was pale and impassive. It seemed cruel to her that his eyes and brows, which she loved, could look so hurting.

"Has the wind made you tired?" she asked. She detected an underneath feeling of weariness about him.

"No, I think not," he answered.

"It must be rough on the road—the wood moans so."

"You can see by the clouds it's a south-west wind; that helps me here."

"You see, I don't cycle, so I don't understand," she murmured.

"Is there need to cycle to know that!" he said.

She thought his sarcasms[12] were unnecessary. They went forward in silence. Round the wild, tussocky[13] lawn at the back of the house was a thorn hedge, under which daffodils were craning forward from among their sheaves of grey-green blades. The cheeks of the flowers were greenish with cold. But still some had burst, and their gold ruffled and glowed. Miriam went on her knees before one cluster, took a wild-looking daffodil between her hands, turned up its face of gold to her, and bowed down, caressing it with her mouth and cheeks and brow. He stood aside, with his hands in his pockets, watching her. One after another she turned up to him the faces of the yellow, bursten flowers appealingly, fondling them lavishly all the while.

"Aren't they magnificent?" she murmured.

"Magnificent! It's a bit thick—they're pretty!"

She bowed again to her flowers at his censure of her praise. He watched her crouching, sipping the flowers with fervid kisses.

"Why must you always be fondling things?" he said irritably.

"But I love to touch them," she replied, hurt.

"Can you never like things without clutching them as if you wanted to pull the heart out of them? Why don't you have a bit more restraint, or reserve, or something?"

She looked up at him full of pain, then continued slowly to stroke her lips against a ruffled flower. Their scent, as she smelled it, was so much kinder than he; it almost made her cry.

"You wheedle the soul out of things," he said. "I would never wheedle—at any rate, I'd go straight."

He scarcely knew what he was saying. These things came from him mechanically. She looked at him. His body seemed one weapon, firm and hard against her.

"You're always begging things to love you," he said, "as if you were a beggar for love. Even the flowers, you have to fawn on them—"

Rhythmically, Miriam was swaying and stroking the flower with her mouth, inhaling the scent which ever after made her shudder as it came to her nostrils.

"You don't want to love—your eternal and abnormal craving is to be loved. You aren't positive, you're negative. You absorb, absorb, as if you must fill yourself up with love, because you've got a shortage somewhere."

She was stunned by his cruelty, and did not hear. He had not the faintest notion of what he was saying. It was as if his fretted, tortured soul, run hot by thwarted passion, jetted off these sayings like sparks from electricity[14]. She did not grasp anything he said. She only sat crouched beneath his cruelty and his hatred of her. She never realised in a flash. Over everything she brooded and brooded.

After tea he stayed with Edgar and the brothers, taking no notice of Miriam. She, extremely unhappy on this looked-for holiday, waited for him. And at last he yielded and came to her. She was determined to track this mood of his to its origin. She counted it not much more than a mood.

"Shall we go through the wood a little way?" she asked him, knowing he never refused a direct request.

They went down to the warren[15]. On the middle path they passed a trap, a narrow horseshoe hedge of small fir-boughs[16], baited with the guts of a rabbit. Paul glanced at it frowning. She caught his eye.

"Isn't it dreadful?" she asked.

"I don't know! Is it worse than a weasel with its teeth in a rabbit's throat? One weasel or many rabbits? One or the other must go!"

He was taking the bitterness of life badly. She was rather sorry for him.

"We will go back to the house," he said. "I don't want to walk out."

They went past the lilac-tree, whose bronze leaf-buds were coming unfastened. Just a fragment remained of the haystack, a monument squared and brown, like a pillar of stone. There was a little bed of hay from the last cutting.

"Let us sit here a minute," said Miriam.

He sat down against his will, resting his back against the hard wall of hay. They faced the amphitheatre[17] of round hills that glowed with sunset, tiny white farms standing out, the meadows golden, the woods dark and yet luminous, tree-tops folded over tree-tops, distinct in the distance. The evening had cleared, and the east was tender with a magenta[18] flush under which the land lay still and rich.

"Isn't it beautiful?" she pleaded.

But he only scowled. He would rather have had it ugly just then.

At that moment a big bull-terrier came rushing up, open-mouthed, pranced his two paws on the youth's shoulders, licking his face. Paul drew back, laughing. Bill was a great relief to him. He pushed the dog aside, but it came leaping back.

"Get out," said the lad, "or I'll dot thee one."

But the dog was not to be pushed away. So Paul had a little battle with the creature, pitching poor Bill away from him, who, however, only floundered tumultuously back again, wild with joy. The two fought together, the man laughing grudgingly, the dog grinning all over. Miriam watched them. There was something pathetic about the man. He wanted so badly to love, to be tender. The rough way he bowled the dog over was really loving. Bill got up, panting with happiness, his brown eyes rolling in his white face, and lumbered back again. He adored Paul. The lad frowned.

"Bill, I've had enough o' thee," he said.

But the dog only stood with two heavy paws, that quivered with love, upon his thigh, and flickered a red tongue at him. He drew back.

"No," he said— "no—I've had enough."

And in a minute the dog trotted off happily, to vary the fun.

He remained staring miserably across at the hills, whose still beauty he begrudged. He wanted to go and cycle with Edgar. Yet he had not the courage to leave Miriam.

"Why are you sad?" she asked humbly.

"I'm not sad; why should I be," he answered. "I'm only normal."

She wondered why he always claimed to be normal when he was disagreeable.

"But what is the matter?" she pleaded, coaxing him soothingly.

"Nothing!"

"Nay!" she murmured.

He picked up a stick and began to stab the earth with it.

"You'd far better not talk," he said.

"But I wish to know—" she replied.

He laughed resentfully.

"You always do," he said.

"It's not fair to me," she murmured.

He thrust, thrust, thrust at the ground with the pointed stick, digging up little clods of earth as if he were in a fever of irritation. She gently and firmly laid her hand on his wrist.

"Don't!" she said. "Put it away."

He flung the stick into the currant-bushes[19], and leaned back. Now he was bottled up.

"What is it?" she pleaded softly.

He lay perfectly still, only his eyes alive, and they full of torment.

"You know," he said at length, rather wearily— "you know—we'd better break off."

It was what she dreaded. Swiftly everything seemed to darken before her eyes.

"Why!" she murmured. "What has happened?"

"Nothing has happened. We only realise where we are. It's no good—"

She waited in silence, sadly, patiently. It was no good being impatient with him. At any rate, he would tell her now what ailed him.

"We agreed on friendship," he went on in a dull, monotonous voice. "How often HAVE we agreed for friendship! And yet—it neither stops there, nor gets anywhere else."

He was silent again. She brooded. What did he mean? He was so wearying. There was something he would not yield. Yet she must be patient with him.

"I can only give friendship—it's all I'm capable of—it's a flaw in my make-up. The thing overbalances to one side—I hate a toppling balance. Let us have done."

There was warmth of fury in his last phrases. He meant she loved him more than he her. Perhaps he could not love her. Perhaps she had not in herself that which he wanted. It was the deepest motive of her soul, this self-mistrust. It was so deep she dared neither realise nor acknowledge. Perhaps she was deficient. Like an infinitely subtle shame, it kept her always back. If it were so, she would do without him. She would never let herself want him. She would merely see.

"But what has happened?" she said.

"Nothing—it's all in myself—it only comes out just now. We're always like this towards Easter-time."

He grovelled so helplessly, she pitied him. At least she never floundered in such a pitiable way. After all, it was he who was chiefly humiliated.

"What do you want?" she asked him.

"Why—I mustn't come often—that's all. Why should I monopolise you when I'm not—You see, I'm deficient in something with regard to you—"

He was telling her he did not love her, and so ought to leave her a chance with another man. How foolish and blind and shamefully clumsy he was! What were other men to her! What were men to her at all! But he, ah! she loved his soul. Was HE deficient in something? Perhaps he was.

"But I don't understand," she said huskily. "Yesterday—"

The night was turning jangled and hateful to him as the twilight faded. And she bowed under her suffering.

"I know," he cried, "you never will! You'll never believe that I can't—can't physically, any more than I can fly up like a skylark—"

"What?" she murmured. Now she dreaded.

"Love you."

He hated her bitterly at that moment because he made her suffer. Love her! She knew he loved her. He really belonged to her. This about not loving her, physically, bodily, was a mere perversity[20] on his part, because he knew she loved him. He was stupid like a child. He belonged to her. His soul wanted her. She guessed somebody had been influencing him. She felt upon him the hardness, the foreignness of another influence.

"What have they been saying at home?" she asked.

"It's not that," he answered.

And then she knew it was. She despised them for their commonness, his people. They did not know what things were really worth.

He and she talked very little more that night. After all he left her to cycle with Edgar.

He had come back to his mother. Hers was the strongest tie in his life. When he thought round, Miriam shrank away. There was a vague, unreal feel about her. And nobody else mattered. There was one place in the world that stood solid and did not melt into unreality: the place where his mother was. Everybody else could grow shadowy, almost non-existent to him, but she could not. It was as if the pivot and pole of his life, from which he could not escape, was his mother.

And in the same way she waited for him. In him was established her life now. After all, the life beyond[21] offered very little to Mrs. Morel. She saw that our chance for DOING is here, and doing counted with her. Paul was going to prove that she had been right; he was going to make a man whom nothing should shift off his feet; he was going to alter the face of the earth in some way which mattered. Wherever he went she felt her soul went with him. Whatever he did she felt her soul stood by him, ready, as it were, to hand him his tools. She could not bear it when he was with Miriam. William was dead. She would fight to keep Paul.

And he came back to her. And in his soul was a feeling of the satisfaction of self-sacrifice because he was faithful to her. She loved him first; he loved her first. And yet it was not enough. His new young life, so strong and imperious, was urged towards something else. It made him mad with restlessness[22]. She saw this, and wished bitterly that Miriam had been a woman who could take this new life of his, and leave her the roots. He fought against his mother almost as he fought against Miriam.

It was a week before he went again to Willey Farm. Miriam had suffered a great deal, and was afraid to see him again. Was she now to endure the ignominy of his abandoning her? That would only be superficial and temporary. He would come back. She held the keys to his soul. But meanwhile, how he would torture her with his battle against her. She shrank from it.

However, the Sunday after Easter he came to tea. Mrs. Leivers was glad to see him. She gathered something was fretting him, that he found things hard. He seemed to drift to her for comfort. And she was good to him. She did him that great kindness of treating him almost with reverence.

He met her with the young children in the front garden.

"I'm glad you've come," said the mother, looking at him with her great appealing[23] brown eyes. "It is such a sunny day. I was just going down the fields for the first time this year."

He felt she would like him to come. That soothed him. They went, talking simply, he gentle and humble. He could have wept with gratitude that she was deferential[24] to him. He was feeling humiliated.

At the bottom of the Mow Close they found a thrush's nest[25].

"Shall I show you the eggs?" he said.

"Do!" replied Mrs. Leivers. "They seem such a sign of spring, and so hopeful."

He put aside the thorns, and took out the eggs, holding them in the palm of his hand.

"They are quite hot—I think we frightened her off them," he said.

"Ay, poor thing!" said Mrs. Leivers.

Miriam could not help touching the eggs, and his hand which, it seemed to her, cradled them so well.

"Isn't it a strange warmth!" she murmured, to get near him.

"Blood heat," he answered.

She watched him putting them back, his body pressed against the hedge, his arm reaching slowly through the thorns, his hand folded carefully over the eggs. He was concentrated on the act. Seeing him so, she loved him; he seemed so simple and sufficient to himself. And she could not get to him.

After tea she stood hesitating at the bookshelf. He took "Tartarin de Tarascon"[26]. Again they sat on the bank of hay at the foot of the stack. He read a couple of pages, but without any heart for it. Again the dog came racing up to repeat the fun of the other day. He shoved his muzzle[27] in the man's chest. Paul fingered his ear for a moment. Then he pushed him away.

"Go away, Bill," he said. "I don't want you."

Bill slunk off, and Miriam wondered and dreaded what was coming. There was a silence about the youth that made her still with apprehension. It was not his furies, but his quiet resolutions that she feared.

Turning his face a little to one side, so that she could not see him, he began, speaking slowly and painfully:

"Do you think—if I didn't come up so much—you might get to like somebody else—another man?"

So this was what he was still harping on.

"But I don't know any other men. Why do you ask?" she replied, in a low tone that should have been a reproach to him.

"Why," he blurted, "because they say I've no right to come up like this—without we mean to marry—"

Miriam was indignant at anybody's forcing the issues between them. She had been furious with her own father for suggesting to Paul, laughingly, that he knew why he came so much.

"Who says?" she asked, wondering if her people had anything to do with it. They had not.

"Mother—and the others. They say at this rate everybody will consider me engaged, and I ought to consider myself so, because it's not fair to you. And I've tried to find out—and I don't think I love you as a man ought to love his wife. What do you think about it?"

Miriam bowed her head moodily. She was angry at having this struggle. People should leave him and her alone.

"I don't know," she murmured.

"Do you think we love each other enough to marry?" he asked definitely. It made her tremble.

"No," she answered truthfully. "I don't think so—we're too young."

"I thought perhaps," he went on miserably, "that you, with your intensity in things, might have given me more—than I could ever make up to you. And even now—if you think it better—we'll be engaged."

Now Miriam wanted to cry. And she was angry, too. He was always such a child for people to do as they liked with.

"No, I don't think so," she said firmly.

He pondered a minute.

"You see," he said, "with me—I don't think one person would ever monopolize me—be everything to me—I think never."

This she did not consider.

"No," she murmured. Then, after a pause, she looked at him, and her dark eyes flashed.

"This is your mother," she said. "I know she never liked me."

"No, no, it isn't," he said hastily. "It was for your sake she spoke this time. She only said, if I was going on, I ought to consider myself engaged." There was a silence. "And if I ask you to come down any time, you won't stop away, will you?"

She did not answer. By this time she was very angry.

"Well, what shall we do?" she said shortly. "I suppose I'd better drop French. I was just beginning to get on with it. But I suppose I can go on alone."

"I don't see that we need," he said. "I can give you a French lesson, surely."

"Well—and there are Sunday nights. I shan't stop coming to chapel, because I enjoy it, and it's all the social life I get. But you've no need to come home with me. I can go alone."

"All right," he answered, rather taken aback. "But if I ask Edgar, he'll always come with us, and then they can say nothing."

There was silence. After all, then, she would not lose much. For all their talk down at his home there would not be much difference. She wished they would mind their own business.

"And you won't think about it, and let it trouble you, will you?" he asked.

"Oh no," replied Miriam, without looking at him.

He was silent. She thought him unstable. He had no fixity of purpose, no anchor of righteousness that held him.

"Because," he continued, "a man gets across his bicycle—and goes to work—and does all sorts of things. But a woman broods."

"No, I shan't bother," said Miriam. And she meant it.

It had gone rather chilly. They went indoors.

"How white Paul looks!" Mrs. Leivers exclaimed. "Miriam, you shouldn't have let him sit out of doors. Do you think you've taken cold, Paul?"

"Oh, no!" he laughed.

But he felt done up. It wore him out, the conflict in himself. Miriam pitied him now. But quite early, before nine o'clock, he rose to go.

"You're not going home, are you?" asked Mrs. Leivers anxiously.

"Yes," he replied. "I said I'd be early." He was very awkward.

"But this IS early," said Mrs. Leivers.

Miriam sat in the rocking-chair, and did not speak. He hesitated, expecting her to rise and go with him to the barn as usual for his bicycle. She remained as she was. He was at a loss.

"Well—good-night, all!" he faltered.

She spoke her good-night along with all the others. But as he went past the window he looked in. She saw him pale, his brows knit slightly in a way that had become constant with him, his eyes dark with pain.

She rose and went to the doorway to wave good-bye to him as he passed through the gate. He rode slowly under the pine-trees, feeling a cur and a miserable wretch. His bicycle went tilting down the hills at random. He thought it would be a relief to break one's neck.

Two days later he sent her up a book and a little note, urging her to read and be busy.

At this time he gave all his friendship to Edgar. He loved the family so much, he loved the farm so much; it was the dearest place on earth to him. His home was not so lovable. It was his mother. But then he would have been just as happy with his mother anywhere. Whereas Willey Farm he loved passionately. He loved the little pokey kitchen, where men's boots tramped, and the dog slept with one eye open for fear of being trodden on; where the lamp hung over the table at night, and everything was so silent. He loved Miriam's long, low parlour, with its atmosphere of romance, its flowers, its books, its high rosewood piano. He loved the gardens and the buildings that stood with their scarlet roofs on the naked edges of the fields, crept towards the wood as if for cosiness, the wild country scooping down a valley and up the uncultured hills of the other side. Only to be there was an exhilaration and a joy to him. He loved Mrs. Leivers, with her unworldliness and her quaint cynicism; he loved Mr. Leivers, so warm and young and lovable; he loved Edgar, who lit up when he came, and the boys and the children and Bill—even the sow Circe and the Indian game-cock called Tippoo. All this besides Miriam. He could not give it up.

So he went as often, but he was usually with Edgar. Only all the family, including the father, joined in charades and games at evening. And later, Miriam drew them together, and they read *Macbeth* out of penny books, taking parts. It was great excitement. Miriam was glad, and Mrs. Leivers was glad, and Mr. Leivers enjoyed it. Then they all learned songs together from *tonic sol-fa*, singing in a circle round the fire. But now Paul was very rarely alone with Miriam. She waited. When she and Edgar and he walked home together from chapel or from the literary society in Bestwood, she knew his talk, so passionate and so unorthodox nowadays, was for her. She did envy Edgar, however, his cycling with Paul, his Friday nights, his days working in the fields. For her Friday nights and her French lessons were gone. She was nearly always alone, walking, pondering in the wood, reading, studying, dreaming, waiting. And he wrote to her frequently.

One Sunday evening they attained to their old rare harmony. Edgar had stayed to Communion—he wondered what it was like—with Mrs. Morel. So Paul came on alone with Miriam to his home. He was more or less under her spell again. As usual, they were discussing the sermon. He was setting now full sail towards Agnosticism[28], but such a religious Agnosticism that Miriam did not suffer so badly. They were at the Renan Vie de Jesus[29] stage. Miriam was the threshing-floor on which he threshed out all his beliefs. While he trampled his ideas upon her soul, the truth came out for him. She alone was his threshing-floor. She alone helped him towards realization. Almost impassive, she submitted to his argument and expounding. And somehow, because of her, he gradually realized where he was wrong. And what he realized, she realized. She felt he could not do without her.

They came to the silent house. He took the key out of the scullery window, and they entered. All the time he went on with his discussion. He lit the gas, mended the fire, and brought her some cakes from the pantry. She sat on the sofa, quietly, with a plate on her knee. She wore a large white hat with some pinkish flowers. It was a cheap hat, but he liked it. Her face beneath was still and pensive, golden-brown and ruddy. Always her ears were hid in her short curls. She watched him.

She liked him on Sundays. Then he wore a dark suit that showed the lithe movement of his body. There was a clean, clear-cut look about him. He went on with his thinking to her. Suddenly he reached for a Bible. Miriam liked the way he reached up—so sharp, straight to the mark. He turned the pages quickly, and read her a chapter of St. John[30]. As he sat in the armchair reading, intent, his voice only thinking, she felt as if he were using her unconsciously as a man uses his tools at some work he is bent on. She loved it. And the wistfulness of his voice was like a reaching to something, and it was as if she were what he reached with. She sat back on the sofa away from him, and yet feeling herself the very instrument his hand grasped. It gave her great pleasure.

Then he began to falter and to get self-conscious. And when he came to the verse, "A woman, when she is in travail, hath sorrow because her hour is come", he missed it out. Miriam had felt him growing uncomfortable. She shrank when the well-known words did not follow. He went on reading, but she did not hear. A grief and shame made her bend her head. Six months ago he would have read it simply. Now there was a scotch in his running with her. Now she felt there was really something hostile between them, something of which they were ashamed.

She ate her cake mechanically. He tried to go on with his argument, but could not get back the right note. Soon Edgar came in. Mrs. Morel had gone to her friends'. The three set off to Willey Farm.

Miriam brooded over his split with her. There was something else he wanted. He could not be satisfied; he could give her no peace. There was between them now always a ground for strife. She wanted to prove him. She believed that his chief need in life was herself. If she could prove it, both to herself and to him, the rest might go; she could simply trust to the future.

So in May she asked him to come to Willey Farm and meet Mrs. Dawes. There was something he hankered after. She saw him, whenever they spoke of Clara Dawes, rouse and get slightly angry. He said he did not like her. Yet he was keen to know about her. Well, he should put himself to the test. She believed that there were in him desires for higher things, and desires for lower, and that the desire for the higher would conquer. At any rate, he should try. She forgot that her "higher" and "lower" were arbitrary.

He was rather excited at the idea of meeting Clara at Willey Farm. Mrs. Dawes came for the day. Her heavy, dun-coloured hair was coiled on top of her head. She wore a white blouse and navy skirt, and somehow, wherever she was, seemed to make things look paltry and insignificant. When she was in the room, the kitchen seemed too small and mean altogether. Miriam's beautiful twilighty parlour looked stiff and stupid. All the Leivers were eclipsed like candles. They found her rather hard to put up with. Yet she was perfectly amiable, but indifferent, and rather hard.

Paul did not come till afternoon. He was early. As he swung off his bicycle, Miriam saw him look round at the house eagerly. He would be disappointed if the visitor had not come. Miriam went out to meet him, bowing her head because of the sunshine. Nasturtiums[31] were coming out crimson under the cool green shadow of their leaves. The girl stood, dark-haired, glad to see him.

"Hasn't Clara come?" he asked.

"Yes," replied Miriam in her musical tone. "She's reading."

He wheeled his bicycle into the barn. He had put on a handsome tie, of which he was rather proud, and socks to match.

"She came this morning?" he asked.

"Yes," replied Miriam, as she walked at his side. "You said you'd bring me that letter from the man at Liberty's[32]. Have you remembered?"

"Oh, dash, no!" he said. "But nag at me till you get it."

"I don't like to nag at you."

"Do it whether or not. And is she any more agreeable?" he continued.

"You know I always think she is quite agreeable."

He was silent. Evidently his eagerness to be early to-day had been the newcomer. Miriam already began to suffer. They went together towards the house. He took the clips off his trousers, but was too lazy to brush the dust from his shoes, in spite of the socks and tie.

Clara sat in the cool parlour reading. He saw the nape of her white neck, and the fine hair lifted from it. She rose, looking at him indifferently. To shake hands she lifted her arm straight, in a manner that seemed at once to keep him at a distance, and yet to fling something to him. He noticed how her breasts swelled inside her blouse, and how her shoulder curved handsomely under the thin muslin at the top of her arm.

"You have chosen a fine day," he said.

"It happens so," she said.

"Yes," he said; "I am glad."

She sat down, not thanking him for his politeness.

"What have you been doing all morning?" asked Paul of Miriam.

"Well, you see," said Miriam, coughing huskily, "Clara only came with father—and so—she's not been here very long."

Clara sat leaning on the table, holding aloof. He noticed her hands were large, but well kept. And the skin on them seemed almost coarse, opaque, and white, with fine golden hairs. She did not mind if he observed her hands. She intended to scorn him. Her heavy arm lay negligently on the table. Her mouth was closed as if she were offended, and she kept her face slightly averted.

"You were at Margaret Bonford's meeting the other evening," he said to her.

Miriam did not know this courteous Paul. Clara glanced at him.

"Yes," she said.

"Why," asked Miriam, "how do you know?"

"I went in for a few minutes before the train came," he answered.

Clara turned away again rather disdainfully.

"I think she's a lovable little woman," said Paul.

"Margaret Bonford!" exclaimed Clara. "She's a great deal cleverer than most men."

"Well, I didn't say she wasn't," he said, deprecating. "She's lovable for all that."

"And, of course, that is all that matters," said Clara witheringly.

He rubbed his head, rather perplexed, rather annoyed.

"I suppose it matters more than her cleverness," he said; "which, after all, would never get her to heaven."

"It's not heaven she wants to get—it's her fair share on earth," retorted Clara. She spoke as if he were responsible for some deprivation which Miss Bonford suffered.

"Well," he said, "I thought she was warm, and awfully nice—only too frail. I wished she was sitting comfortably in peace—"

"'Darning her husband's stockings,'" said Clara scathingly.

"I'm sure she wouldn't mind darning even my stockings," he said. "And I'm sure she'd do them well. Just as I wouldn't mind blacking her boots if she wanted me to."

But Clara refused to answer this sally of his. He talked to Miriam for a little while. The other woman held aloof.

"Well," he said, "I think I'll go and see Edgar. Is he on the land?"

"I believe," said Miriam, "he's gone for a load of coal. He should be back directly."

"Then," he said, "I'll go and meet him."

Miriam dared not propose anything for the three of them. He rose and left them.

On the top road, where the gorse was out, he saw Edgar walking lazily beside the mare, who nodded her white-starred forehead as she dragged the clanking load of coal. The young farmer's face lighted up as he saw his friend. Edgar was good-looking, with dark, warm eyes. His clothes were old and rather disreputable, and he walked with considerable pride.

"Hello!" he said, seeing Paul bareheaded. "Where are you going?"

"Came to meet you. Can't stand 'Nevermore.'"

Edgar's teeth flashed in a laugh of amusement.

"Who is 'Nevermore'?" he asked.

"The lady—Mrs. Dawes—it ought to be Mrs. The Raven that quothed 'Nevermore.'"

Edgar laughed with glee.

"Don't you like her?" he asked.

"Not a fat lot," said Paul. "Why, do you?"

"No!" The answer came with a deep ring of conviction. "No!" Edgar pursed up his lips. "I can't say she's much in my line." He mused a little. Then: "But why do you call her 'Nevermore'?" he asked.

"Well," said Paul, "if she looks at a man she says haughtily 'Nevermore,' and if she looks at herself in the looking-glass she says disdainfully 'Nevermore,' and if she thinks back she says it in disgust, and if she looks forward she says it cynically."

Edgar considered this speech, failed to make much out of it, and said, laughing: "You think she's a man-hater?"

"SHE thinks she is," replied Paul.

"But you don't think so?"

"No," replied Paul.

"Wasn't she nice with you, then?"

"Could you imagine her NICE with anybody?" asked the young man.

Edgar laughed. Together they unloaded the coal in the yard. Paul was rather self-conscious, because he knew Clara could see if she looked out of the window. She didn't look.

On Saturday afternoons the horses were brushed down and groomed. Paul and Edgar worked together, sneezing with the dust that came from the pelts of Jimmy and

Flower.

"Do you know a new song to teach me?" said Edgar.

He continued to work all the time. The back of his neck was sun-red when he bent down, and his fingers that held the brush were thick. Paul watched him sometimes.

"'Mary Morrison'?" suggested the younger.

Edgar agreed. He had a good tenor voice, and he loved to learn all the songs his friend could teach him, so that he could sing whilst he was carting. Paul had a very indifferent baritone voice, but a good ear. However, he sang softly, for fear of Clara. Edgar repeated the line in a clear tenor. At times they both broke off to sneeze, and first one, then the other, abused his horse.

Miriam was impatient of men. It took so little to amuse them—even Paul. She thought it anomalous in him that he could be so thoroughly absorbed in a triviality.

It was tea-time when they had finished.

"What song was that?" asked Miriam.

Edgar told her. The conversation turned to singing.

"We have such jolly times," Miriam said to Clara.

Mrs. Dawes ate her meal in a slow, dignified way. Whenever the men were present she grew distant.

"Do you like singing?" Miriam asked her.

"If it is good," she said.

Paul, of course, coloured.

"You mean if it is high-class and trained?" he said.

"I think a voice needs training before the singing is anything," she said.

"You might as well insist on having people's voices trained before you allowed them to talk," he replied. "Really, people sing for their own pleasure, as a rule."

"And it may be for other people's discomfort."

"Then the other people should have flaps to their ears," he replied.

The boys laughed. There was a silence. He flushed deeply, and ate in silence.

After tea, when all the men had gone but Paul, Mrs. Leivers said to Clara:

"And you find life happier now?"

"Infinitely."

"And you are satisfied?"

"So long as I can be free and independent."

"And you don't MISS anything in your life?" asked Mrs. Leivers gently.

"I've put all that behind me."

Paul had been feeling uncomfortable during this discourse. He got up.

"You'll find you're always tumbling over the things you've put behind you," he said. Then he took his departure to the cowsheds. He felt he had been witty, and his manly pride was high. He whistled as he went down the brick track.

Miriam came for him a little later to know if he would go with Clara and her for a walk. They set off down to Strelley Mill Farm. As they were going beside the brook, on the Willey Water side, looking through the brake at the edge of the wood, where pink campions[33] glowed under a few sunbeams, they saw, beyond the tree-trunks and the thin hazel bushes, a man leading a great bay horse through the gullies. The big red beast seemed to dance romantically through that dimness of green hazel drift, away there where the air was shadowy, as if it were in the past, among the fading bluebells that might have bloomed for Deidre or Iseult.

The three stood charmed.

"What a treat to be a knight," he said, "and to have a pavilion here."

"And to have us shut up safely?" replied Clara.

"Yes," he answered, "singing with your maids at your broidery. I would carry your banner of white and green and heliotrope. I would have 'W. S. P. U.' emblazoned on my shield, beneath a woman rampant."

"I have no doubt," said Clara, "that you would much rather fight for a woman than let her fight for herself."

"I would. When she fights for herself she seems like a dog before a looking-glass, gone into a mad fury with its own shadow."

"And YOU are the looking-glass?" she asked, with a curl of the lip.

"Or the shadow," he replied.

"I am afraid," she said, "that you are too clever."

"Well, I leave it to you to be GOOD," he retorted, laughing. "Be good, sweet maid, and just let ME be clever."

But Clara wearied of his flippancy. Suddenly, looking at her, he saw that the upward lifting of her face was misery and not scorn. His heart grew tender for everybody. He turned and was gentle with Miriam, whom he had neglected till then.

At the wood's edge they met Limb, a thin, swarthy man of forty, tenant of Strelley Mill, which he ran as a cattle-raising farm. He held the halter of the powerful stallion indifferently, as if he were tired. The three stood to let him pass over the stepping-stones of the first brook. Paul admired that so large an animal should walk on such springy toes, with an endless excess of vigour. Limb pulled up before them.

"Tell your father, Miss Leivers," he said, in a peculiar piping voice, "that his young beas'es 'as broke that bottom fence three days an' runnin'."

"Which?" asked Miriam, tremulous.

The great horse breathed heavily, shifting round its red flanks, and looking suspiciously with its wonderful big eyes upwards from under its lowered head and falling mane.

"Come along a bit," replied Limb, "an' I'll show you."

The man and the stallion went forward. It danced sideways, shaking its white fetlocks and looking frightened, as it felt itself in the brook.

"No hanky-panky[34] in'," said the man affectionately to the beast.

It went up the bank in little leaps, then splashed finely through the second brook. Clara, walking with a kind of sulky abandon, watched it half-fascinated, half-contemptuous. Limb stopped and pointed to the fence under some willows.

"There, you see where they got through," he said. "My man's druv 'em back three times."

"Yes," answered Miriam, colouring as if she were at fault.

"Are you comin' in?" asked the man.

"No, thanks; but we should like to go by the pond."

"Well, just as you've a mind," he said.

The horse gave little whinneys of pleasure at being so near home.

"He is glad to be back," said Clara, who was interested in the creature.

"Yes—'e 's been a tidy step to-day."

They went through the gate, and saw approaching them from the big farmhouse a smallish, dark, excitable-looking woman of about thirty-five. Her hair was touched with grey, her dark eyes looked wild. She walked with her hands behind her back. Her brother went forward. As it saw her, the big bay stallion whinneyed again. She came up excitedly.

"Are you home again, my boy!" she said tenderly to the horse, not to the man. The great beast shifted round to her, ducking his head. She smuggled into his mouth the wrinkled yellow apple she had been hiding behind her back, then she kissed him near the eyes. He gave a big sigh of pleasure. She held his head in her arms against her breast.

"Isn't he splendid!" said Miriam to her.

Miss Limb looked up. Her dark eyes glanced straight at Paul.

"Oh, good-evening, Miss Leivers," she said. "It's ages since you've been down."

Miriam introduced her friends.

"Your horse IS a fine fellow!" said Clara.

"Isn't he!" Again she kissed him. "As loving as any man!"

"More loving than most men, I should think," replied Clara.

"He's a nice boy!" cried the woman, again embracing the horse.

Clara, fascinated by the big beast, went up to stroke his neck.

"He's quite gentle," said Miss Limb. "Don't you think big fellows are?"

"He's a beauty!" replied Clara.

She wanted to look in his eyes. She wanted him to look at her.

"It's a pity he can't talk," she said.

"Oh, but he can—all but," replied the other woman.

Then her brother moved on with the horse.

"Are you coming in? DO come in, Mr. —I didn't catch it."

"Morel," said Miriam. "No, we won't come in, but we should like to go by the mill-pond."

"Yes—yes, do. Do you fish, Mr. Morel?"

"No," said Paul.

"Because if you do you might come and fish any time," said Miss Limb. "We scarcely see a soul from week's end to week's end. I should be thankful."

"What fish are there in the pond?" he asked.

They went through the front garden, over the sluice, and up the steep bank to the pond, which lay in shadow, with its two wooded islets. Paul walked with Miss Limb.

"I shouldn't mind swimming here," he said.

"Do," she replied. "Come when you like. My brother will be awfully pleased to talk with you. He is so quiet, because there is no one to talk to. Do come and swim."

Clara came up.

"It's a fine depth," she said, "and so clear."

"Yes," said Miss Limb.

"Do you swim?" said Paul. "Miss Limb was just saying we could come when we liked."

"Of course there's the farm-hands," said Miss Limb.

They talked a few moments, then went on up the wild hill, leaving the lonely, haggard-eyed woman on the bank.

The hillside was all ripe with sunshine. It was wild and tussocky, given over to rabbits. The three walked in silence. Then:

"She makes me feel uncomfortable," said Paul.

"You mean Miss Limb?" asked Miriam. "Yes."

"What's a matter with her? Is she going dotty with being too lonely?"

"Yes," said Miriam. "It's not the right sort of life for her. I think it's cruel to bury her there. I really ought to go and see her more. But—she upsets me."

"She makes me feel sorry for her—yes, and she bothers me," he said.

"I suppose," blurted Clara suddenly, "she wants a man."

The other two were silent for a few moments.

"But it's the loneliness sends her cracked," said Paul.

Clara did not answer, but strode on uphill. She was walking with her hand hanging, her legs swinging as she kicked through the dead thistles and the tussocky grass, her arms hanging loose. Rather than walking, her handsome body seemed to be blundering up the hill. A hot wave went over Paul. He was curious about her. Perhaps life had been cruel to her. He forgot Miriam, who was walking beside him talking to him. She glanced at him, finding he did not answer her. His eyes were fixed ahead on

Clara.

"Do you still think she is disagreeable?" she asked.

He did not notice that the question was sudden. It ran with his thoughts.

"Something's the matter with her," he said.

"Yes," answered Miriam.

They found at the top of the hill a hidden wild field, two sides of which were backed by the wood, the other sides by high loose hedges of hawthorn and elder bushes. Between these overgrown bushes were gaps that the cattle might have walked through had there been any cattle now. There the turf was smooth as velveteen, padded and holed by the rabbits. The field itself was coarse, and crowded with tall, big cowslips that had never been cut. Clusters of strong flowers rose everywhere above the coarse tussocks of bent. It was like a roadstead crowded with tan, fairy shipping.

"Ah!" cried Miriam, and she looked at Paul, her dark eyes dilating. He smiled. Together they enjoyed the field of flowers. Clara, a little way off, was looking at the cowslips disconsolately. Paul and Miriam stayed close together, talking in subdued tones. He kneeled on one knee, quickly gathering the best blossoms, moving from tuft to tuft restlessly, talking softly all the time. Miriam plucked the flowers lovingly, lingering over them. He always seemed to her too quick and almost scientific. Yet his bunches had a natural beauty more than hers. He loved them, but as if they were his and he had a right to them. She had more reverence for them: they held something she had not.

The flowers were very fresh and sweet. He wanted to drink them. As he gathered them, he ate the little yellow trumpets. Clara was still wandering about disconsolately. Going towards her, he said:

"Why don't you get some?"

"I don't believe in it. They look better growing."

"But you'd like some?"

"They want to be left."

"I don't believe they do."

"I don't want the corpses of flowers about me," she said.

"That's a stiff, artificial notion," he said. "They don't die any quicker in water than on their roots. And besides, they LOOK nice in a bowl—they look jolly. And you only call a thing a corpse because it looks corpse-like."

"Whether it is one or not?" she argued.

"It isn't one to me. A dead flower isn't a corpse of a flower."

Clara now ignored him.

"And even so—what right have you to pull them?" she asked.

"Because I like them, and want them—and there's plenty of them."

"And that is sufficient?"

"Yes. Why not? I'm sure they'd smell nice in your room in Nottingham."

"And I should have the pleasure of watching them die."

"But then—it does not matter if they do die."

Whereupon he left her, and went stooping over the clumps of tangled flowers which thickly sprinkled the field like pale, luminous foam-clots. Miriam had come close. Clara was kneeling, breathing some scent from the cowslips.

"I think," said Miriam, "if you treat them with reverence you don't do them any harm. It is the spirit you pluck them in that matters."

"Yes," he said. "But no, you get 'em because you want 'em, and that's all." He held out his bunch.

Miriam was silent. He picked some more.

"Look at these!" he continued; "sturdy and lusty like little trees and like boys with fat legs."

Clara's hat lay on the grass not far off. She was kneeling, bending forward still to smell the flowers. Her neck gave him a sharp pang, such a beautiful thing, yet not proud of itself just now. Her breasts swung slightly in her blouse. The arching curve of her back was beautiful and strong; she wore no stays. Suddenly, without knowing, he was scattering a handful of cowslips over her hair and neck, saying:

"Ashes to ashes, and dust to dust,

If the Lord won't have you the devil must."

The chill flowers fell on her neck. She looked up at him, with almost pitiful, scared grey eyes, wondering what he was doing. Flowers fell on her face, and she shut her eyes.

Suddenly, standing there above her, he felt awkward.

"I thought you wanted a funeral," he said, ill at ease.

Clara laughed strangely, and rose, picking the cowslips from her hair. She took up her hat and pinned it on. One flower had remained tangled in her hair. He saw, but would not tell her. He gathered up the flowers he had sprinkled over her.

At the edge of the wood the bluebells had flowed over into the field and stood there like flood-water. But they were fading now. Clara strayed up to them. He wandered after her. The bluebells pleased him.

"Look how they've come out of the wood!" he said.

Then she turned with a flash of warmth and of gratitude.

"Yes," she smiled.

His blood beat up.

"It makes me think of the wild men of the woods, how terrified they would be when they got breast to breast with the open space."

"Do you think they were?" she asked.

"I wonder which was more frightened among old tribes—those bursting out of their darkness of woods upon all the space of light, or those from the open tiptoeing into the forests."

"I should think the second," she answered.

"Yes, you DO feel like one of the open space sort, trying to force yourself into the dark, don't you?"

"How should I know?" she answered queerly.

The conversation ended there.

The evening was deepening over the earth. Already the valley was full of shadow. One tiny square of light stood opposite at Crossleigh Bank Farm. Brightness was swimming on the tops of the hills. Miriam came up slowly, her face in her big, loose bunch of flowers, walking ankle-deep through the scattered froth of the cowslips. Beyond her the trees were coming into shape, all shadow.

"Shall we go?" she asked.

And the three turned away. They were all silent. Going down the path they could see the light of home right across, and on the ridge of the hill a thin dark outline with little lights, where the colliery village touched the sky.

"It has been nice, hasn't it?" he asked.

Miriam murmured assent. Clara was silent.

"Don't you think so?" he persisted.

But she walked with her head up, and still did not answer. He could tell by the way she moved, as if she didn't care, that she suffered.

At this time Paul took his mother to Lincoln. She was bright and enthusiastic as ever, but as he sat opposite her in the railway carriage, she seemed to look frail. He had a momentary sensation as if she were slipping away from him. Then he wanted to get hold of her, to fasten her, almost to chain her. He felt he must keep hold of her with his hand.

They drew near to the city. Both were at the window looking for the cathedral.

"There she is, mother!" he cried.

They saw the great cathedral lying couchant above the plain.

"Ah!" she exclaimed. "So she is!"

He looked at his mother. Her blue eyes were watching the cathedral quietly. She seemed again to be beyond him. Something in the eternal repose of the uplifted cathedral, blue and noble against the sky, was reflected in her, something of the fatality. What was, WAS. With all his young will he could not alter it. He saw her face, the skin still fresh and pink and downy, but crow's-feet near her eyes, her eyelids steady, sinking a little, her mouth always closed with disillusion; and there was on her the same eternal look, as if she knew fate at last. He beat against it with all the strength of his soul.

"Look, mother, how big she is above the town! Think, there are streets and streets below her! She looks bigger than the city altogether."

"So she does!" exclaimed his mother, breaking bright into life again. But he had seen her sitting, looking steady out of the window at the cathedral, her face and eyes fixed, reflecting the relentlessness of life. And the crow's-feet near her eyes, and her mouth shut so hard, made him feel he would go mad.

They ate a meal that she considered wildly extravagant.

"Don't imagine I like it," she said, as she ate her cutlet. "I DON'T like it, I really don't! Just THINK of your money wasted!"

"You never mind my money," he said. "You forget I'm a fellow taking his girl for an outing."

And he bought her some blue violets.

"Stop it at once, sir!" she commanded. "How can I do it?"

"You've got nothing to do. Stand still!"

And in the middle of High Street he stuck the flowers in her coat.

"An old thing like me!" she said, sniffing.

"You see," he said, "I want people to think we're awful swells. So look ikey."

"I'll jowl your head," she laughed.

"Strut!" he commanded. "Be a fantail pigeon."

It took him an hour to get her through the street. She stood above Glory Hole, she stood before Stone Bow, she stood everywhere, and exclaimed.

A man came up, took off his hat, and bowed to her.

"Can I show you the town, madam?"

"No, thank you," she answered. "I've got my son."

Then Paul was cross with her for not answering with more dignity.

"You go away with you!" she exclaimed. "Ha! that's the Jew's House. Now, do you remember that lecture, Paul—?"

But she could scarcely climb the cathedral hill. He did not notice. Then suddenly he found her unable to speak. He took her into a little public-house, where she rested.

"It's nothing," she said. "My heart is only a bit old; one must expect it."

He did not answer, but looked at her. Again his heart was crushed in a hot grip. He wanted to cry, he wanted to smash things in fury.

They set off again, pace by pace, so slowly. And every step seemed like a weight on his chest. He felt as if his heart would burst. At last they came to the top. She stood enchanted, looking at the castle gate, looking at the cathedral front. She had quite forgotten herself.

"Now THIS is better than I thought it could be!" she cried.

But he hated it. Everywhere he followed her, brooding. They sat together in the cathedral. They attended a little service in the choir. She was timid.

"I suppose it is open to anybody?" she asked him.

"Yes," he replied. "Do you think they'd have the damned cheek to send us away."

"Well, I'm sure," she exclaimed, "they would if they heard your language."

Her face seemed to shine again with joy and peace during the service. And all the time he was wanting to rage and smash things and cry.

Afterwards, when they were leaning over the wall, looking at the town below, he blurted suddenly:

"Why can't a man have a YOUNG mother? What is she old for?"

"Well," his mother laughed, "she can scarcely help it."

"And why wasn't I the oldest son? Look—they say the young ones have the advantage—but look, THEY had the young mother. You should have had me for your eldest son."

"I didn't arrange it," she remonstrated. "Come to consider, you're as much to blame as me."

He turned on her, white, his eyes furious.

"What are you old for!" he said, mad with his impotence. "WHY can't you walk? WHY can't you come with me to places?"

"At one time," she replied, "I could have run up that hill a good deal better than you."

"What's the good of that to ME?" he cried, hitting his fist on the wall. Then he became plaintive. "It's too bad of you to be ill. Little, it is—"

"Ill!" she cried. "I'm a bit old, and you'll have to put up with it, that's all."

They were quiet. But it was as much as they could bear. They got jolly again over tea. As they sat by Brayford, watching the boats, he told her about Clara. His mother asked him innumerable questions.

"Then who does she live with?"

"With her mother, on Bluebell[35] Hill."

"And have they enough to keep them?"

"I don't think so. I think they do lace work."

"And wherein lies her charm, my boy?"

"I don't know that she's charming, mother. But she's nice. And she seems straight, you know—not a bit deep, not a bit."

"But she's a good deal older than you."

"She's thirty, I'm going on twenty-three."

"You haven't told me what you like her for."

"Because I don't know—a sort of defiant way she's got—a sort of angry way."

Mrs. Morel considered. She would have been glad now for her son to fall in love with some woman who would—she did not know what. But he fretted so, got so furious suddenly, and again was melancholic. She wished he knew some nice woman—She did not know what she wished, but left it vague. At any rate, she was not hostile to the idea of Clara.

Annie, too, was getting married. Leonard had gone away to work in Birmingham[36]. One week-end when he was home she had said to him:

"You don't look very well, my lad."

"I dunno[37]," he said. "I feel anyhow or nohow, ma."

He called her "ma" already in his boyish fashion.

"Are you sure they're good lodgings?" she asked.

"Yes—yes. Only—it's a winder when you have to pour your own tea out—an' nobody to grouse if you team it in your saucer and sup it up. It somehow takes a' the taste out of it."

Mrs. Morel laughed.

"And so it knocks you up?" she said.

"I dunno. I want to get married," he blurted, twisting his fingers and looking down at his boots. There was a silence.

"But," she exclaimed, "I thought you said you'd wait another year."

"Yes, I did say so," he replied stubbornly.

Again she considered.

"And you know," she said, "Annie's a bit of a spendthrift[38]. She's saved no more than eleven pounds. And I know, lad, you haven't had much chance."

He coloured[39] up to the ears.

"I've got thirty-three quid," he said.

"It doesn't go far," she answered.

He said nothing, but twisted his fingers.

"And you know," she said, "I've nothing—"

"I didn't want, ma!" he cried, very red, suffering and remonstrating.

【注释】

1. renunciation：（因道德或宗教原因）克己，自我克制。

2. Easter：复活节，在每年春分月圆后第一个星期日（通常在3月21日或之后几天），是西方的重要节日，是纪念耶稣基督在十字架受刑死后复活的节日。

3. in suspense：悬而未决，处于焦灼等待状态，心神不宁。

4. 译文为：今天他走进来时双唇紧闭，举止冷酷，带着一种懒散、嘲讽的神情。

5. Mary, Queen of Scots：苏格兰女王玛丽·斯图亚特（1542 - 1587），出生六天后即位为苏格兰女王，1558年成为法国王后。1560年丈夫去世，次年回苏格兰亲政。她是狂热的天主教徒，为苏格兰贵族和加尔文教所不满。1567年被废黜，次年逃入英格兰，被伊丽莎白女王囚禁，最终以图谋弑君罪被斩首。16

及 17 世纪的时尚就是穿镶着小轮状绉的高领。

6. Primitive Methodist Chapel：Methodism 指的是卫理公会，又称为卫斯理宗，是基督教新教主要宗派之一。由英国牧师 John Wesley 和其弟 Charles Wesley 于 1738 年在伦敦所创立，该会主张圣洁生活和改善社会，注重在群众中进行传教活动，非常注重个人对教义的接受，主张个人对上帝的信仰。后来卫理公会又发展分出好几个分支，Primitive Methodist Chapel 是其中的一支。该分支于 1811 年创立，也成为卫斯理会守旧派，比较注重在工人阶级中的影响。

7. Mrs. Leivers：是 Miriam 的母亲，也是 Morel 家的朋友。

8. take-off：夸张的模仿。

9. a spark of warmth：一丝激动。

10. daffodil：黄水仙。

11. the budding damson-trees：正在发芽的西洋李子树。

12. sarcasm：讥讽，挖苦。

13. tussocky：草丛的，多丛的。

14. jetted off these saying like sparks from electricity：他的言语就像电火花一样机械地迸发出来。作者劳伦斯在这主要是想强调 Paul 似乎自己不知所云。

15. warren：兔穴；人口拥挤的地区，易迷路的场所。这里指的是一片专门留给兔子生长的地方。

16. fir-bough：枞树树枝。

17. amphitheatre：露天场地。

18. magenta：紫红，洋红。

19. currant-bushes：醋栗灌木。

20. perversity：倔强，任性。

21. the life beyond：指来世，死后在天堂的生活。

22. restlessness：心神不宁，坐立不安。

23. appealing：吸引人的，动人的。

24. deferential：恭敬的，惯于顺从的。

25. thrush's nest：画眉鸟鸟巢。

26. Tartarin de Tarascon：法国 19 世纪现实主义作家阿尔封斯·都德的长篇小说《塔拉斯孔城的达达兰》（1872—1890）。阿尔封斯·都德最为国人熟知的作品是《最后一课》。

27. muzzle：动物的鼻口。

28. Agnosticism：不可知论，是一种唯心主义的认识论，认为除了感觉或现象之外，世界本身是无法认识的。它否认社会发展的客观规律，否认社会实践的作用。

29. The Renan Vie de Jesus：Renan 指的是法国哲学家雷南（Ernest Joseph Renan）（1823 - 1892）。Vie de Jesus 是雷南的一本书《耶稣传》，书的英文名为：*Life of Jesus*（1863）。当时《耶稣传》在法国引起了轰动，全国的人都在寻找耶稣到底是谁。

30. St. John：圣经中的《约翰福音》。
31. Nasturtiums：（植物）旱金莲花。
32. Liberty：是一家位于英国伦敦梅费尔的皇家保证店，从 Oxford Circus 地铁站出来步行约 3 分钟可到达。Liberty 从 19 世纪晚期建立时就以进口日本及东方世界的织品、家具与饰品而闻名，"东方市场"（Easter Bazaar）的称号从那时起就不胫而走。
33. campions：剪秋罗属植物。
34. hanky-panky：【口语】阴谋诡计，把戏，花招，无聊言行。
35. bluebell：野风信子。
36. Birmingham：伯明翰（英国一座城市）。
37. I dunno：【口语】我不知道。
38. spendthrift：挥霍无度的，浪费的。
39. coloured：（因尴尬而）脸红。

Questions for discussion：

1. Lawrence uses the art of symbolism in his novels. He always uses the description of nature to imply the characters' inner qualities of human nature. In these excerpt, there are some examples. Please find some examples, and then think of the effect of these sentences contained in these examples.

2. What do you think of the relationship between Paul and Miriam? Is it the true love? And what kind of influence does Paul's mother exert on their relationship?

3. What do you think of the relationship between the mother, Paul and Miriam? And how would you think of the human nature of Miriam and Paul?

名言摘录

The family you came from isn't as important as the family you are going to have.

——*D. H. Lawrence*

小 说 术 语

1. **Allegory**: a technique whereby abstract qualities are given human shape; in a story there would usually be a second distinct meaning partially hidden behind its literal or visible meaning.

2. **Analepsis**: a technique by which events of a story that should happen later are related at an earlier time. This is often referred to as retrospection or flashback.

3. **Antagonist**: the chief fictional character who is opposed to the protagonist or hero(ine) in a narrative work. The antagonist is usually a villain; yet when the protagonist is evil, the antagonist could be virtuous.

4. **Anti-hero or Anti-heroine**: a main character in a novel who lacks the qualities of traditional heroes and heroines in romances and epics. In Joyce's novel *Ulysses*, Leopold Bloom is such an antiheroic character.

5. **Bildungsroman**: This German term designates a kind of novel that traces the maturational processes of fictional characters. Dickens's novel *David Copperfield* is a good example of this genre.

6. **Context**: the parts surrounding a particular text, giving it fuller meaning. The context could be understood to adjacent linguistic signs or the biographical, social, cultural, and historical circumstances in which it is made.

7. **Dialogue**: verbal exchanges between or among characters in the novel.

8. **Embedded narrative**: a tale within a tale. It is a literary form that is also referred to as frame narrative. Chaucer's *Canterbury Tales* is a good example of this type.

9. **First-person narrative**: a mode of story-telling in which the narrator "I" recounts his/her story, often as a witness or participant. Charlotte Bronte's *Jane Eyre* is a good example of this type.

10. **Focalization**: a narratological term for point of view. It signifies the

perspective through which the events are represented. The traditional omniscient narrator is said to be non-focalized; yet events perceived from the limited perspective of characters are "internally focalized".

11. **Intertextuality**: a term that designates the various relationships that a particular text may have with other texts. The relationships may include allusion, adaptation, translation, etc.

12. **Leitmotif**: a term that designates a frequently repeated phrase, image, symbol, or situation in a literary work, the recurrence of which usually indicates or supports a theme. The repeated references to rings and arches in D. H. Lawrence's novel *The Rainbow* are examples of the use of a leitmotif.

13. **Metafiction**: a kind of fiction that openly talks about its own fictitious status, so that it has self-consciousness about themselves as fictions. In modern novels, novelists may argue about the fictitious nature of his work or discuss the technical troubles they encounter in the process of writing a novel. A good example is John Fowles's *The French Lieutenant's Woman*.

14. **Prolepsis**: a Greek for anticipation. In the novel, it means a "flashforward" or telling a story in advance of its appearance in chronological order.

15. **Third-person narrative**: a mode of storytelling in which the narrator is not a character within the novel, so that all characters within the story are referred to as "he", "she", or "they", though the narrator may occasionally use "we" to convey the voice of the community. Third-person narrators are often omniscient narrators but they may also appear to have limited knowledge of certain events.

16. **Narratology**: a research subject that concerns itself with the study of narrative, with emphasis on the characteristics common to all narratives. It concerns itself less with the details of a particular narrative than with the general principles or building blocks that make the narrative act possible. Narratology as a modern theory is often associated with structuralism.

第三章　英国戏剧选编

导　言

　　戏剧文学是集文学、表演、美术、音乐、舞蹈等多种艺术成分为一体的综合艺术形式。英国的戏剧起源于中世纪教堂的弥撒。9 世纪复活节弥撒中有一段被称为"你找谁"的插曲，一位教士装扮天使守护基督的坟墓，另外 3 位教士装扮成 3 个叫玛丽的妇女来朝拜圣墓，他们对话性的轮唱和表演动作，已具有戏剧的雏形，并由此发展成一种作为教堂礼拜仪式组成部分而演出的戏剧，称为"礼拜剧"。礼拜剧在发展过程中逐步世俗化，从 13 世纪起，由市民代替教士，由拉丁语改用方言，并转移到教堂外演出，情节也日益复杂，增加了市俗的喜剧成分，成为独立的戏剧形式。中世纪英国戏剧脱胎于教堂礼拜仪式，以后逐步摆脱教会影响和宗教色彩。从礼拜剧到奇迹剧，到道德剧，再到插剧的演变过程就是世俗化不断加深的过程，直至文艺复兴戏剧兴起。

　　英国戏剧的第一个黄金时期出现在文艺复兴时代。从 1498 年都铎王朝的建立到 1642 年的资产阶级革命，是英国的文艺复兴时期第一个高峰。而戏剧即代表了此阶段英国文学的最高成就。以克里斯托弗·马洛（1564—1593）为代表的大学才子们借鉴了古罗马戏剧家的"复仇悲剧"模式，在伊丽莎白时代初期流行一时的通俗剧的基础上，创造了一种表现悲剧主人公个人事迹的传奇悲剧。在这些悲剧中，主人公向中世纪社会的清规戒律发起挑战。他们冒着犯下可怕的罪恶和受苦受难的危险，拓展了人们的精神境界，威慑了上天，在战争与抗争中直面死亡。对伊丽莎白时代的英国观众而言，这些悲剧主人公的行为在很大程度上代表了当时具有英雄主义色彩的价值取向。其中，马洛奔放的激情、鲜明的人物性格和探索一切的巨人思想，为英国戏剧作出了独特的贡献。

　　文艺复兴时期的英国戏剧舞台高度繁荣与发展，其中最有影响的贡献即是莎士比亚（1564—1616）戏剧。莎剧一向被认为是西方乃至人类文明和文化的一座高峰，它代表着文艺复兴时期戏剧的杰出典范。他的作品几乎涉及当时所有的重大社会问题，集中表现了人文主义思想，是戏剧化的民族史诗。其中，《哈姆雷特》创作于 1601 年，代表了莎士比亚戏剧的最高成就。莎翁将简单的复仇故事深化成复杂的性格悲剧，显示出更深刻的人性思考的容量，其并行交叉的复杂情节，广阔的社会场景，尤其是对主人公内心冲突的深刻描写，生动地展示了宏伟壮丽的人生画面，而"生存还是毁灭"、"人是万物的灵长"等独白更成为文学史上的经典。莎士比亚的代表作有悲剧《哈姆雷特》、《奥赛罗》、《李尔王》、《麦克白》，喜剧《威尼斯商人》等和一百多首十四行诗。本·琼森说："他不属于一个时代,而属于所有世纪。"

文艺复兴之后,英国戏剧继续发展。在 17—18 世纪,无论是古典主义文学还是启蒙主义文学,英国戏剧已失去了早期尖锐的个人主义色彩及革命性,成为上层人物的时髦的娱乐。从"光荣革命"到"戏剧检查法"阶段,资本主义在英国确立和稳步发展,但戏剧发展平平。直至 19 世纪初浪漫主义运动在欧洲兴起,对戏剧的影响则是产生了统治了英国舞台的情节剧。

19 世纪末到 20 世纪初,英国戏剧逐渐开始复兴。90 年代初,萧伯纳的重要剧本《鳏夫的房产》(1892)、《华伦夫人的职业》(1894)、《巴巴拉少校》(1905) 相继问世,它们不同于流行的情节剧,比前人的作品前进了一大步。萧伯纳揭露了当代社会的尖锐矛盾,在矛盾冲突中表现人物个性,在幽默风趣中寄寓深刻的讽刺。当时英国出现了各种思潮,社会主义、费边主义、女权主义等各自提出社会主张,进行激烈的争论。他笔下的人物机智俏皮,常常在似非而是的反语中揭示真理。他似乎在戏剧中开玩笑,但在玩笑之中揭示出"英国社会出了什么毛病"。萧伯纳正是以莎士比亚为代表的民族戏剧优秀传统的继承者。

与萧伯纳同时代的王尔德另树一帜。王尔德是唯美主义的鼓吹者,但在他的喜剧创作中,却表现出一种现实主义的批判态度。他的《温德米尔夫人的扇子》(1892)、《认真的重要》(1895)等剧作对上层社会的虚伪进行了揭露和嘲讽,但其中尚有情节剧的痕迹。王尔德反对英国戏剧中存在已久的粗制滥造现象,在创作上刻意求工,语言机智风趣,情节的发展出人意料而又轻松自然。风俗喜剧在王尔德的笔下发出了光辉。

20 世纪的英国戏剧重新呈现出繁荣发展的趋势,当代英国剧作家对创新一直孜孜不倦。其中,代表人物爱尔兰剧作家萨缪尔·贝克特(1906—1989),让英国戏剧在新时代呈现出新的特性。贝克特写了数部反映战后西方世界中人类生存和心理状况的先锋戏剧。在剧中,他颠覆戏剧传统要素,开创了一种戏剧新形式"荒诞派戏剧"。他的代表作《等待戈多》从情节、角色、对话、行动及布景等各方面都表现出人的"疏离"这一主题。贝克特因"他那具有新奇形式的小说和戏剧作品使现代人从精神贫困中得到振奋",并且他的戏剧"具有希腊悲剧的净化作用",从而获得 1969 年诺贝尔文学奖。

"二战"以后,以 J. J. 奥斯本(1929—)的《愤怒的回顾》(1956)为标志,出现了英国戏剧的所谓"新潮流"。剧中主人公吉米·波特对周围环境的厌恶反映了战后英国青年的心理,紧张的戏剧性和生动的对话也很有特色,所以此剧立即引起普遍的共鸣和广泛的注意。

1 The Tragical History of the Life and Death of Doctor Faustus

Christopher Marlowe

ACT II, Scene I
(*Enter FAUSTUS in his study*)
FAUSTUS: Now, Faustus, must thou needs be damned;
  Canst thou not be saved!
  What boots it then to think on God or heaven?
  Away with such vain fancies, and despair—
  Despair in God and trust in Belzebub!
  Now go not backward. Faustus, be resolute!
  Why waver'st thou? O, something soundeth in mine ear,
  "Abjure this magic, turn to God again!"
  Ay, and Faustus will turn to God again.
  To God? He loves thee not;
  The god thou serv'st is thine own appetite,
  Wherein is fixed the love of Belzebub!
  To him I'll build an altar and a church,
  And offer lukewarm blood of new-born babes.
(*Enter Good Angel and Bad Angel*)
BAD ANGEL: Go forward, Faustus, in that famous art.
GOOD ANGEL: Sweet Faustus, leave that execrable art.
FAUSTUS: Contrition, prayer, repentance! What of these?
GOOD ANGEL: O, they are means to bring thee unto Heaven!
BAD ANGEL: Rather illusions—fruits of lunacy,
  That makes men foolish that do trust them most.
GOOD ANGEL: Sweet Faustus, think of Heaven and heavenly things.
BAD ANGEL: No, Faustus, think of honour and of wealth.
(*Exeunt Angels.*)
FAUSTUS: Wealth!
  Why, the signory of Embden[1] shall be mine!
  When Mephistophilis shall stand by me,
  What power can hurt thee? Faustus, thou art safe.
  Cast no more doubts! Come, Mephistophilis,

    And bring glad tidings from great Lucifer.
    Is't not midnight? Come, Mephistophilis,
    Veni, veni, Mephistophile![2]
(*Enter* MEPHISTOPHILIS.)
    Now tell me, what saith Lucifer thy lord?
MEPHIST: That I shall wait on Faustus whilst he lives,
    So he will buy my service with his soul.
FAUSTUS: Already Faustus hath hazarded that for thee.
MEPHIST: But, Faustus, thou must bequeath it solemnly,
    And write a deed of gift with thine own blood,
    For that security craves great Lucifer.
    If thou deny it, I will back to hell.
FAUSTUS: Stay Mephistophilis and tell me
    What good will my soul do thy lord?
MEPHIST: Enlarge his kingdom.
FAUSTUS: Is that the reason why he tempts us thus?
MEPHIST: *Solamen miseris socios habuisse doloris.*[3]
FAUSTUS: Why, have you any pain that tortures others?
MEPHIST: As great as have the human souls of men.
    But tell me, Faustus, shall I have thy soul?
    And I will be thy slave, and wait on thee,
    And give thee more than thou hast wit to ask.
FAUSTUS: Ay, Mephistophilis, I give it thee.
MEPHIST: Then, Faustus, stab thy arm courageously
    And bind thy soul that at some certain day
    Great Lucifer may claim it as his own.
    And then be thou as great as Lucifer.
FAUSTUS: [Stabbing his arm.]
    Lo, Mephistophilis, for love of thee,
    Faustus hath cut his arm and with my proper[4] blood
    Assure my soul to be great Lucifer's,
    Chief lord and regent of perpetual night.
    View here the blood that trickles from mine arm,
    And let it be propitious for my wish.
MEPHIST: But Faustus, thou must
    Write it in manner of a deed of gift.
FAUSTUS: Ay, so I will—But, Mephistophilis,
    My blood congeals and I can write no more.
MEPHIST: I'll fetch thee fire to dissolve it straight.

(*Exit.*)

FAUSTUS: What might the staying of my blood portend?
  Is it unwilling I should write this bill?
  Why streams it not, that I may write afresh:
    "Faustus gives to thee his soul"? O there it stayed!
  Why should'st thou not? Is not thy soul thine own?
  Then write again: "Faustus gives to thee his soul."
(*Re-enter MEPHISTOPHILIS with a chafer[5] of coals.*)

MEPHIST: See Faustus, Here's fire. Come, set it on.

FAUSTUS: So now the blood begins to clear again.
  Now will I make an end immediately.

MEPHIST: O, what will not I do to obtain his soul?

FAUSTUS: *Consummatum est*![6] this bill is ended,
  And Faustus hath bequeathed his soul to Lucifer.
  But what is this inscription on mine arm?
  Homo, fuge![7] Whither should I fly?
  If unto God, he'll throw me down to hell.
  My senses are deceived; here's nothing writ:
  I see it plain! Even here is writ
  Homo, fuge! Yet shall not Faustus fly.

MEPHIST: I'll fetch him somewhat to delight his mind.

(*Exit.*)

(*Re-enter MEPHISTOPHILIS with Devils, who give crowns and rich apparel to FAUSTUS, dance, and then depart.*)

FAUSTUS: Speak, Mephistophilis, what means this show?

MEPHIST: Nothing, Faustus, but to delight thy mind
  And to show thee what magic can perform.

FAUSTUS: But may I raise up spirits when I please?

MEPHIST: Ay, Faustus, and do greater things than these.

FAUSTUS: Then Mephistophilis, receive this scroll,
  A deed of gift of body and of soul:
  But yet conditionally that thou perform
  All covenants and articles prescribed between us both.

MEPHIST: Faustus, I swear by hell and Lucifer
  To effect all promises between us both.

FAUSTUS: Then hear me read them:
  On these conditions following:
  First, that Faustus may be a spirit in form and substance.
  Secondly, that Mephistophilis shall be his servant, and at his command.

Thirdly, that Mephistophilis shall do for him and bring him whatsoever he desires.

Fourthly, that he shall be in his chamber or house invisible.

Lastly, that he shall appear to the said John Faustus, at all times in what form or shape soever he pleases:

I, John Faustus of Wertenberg, Doctor, by these presents do give both body and soul to Lucifer, Prince of the East, and his minister, Mephistophilis, and furthermore grant unto them that, twenty-four years being expired, the articles above-written being inviolate[8], full power to fetch or carry the said John Faustus, body and soul, flesh, blood, or goods, into their habitation wheresoever.

By me, John Faustus.

MEPHIST: Speak, Faustus, do you deliver this as your deed?

FAUSTUS: Ay, take it, and the Devil give thee good on it!

MEPHIST: Now, Faustus, ask what thou wilt.

FAUSTUS: First will I question with thee about hell.

Tell me where is the place that men call hell?

MEPHIST: Under the heavens.

FAUSTUS: Ay, but whereabouts?

MEPHIST: Within the bowels of these elements,

Where we are tortured and remain forever;

Hell hath no limits, nor is circumscribed

In one self place; for where we are is hell,

And where hell is there must we ever be.

And, to conclude, when all the world dissolves,

And every creature shall be purified,

All places shall be hell that is not Heaven!

FAUSTUS: Come, I think hell's a fable.

MEPHIST: Ay, think so still, till experience change thy mind.

FAUSTUS: Why, think'st thou, then, that Faustus shall be damned?

MEPHIST: Ay, of necessity, for here's the scroll

Wherein thou hast given thy soul to Lucifer.

FAUSTUS: Ay, and body too; but what of that?

Think'st thou that Faustus is so fond[9] to imagine

That, after this life, there is any pain?

No, these are trifles and mere old wives' tales.

MEPHIST: But, Faustus, I am an instance to prove the contrary,

For I am damned, and am now in hell.

FAUSTUS: How! Now in hell?

Nay, and this be hell, I'll willingly be damned here;

What, sleeping, eating, walking, disputing?
But, leaving off this, let me have a wife,
The fairest maid in Germany,
For I am wanton and lascivious,
And cannot live without a wife.

MEPHIST: How—a wife?
I prithee, Faustus, talk not of a wife.

FAUSTUS: Nay, sweet Mephistophilis, fetch me one, for I will have one.

MEPHIST: Well—thou wilt have one? Sit there till I come:
I'll fetch thee a wife in the Devil's name.

(*Exit.*)

(*Re-enter MEPHISTOPHILIS with a Devil dressed like a woman, with fireworks.*)

MEPHIST: Tell me, Faustus, how dost thou like thy wife?

FAUSTUS: A plague on her for a hot whore!

MEPHIST: Marriage is but a ceremonial toy[10];
If thou lovest me, think no more of it.
I'll cull thee out the fairest courtesans,
And bring them every morning to thy bed;
She whom thine eye shall like, thy heart shall have,
Be she as chaste as was Penelope[11],
As wise as Saba[12], or as beautiful
As was bright Lucifer before his fall.
Here, take this book, peruse it thoroughly:
The iterating[13] of these lines brings gold;
The framing[14] of this circle on the ground
Brings whirlwinds, tempests, thunder and lightning;
Pronounce this thrice devoutly to thyself,
And men in harness[15] shall appear to thee,
Ready to execute what thou desir'st.

FAUSTUS: Thanks, Mephistophilis for this sweet book.
This will I keep as chary as my life.

【注释】

1. signory of Emden: lordship of the rich German port at the mouth of the Ems. 埃姆顿城的权贵

2. Veni, veni, Mephostophile: (Latin) Come, come, Mephostophilis. （拉丁）来啊，来啊，摩菲斯特

3. Solamen...doloris: (Latin) Misery loves company. （拉丁）落难人遇上落难人会觉得安慰

4. proper: own. 拥有
5. chafer: portable grate. 计量单位：盆
6. Consummatum est: (Latin) It is finished! (a blasphemous repetition of Christ's words on the Cross) (拉丁) 写好了
7. Homo fuge!: (Latin) Fly, man! (拉丁) 你逃呀
8. inviolate: unviolated. 不可撤销
9. fond: foolish. 愚蠢
10. toy: trifle. 把戏
11. Penelope: wife of Ulysses, famed for her fidelity. 珀尼洛普（奥德修斯的妻子）
12. Saba: the Queen of Sheba. 示巴女王
13. iterating: repetition. 反复诵读
14. framing: drawing. 画
15. harness: armor. 全副武装

Questions for discussion:

1. What is the function of the Good Angel and the Bad Angel in the play? How are the Good Angel and the Bad Angel related to earlier morality plays? What else in the play is a holdover from the morality plays?

2. What makes Faustus desire to repent? Why do you think he fails to repent?

3. Is Faustus misled by the devils, or is he willfully blind to the reality of his situation?

4. One view of Faustus's story is that he presents some of the intellectual aspirations and impulses to power of a "Renaissance man." Another view sees him as an example of just punishment inflicted upon a godless sinner as in medieval time. Explain these two.

名言摘录

The mind can make a heaven out of hell or a hell out of heaven.

——*Victor Hugo*

2 Hamlet

William Shakespeare

Act III, Scene one[1]
To be, or not to be[2], —that is the question:
Whether 'tis nobler in the mind to suffer
The slings and arrows of outrageous[3] fortune,
Or to take arms against a sea of troubles,
And by opposing end them[4]? To die: to sleep;
No more; and by a sleep to say we end
The heart-ache and the thousand natural shocks
That flesh is heir to[5], 'tis a consummation
Devoutly to be wish'd. To die, to sleep;
To sleep: perchance[6] to dream: ay[7], there's the rub[8];
For in that sleep of death what dreams may come
When we have shuffled off this mortal coil[9],
Must give us pause: there's the respect
That makes calamity of so long life[10];
For who would bear the whips and scorns of time,
The oppressor's wrong, the proud man's contumely[11],
The pangs of despised love, the law's delay[12],
The insolence of office[13], and the spurns[14]
That patient merit of the unworthy takes[15],
When he himself might his quietus make[16]
With a bare bodkin[17]? who would fardels[18] bear,
To grunt[19] and sweat under a weary life,
But that the dread of something after death,
The undiscover'd country[20] from whose bourn[21]
No traveller returns, puzzles the will
And makes us rather bear those ills we have
Than fly to others[22] that we know not of?
Thus conscience does make cowards of us all;
And thus the native hue of resolution
Is sicklied o'er with the pale cast of thought[23],
And enterprises of great pith and moment[24]

With this regard, their currents turn awry[25],
And lose the name of action[26]. —Soft you now!
The fair Ophelia! Nymph, in thy orisons
Be all my sins remember'd.

【注释】

1. *Hamlet* is Shakespeare's masterpiece, which is considered as the summit of his art. It was probably written around the year 1601—1602. The story of Hamlet came from an old Danish legend.

2. To be, or not to be: to endure or to resist; to live or to die. 活，还是不活

3. outrageous: cruel, furious. 残暴的

4. end them: put an end to the troubles. 结束苦难

5. heir to: certain to receive. 与生俱来的

6. perchance: possibly. 可能

7. ay: yes. 哎

8. there's the rub: there lies the difficulties. 这就是问题所在

9. shuffled off this mortal coil: ended this life. ("mortal coil" refers to turmoil of mortality.) 结束这个生命

10. Makes calamity of so long life: makes a long life seem to be a great misfortune. 使漫长的生活变成无数不幸

11. contumely: insolence, contempt. 轻视

12. the law's delay: law which can't defend the people. 法律不能得到执行

13. office: people of high rank. 官吏

14. spurns: insults. 污辱

15. That patient merit of the unworthy takes: that people of worth and fortitude endure at the hands of the unworthy. 小人的轻视

16. might his quietus make: might end his life. 可能结束生命

17. bare bodkin: mere dagger. 一把刀

18. fardels: burdens. 负担

19. grunt: groan. 呻吟

20. the undiscovered country: death. 死亡

21. hourn: boundary. 疆界

22. fly to others: go to others. 飞到另一个（国度）

23. the native hue of resolution/Is sickled o'er with the pale cast of thought: A natural decision becomes weakened by melancholy thought. 决心的色彩被苍白的理性所车黯淡

24. pith and moment: actions of great importance. 伟大的事业

25. their currents turn awry: turn awry their currents. 改变了航道

26. lose the name of action: fail to be put into action. 失去了行动的可能

Questions for discussion:

1. What is Hamlet's famous "hesitation"? How do you understand the "hesitation"?

2. Why is sleep so frightening, according to Hamlet, since it can "end the heartache and the thousand natural shocks"?

3. Hamlet as a dramatic character is uniquely defined by his soliloquies. What can you learn about Hamlet from the above soliloquy? Why does he wait so long to act after promising his father's ghost that he will avenge his murder? What are the reasons for his hesitation in the play?

3 The Merchant of Venice

William Shakespeare

Act 3, Scene I

SHYLOCK: To bait fish withal[1]: if it will feed nothing else, it will feed my revenge. He hath[2] disgraced me, and hindered me half a million; laughed at my losses, mocked at my gains, scorned my nation, thwarted my bargains, cooled my friends, heated mine enemies; and what's his reason? I am a Jew. Hath not a Jew eyes? hath not a Jew hands, organs, dimensions, senses, affections, passions? fed with the same food, hurt with the same weapons, subject to the same diseases, healed by the same means, warmed and cooled by the same winter and summer, as a Christian is?

If you prick us, do we not bleed? if you tickle us, do we not laugh? if you poison us, do we not die? and if you wrong us, shall we not revenge? If we are like you in the rest, we will resemble you in that. If a Jew wrong a Christian, what is his humility? Revenge. If a Christian wrong a Jew, what should his sufferance be by Christian example? Why, revenge. The villany[3] you teach me, I will execute[4], and it shall go hard but I will better[5] the instruction.

【注释】
1. withal: 此外，依然。
2. hath: （古英语）has
3. villany: evilness. 邪恶
4. execute: do. 执行
5. better: do it better than. 做得更好

Questions for discussion:

1. How do you view Shylock's anger?
2. Is Shylock a man more sinned against than sinning, more wronged than wronging others?
3. How do you understand the cultural background for Jews at Shakespearean time?
4. What's Shakespeare's attitude towards Jews?

4 Samson Agonistes

John Milton

(*Lines* 1596 – 1707)

Messenger: Occasions drew me early to this City,
And, as the gates I entered with Sun-rise,
The morning Trumpets Festival proclaim'd
Through each high street: little I had dispatch'd
When all abroad was rumour'd that this day
Samson should be brought forth to shew[1] the people
Proof of his mighty strength in feats and games;
I sorrow'd at his captive state, but minded
Not to be absent at that spectacle.
The building was a spacious Theatre
Half round on two main Pillars vaulted high,
With seats where all the Lords and each degree
Of sort, might sit in order to behold,
The other side was open, where the throng
On banks and scaffolds under Skie[2] might stand;
I among these aloof obscurely stood.
The Feast and noon grew high, and Sacrifice
Had fill'd their hearts with mirth, high cheer and wine,
When to their sports they turned. Immediately
Was Samson as a public servant brought,
In their state Livery clad; before him Pipes
And Timbrels, on each side went armed guards,
Both horse and foot before him and behind
Archers, and Slingers, Cataphracts and Spears.
At sight of him the people with a shout
Rifted the Air clamouring their god with praise,
Who had made their dreadful enemy their thrall.
He patient but undaunted where they led him,
Came to the place, and what was set before him
Which without help of eye, might be assayed,

To heave, pull, draw, or break, he still performed
All with incredible, stupendious force,
None daring to appear Antagonist.
At length for intermission sake they led him
Between the pillars; he his guide requested
(For so from such as nearer stood we heard)
As over-tired to let him lean a while
With both his arms on those two massie³ Pillars
That to the arched roof gave main support.
He unsuspitious led him; which when Samson
Felt in his arms, with head a while enclin'd,
And eyes fast fixt⁴ he stood, as one who pray'd,
Or some great matter in his mind revolv'd.
At last with head erect thus cried aloud,
Hitherto, Lords, what your commands impos'd
I have performed, as reason was, obeying,
Not without wonder or delight beheld.
Now of my own accord such other trial
I mean to shew you of my strength, yet greater;
As with amaze shall strike all who behold.
This uttered, straining all his nerves he bowed,
As with the force of winds and waters pent,
When Mountains tremble, those two massie Pillars
With horrible convulsion to and fro,
He tugged, he shook, till down thy came and drew
The whole roof after them, with burst of thunder
Upon the heads of all who sate beneath,
Lords, Ladies, Captains, Councellors, or Priests,
Their choice nobility and flower, not only
Of this but each Philistian City round
Met from all parts to solemnize this Feast.
Samson with these immixed, inevitably
Pulled down the same destruction on himself;
The vulgar only scaped who stood without.

Chorus: O dearly-bought revenge, yet glorious!
Living or dying thou hast fulfilled
The work for which thou wast foretold
To Israel, and now liest victorious
Among thy slain self-killed

     Not willingly, but tangled in the fold
     Of dire necessity, whose law in death conjoined
     Thee with thy slaughtered foes in number more
     Then all thy life had slain before.
Semichorus: While their hearts were jocund and sublime[5],
     Drunk with Idolatry, drunk with Wine,
     And fat regorged[6] of Bulls and Goats,
     Chaunting their Idol, and preferring
     Before our Living Dread who dwells
     In Silo[7] his bright Sanctuary,
     Among them he a spirit of phrenzy[8] sent,
     Who hurt their minds,
     And urged them on with mad desire
     To call in hast for their destroyer;
     They only set on sport and play
     Unweetingly importuned
     Their own destruction to come speedy upon them.
     So fond are mortal men
     Fallen into wrath divine,
     As their own ruin on themselves to invite,
     Insensate left, or to sense reprobate,
     And with blindness internal struck.
Semichorus: But he though blind of sight,
     Despis'd and thought extinguished quite,
     With inward eyes illuminated
     His fiery virtue roused
     From under ashes into sudden flame,
     And as an evening Dragon[9] came,
     Assailant on the perched roosts,
     And nests in order ranged
     Of tame villatic[10] Fowl; but as an Eagle
     His cloudless thunder bolted on their heads.
     So Virtue given for lost,
     Depressed, and overthrown, as seemed,
     Like that self-begotten bird[11]
     In the Arabian woods embossed[12]
     That no second knows nor third,
     And lay ere while a Holocaust,
     From out her ashie[13] womb now teemed

Revives, reflourishes, then vigorous most
When most unactive[14] deemed,
And though her body die, her fame survives,
A secular bird ages of lives[15].

【注释】

1. shew: show. 展示
2. Skie: sky. 天空
3. massie: massy. 厚重的
4. fixt: fixed. 修补好的
5. sublime: lifted up and is not a term of praise. 洋洋自得
6. regorged: it conveys the idea of excess. Animal fat was forbidden to the Israelites, so there is an extra touch of disgust and self-righteousness in the Chorus's mention of this detail. 横溢，多余
7. Silo: where the Ark of the Covenant was kept in Israel. 圣经里保存诺亚方舟的地方
8. phrenzy: frenzy. 狂暴的
9. dragon: snake. 蛇
10. villatic: farmyard. 村庄
11. self-begotten bird: mythical Phoenix of Arabia, of which there was never more than one in the world at a time because it died by burning to death in its nest and then rose form its own ashes. 凤凰
12. embossed: sheltered. 遮蔽的
13. ashie: ashes. 灰烬
14. unactive: inactive. 不活跃的
15. a secular bird ages of lives: it lives forever, but in many different lives. 在不停轮回中永生

Questions for discussion:

1. Having just heard the messenger describe how Samson destroyed himself and the Philistines together, the Chorus rejoice in his "dearly-bought revenge, yet glorious". Milton splits them into two groups—two semichoruses. What exactly do those two semichoruses talk about?
2. What's the relation between Samson and chorus?
3. Talk about your opinion on Samson.
4. What's the Philistines' attitude to the gods?

名言摘录

The best apology against false accusers is silence and sufferance, and honest deeds set against dishonest words.

5 The Importance of Being Earnest[1]

Oscar Wilde

ACT I

(*Enter LANE.*)
Lady BRACKNELL[2] and Miss FAIRFAX.
(*ALGERNON goes forward to meet them. Enter LADY BRACKNELL and GWENDOLEN.*)

LADY BRACKNELL: Good afternoon, dear Algernon, I hope you are behaving very well.

ALGERNON: I'm feeling very well, Aunt Augusta.

LADY BRACKNELL: That's not quite the same thing. In fact the two things rarely go together. (*Sees JACK and bows to him with icy coldness.*)

ALGERNON: (*To GWENDOLEN.*) Dear me, you are smart!

GWENDOLEN: I am always smart! Am I not, Mr. Worthing?

JACK: You're quite perfect, Miss Fairfax.

GWENDOLEN: Oh! I hope I am not that. It would leave no room for developments, and I intend to develop in many directions. (*GWENDOLEN and JACK sit down together in the corner.*)

LADY BRACKNELL: I'm sorry if we are a little late, Algernon, but I was obliged to call on dear Lady Harbury. I hadn't been there since her poor husband's death. I never saw a woman so altered; she looks quite twenty years younger. And now I'll have a cup of tea, and one of those nice cucumber sandwiches you promised me.

ALGERNON: Certainly, Aunt Augusta. (*Goes over to tea-table.*)

LADY BRACKNELL: Won't you come and sit here, Gwendolen?

GWENDOLEN: Thanks, mamma, I'm quite comfortable where I am.

ALGERNON: (*Picking up empty plate in horror.*) Good heavens! Lane! Why are there no cucumber sandwiches? I ordered them specially.

LANE: (*Gravely.*) There were no cucumbers in the market this morning, sir. I went down twice.

ALGERNON: No cucumbers!

LANE: No, sir. Not even for ready money.

ALGERNON: That will do, Lane, thank you.

LANE: Thank you, sir. (*Goes out.*)

ALGERNON: I am greatly distressed, Aunt Augusta, about there being no cucumbers, not even for ready money.

LADY BRACKNELL: It really makes no matter, Algernon. I had some crumpets with Lady Harbury, who seems to me to be living entirely for pleasure now.

ALGERNON: I hear her hair has turned quite gold from grief.

LADY BRACKNELL: It certainly has changed its colour. From what cause I, of course, cannot say. (*ALGERNON crosses and hands tea.*) Thank you. I've quite a treat for you to-night, Algernon. I am going to send you down with Mary Farquhar. She is such a nice woman, and so attentive to her husband. It's delightful to watch them.

ALGERNON: I am afraid, Aunt Augusta, I shall have to give up the pleasure of dining with you to-night after all.

LADY BRACKNELL: (*Frowning.*) I hope not, Algernon. It would put my table completely out. Your uncle would have to dine upstairs. Fortunately he is accustomed to that.

ALGERNON: It is a great bore, and, I need hardly say, a terrible disappointment to me, but the fact is I have just had a telegram to say that my poor friend Bunbury is very ill again. (*Exchanges glances with JACK.*) They seem to think I should be with him.

LADY BRACKNELL: It is very strange. This Mr. Bunbury seems to suffer from curiously bad health.

ALGERNON: Yes; poor Bunbury is a dreadful invalid.

LADY BRACKNELL: Well, I must say, Algernon, that I think it is high time that Mr. Bunbury made up his mind whether he was going to live or to die. This shilly-shallying with the question is absurd. Nor do I in any way approve of the modern sympathy with invalids. I consider it morbid. Illness of any kind is hardly a thing to be encouraged in others. Health is the primary duty of life. I am always telling that to your poor uncle, but he never seems to take much notice … as far as any improvement in his ailment goes. I should be much obliged if you would ask Mr. Bunbury, from me, to be kind enough not to have a relapse on Saturday, for I rely on you to arrange my music for me. It is my last reception, and one wants something that will encourage conversation, particularly at the end of the season when every one has practically said whatever they had to say, which, in most cases, was probably not much.

ALGERNON: I'll speak to Bunbury, Aunt Augusta, if he is still conscious, and I think I can promise you he'll be all right by Saturday. Of course the music is a great difficulty. You see, if one plays good music, people don't listen, and if one plays bad music people don't talk. But I'll ran over the programme I've drawn out, if you will kindly come into the next room for a moment.

LADY BRACKNELL: Thank you, Algernon. It is very thoughtful of you. (*Rising, and following ALGERNON.*) I'm sure the programme will be delightful, after a few expurgations. French songs I cannot possibly allow. People always seem to think that they are improper, and either look shocked, which is vulgar, or laugh, which is worse. But German sounds a thoroughly respectable language, and indeed, I believe is so. Gwendolen, you will accompany me.

GWENDOLEN: Certainly, mamma.

(*LADY BRACKNELL and ALGERNON go into the music-room, GWENDOLEN remains behind.*)

JACK: Charming day it has been, Miss Fairfax.

GWENDOLEN: Pray don't talk to me about the weather, Mr. Worthing. Whenever people talk to me about the weather, I always feel quite certain that they mean something else. And that makes me so nervous.

JACK: I do mean something else.

GWENDOLEN: I thought so. In fact, I am never wrong.

JACK: And I would like to be allowed to take advantage of Lady Bracknell's temporary absence ...

GWENDOLEN: I would certainly advise you to do so. Mamma has a way of coming back suddenly into a room that I have often had to speak to her about.

JACK: (*Nervously.*) Miss Fairfax, ever since I met you I have admired you more than any girl ... I have ever met since ... I met you.

GWENDOLEN: Yes, I am quite well aware of the fact. And I often wish that in public, at any rate, you had been more demonstrative. For me you have always had an irresistible fascination. Even before I met you I was far from indifferent to you. (*JACK looks at her in amazement.*) We live, as I hope you know, Mr Worthing, in an age of ideals. The fact is constantly mentioned in the more expensive monthly magazines, and has reached the provincial pulpits, I am told; and my ideal has always been to love some one of the name of Ernest. There is something in that name that inspires absolute confidence. The moment Algernon first mentioned to me that he had a friend called Ernest, I knew I was destined to love you.

JACK: You really love me, Gwendolen?

GWENDOLEN: Passionately!

JACK: Darling! You don't know how happy you've made me.

GWENDOLEN: My own Ernest!

JACK: But you don't really mean to say that you couldn't love me if my name wasn't Ernest?

GWENDOLEN: But your name is Ernest.

JACK: Yes, I know it is. But supposing it was something else? Do you mean to say you couldn't love me then?

GWENDOLEN: (*Glibly.*) Ah! that is clearly a metaphysical speculation, and like most metaphysical speculations has very little reference at all to the actual facts of real life, as we know them.

JACK: Personally, darling, to speak quite candidly, I don't much care about the name of Ernest ... I don't think the name suits me at all.

GWENDOLEN: It suits you perfectly. It is a divine name. It has a music of its own. It produces vibrations.

JACK: Well, really, Gwendolen, I must say that I think there are lots of other much nicer names. I think Jack, for instance, a charming name.

GWENDOLEN: Jack? ... No, there is very little music in the name Jack, if any at all, indeed. It does not thrill. It produces absolutely no vibrations ... I have known several Jacks, and they all, without exception, were more than usually plain. Besides, Jack is a notorious domesticity for John! And I pity any woman who is married to a man called John. She would probably never be allowed to know the entrancing pleasure of a single moment's solitude. The only really safe name is Ernest

JACK: Gwendolen, I must get christened at once—I mean we must get married at once. There is no time to be lost.

GWENDOLEN: Married, Mr. Worthing?

JACK: (*Astounded.*) Well ... surely. You know that I love you, and you led me to believe, Miss Fairfax, that you were not absolutely indifferent to me.

GWENDOLEN: I adore you. But you haven't proposed to me yet. Nothing has been said at all about marriage. The subject has not even been touched on.

JACK: Well ... may I propose to you now?

GWENDOLEN: I think it would be an admirable opportunity. And to spare you any possible disappointment, Mr. Worthing, I think it only fair to tell you quite frankly before-hand that I am fully determined to accept you.

JACK: Gwendolen!

GWENDOLEN: Yes, Mr. Worthing, what have you got to say to me?

JACK: You know what I have got to say to you.

GWENDOLEN: Yes, but you don't say it.

JACK: Gwendolen, will you marry me? (*Goes on his knees.*)

GWENDOLEN: Of course I will, darling. How long you have been about it! I am afraid you have had very little experience in how to propose.

JACK: My own one, I have never loved any one in the world but you.

GWENDOLEN: Yes, but men often propose for practice. I know my brother Gerald does. All my girl-friends tell me so. What wonderfully blue eyes you have, Ernest! They are quite, quite, blue. I hope you will always look at me just like that, especially when there are other people present. (*Enter LADY BRACKNELL.*)

LADY BRACKNELL: Mr. Worthing! Rise, sir, from this semi-recumbent posture. It is most indecorous.

GWENDOLEN: Mamma! (*He tries to rise; she restrains him.*) I must beg you to retire. This is no place for you. Besides, Mr. Worthing has not quite finished yet.

LADY BRACKNELL: Finished what, may I ask?

GWENDOLEN: I am engaged to Mr. Worthing, mamma. (*They rise together.*)

LADY BRACKNELL: Pardon me, you are not engaged to any one. When you do become engaged to some one, I, or your father, should his health permit him, will inform you of the fact. An engagement should come on a young girl as a surprise, pleasant or unpleasant, as the case may be. It is hardly a matter that she could be allowed to arrange for herself ... And now I have a few questions to put to you, Mr. Worthing. While I am making these inquiries, you, Gwendolen, will wait for me below in the carriage.

GWENDOLEN: (*Reproachfully.*) Mamma!

LADY BRACKNELL: In the carriage, Gwendolen! (*GWENDOLEN goes to the door. She and JACK blow kisses to each other behind LADY BRACKNELL'S back. LADY BRACKNELL looks vaguely about as if she could not understand what the noise was. Finally turns round.*) Gwendolen, the carriage!

GWENDOLEN: Yes, mamma. (*Goes out, looking back at JACK.*)

LADY BRACKNELL: (*Sitting down.*) You can take a seat, Mr. Worthing. (*Looks in her pocket for note-book and pencil.*)

JACK: Thank you, Lady Bracknell, I prefer standing.

LADY BRACKNELL: (*Pencil and note-book in hand.*) I feel bound to tell you that you are not down on my list of eligible young men, although I have the same list as the dear Duchess of Bolton has. We work together, in fact. However, I am quite ready to enter your name, should your answers be what a really affectionate mother requires. Do you smoke?

JACK: Well, yes, I must admit I smoke.

LADY BRACKNELL: I am glad to hear it. A man should always have an occupation of some kind. There are far too many idle men in London as it is. How old are you?

JACK: Twenty-nine.

LADY BRACKNELL: A very good age to be married at. I have always been of opinion that a man who desires to get married should know either everything or nothing. Which do you know?

JACK: (*After some hesitation.*) I know nothing, Lady Bracknell.

LADY BRACKNELL: I am pleased to hear it. I do not approve of anything that tampers with natural ignorance. Ignorance is like a delicate exotic fruit; touch it and the bloom is gone. The whole theory of modern education is radically unsound. Fortunately in England, at any rate, education produces no effect whatsoever. If it did, it would prove a serious danger to the upper classes, and probably lead to acts of violence in Grosvenor Square. What is your income?

JACK: Between seven and eight thousand a year.

LADY BRACKNELL: (*Makes a note in her book.*) In land, or in investments?

JACK: In investments, chiefly.

LADY BRACKNELL: That is satisfactory. What between the duties expected of one during one's lifetime, and the duties exacted from one after one's death, land has ceased to be either a profit or a pleasure. It gives one position, and prevents one from keeping it up. That's all that can be said about land.

JACK: I have a country house with some land, of course, attached to it, about fifteen hundred acres, I believe; but I don't depend on that for my real income. In fact, as far as I can make out, the poachers are the only people who make anything out of it.

LADY BRACKNELL: A country house! How many bedrooms? Well, that point can be cleared up afterwards. You have a town house, I hope? A girl with a simple, unspoiled nature, like Gwendolen, could hardly be expected to reside in the country.

JACK: Well, I own a house in Belgrave Square, but it is let by the year to Lady Bloxham. Of course, I can get it back whenever I like, at six months' notice.

LADY BRACKNELL: Lady Bloxham? I don't know her.

JACK: Oh, she goes about very little. She is a lady considerably advanced in years.

LADY BRACKNELL: Ah, nowadays that is no guarantee of respectability of character. What number in Belgrave Square?

JACK: 149.

LADY BRACKNELL: (*Shaking her head.*) The unfashionable side. I thought there was something. However, that could easily be altered.

JACK: Do you mean the fashion, or the side?

LADY BRACKNELL: (*Sternly.*) Both, if necessary, I presume. What are your politics?

JACK: Well, I am afraid I really have none. I am a Liberal Unionist.

LADY BRACKNELL: Oh, they count as Tories. They dine with us. Or come in the evening, at any rate. Now to minor matters. Are your parents living?

JACK: I have lost both my parents.

LADY BRACKNELL: To lose one parent, Mr. Worthing, may be regarded as a misfortune; to lose both looks like carelessness. Who was your father? He was evidently a man of some wealth. Was he born in what the Radical papers call the purple of commerce, or did he rise from the ranks of the aristocracy?

JACK: I am afraid I really don't know. The fact is, Lady Bracknell, I said I had lost my parents. It would be nearer the truth to say that my parents seem to have lost me ... I don't actually know who I am by birth. I was ... well, I was found.

LADY BRACKNELL: Found!

JACK: The late Mr. Thomas Cardew, an old gentleman of a very charitable and kindly disposition, found me, and gave me the name of Worthing, because he happened to have a first-class ticket for Worthing in his pocket at the time. Worthing is a place in Sussex. It is a seaside resort.

LADY BRACKNELL: Where did the charitable gentleman who had a first-class ticket for this seaside resort find you?

JACK: (*Gravely.*) In a hand-bag.

LADY BRACKNELL: A hand-bag?

JACK: (*Very seriously.*) Yes, Lady Bracknell. I was in a hand-bag—a somewhat large, black leather hand-bag, with handles to it—an ordinary hand-bag in fact.

LADY BRACKNELL: In what locality did this Mr. James, or Thomas, Cardew come across this ordinary hand-bag?

JACK: In the cloak-room at Victoria Station. It was given to him in mistake for his own.

LADY BRACKNELL: The cloak-room at Victoria Station?

JACK: Yes. The Brighton line.

LADY BRACKNELL: The line is immaterial. Mr. Worthing, I confess I feel somewhat bewildered by what you have just told me. To be born, or at any rate bred, in a hand-bag, whether it had handles or not, seems to me to display a contempt for the ordinary decencies of family life that reminds one of the worst excesses of the French Revolution. And I presume you know what that unfortunate movement led to? As for the particular locality in which the hand-bag was found, a cloak-room at a railway station might serve to conceal a social indiscretion—has probably, indeed, been used for that purpose before now—but it could hardly be regarded as an assured basis for a recognised position in good society.

JACK: May I ask you then what you would advise me to do? I need hardly say I would do anything in the world to ensure Gwendolen's happiness.

LADY BRACKNELL: I would strongly advise you, Mr. Worthing, to try and acquire some relations as soon as possible, and to make a definite effort to produce at any rate one parent, of either sex, before the season is quite over.

JACK: Well, I don't see how I could possibly manage to do that. I can produce the hand-bag at any moment. It is in my dressing-room at home. I really think that should satisfy you, Lady Bracknell.

LADY BRACKNELL: Me, sir! What has it to do with me? You can hardly imagine that I and Lord Bracknell would dream of allowing our only daughter—a girl brought up with the utmost care—to marry into a cloak-room, and form an alliance with a parcel? Good morning, Mr. Worthing!

(*LADY BRACKNELL sweeps out in majestic indignation.*)

JACK: Good morning! (*ALGERNON, from the other room, strikes up the Wedding March. Jack looks perfectly furious, and goes to the door.*) For goodness' sake don't play that ghastly tune, Algy. How idiotic you are!

(*The music stops and ALGERNON enters cheerily.*)

【注释】

1. *The Importance of Being Earnest* opened in the West End of London in February 1894 during an era when many of the religious, social, political, and economic structures were experiencing change—The Victorian Age (the last 25 - 30 years of the 1800s). The English aristocracy was dominant, snobbish and rich—far removed from the British middle class and poor. They were aware of the culture and atmosphere of the West End. The West End was also a red-light district that could provide any pleasure. It was a virtual garden of delights, and the patrons could understand the need for married men to invent Ernests and Bunburys so that they could frolic in this world.

2. Lady Bracknell. 这里所选的第一幕中伯爵夫人 Lady Bracknell 发现 John 正向自己女儿求婚后盘问 John 的一场。Lady Bracknell is the most memorable character and one who has a tremendous impact on the audience is Lady Augusta Bracknell. Wilde's audience would have identified most with her titled position and bearing. Wilde humorously makes her the tool of the conflict, and much of the satire. 布莱克纳尔女士是剧中最让人的印象深刻的角色。观众难以忘记她的高高在上和盛气凌人，王尔德用诙谐的笔法使她成为矛盾和讽刺的中心人物之一。

Questions for discussion:

1. What attitudes toward marriage do Wilde's characters explore?
2. How is conflict developed in the play?
3. Why doesn't Lady Bracknell approve of the love between Jack and Gwendolen at first? What are her requirements for a proper suitor for her girl? What role does she play in the development of the comic action?

名言摘录

1. A dreamer is one who can only find his way by moonlight, and his punishment is that he sees the dawn before the rest of the world.
2. A little sincerity is a dangerous thing, and a great deal of it is absolutely fatal.
3. All women become like their mothers. That is their tragedy. No man does. That's his.
4. Always forgive your enemies. Nothing annoys them so much.

6 Major Barbara[1]

George Bernard Shaw

Act II

(*The yard of the West Ham shelter of the Salvation Army is a cold place on a January morning. Andrew Undershaft comes to visit the yard where Barbara works, and decided to give five thousand pounds to the Salvation Army, and just when he is about to sign on the paper...*)

BARBARA   Stop. (*Undershaft stops writing: they all turn to her in surprise*). Mrs Baines: are you really going to take this money?

MRS BAINES   (*astonished*) Why not, dear?

BARBARA   Why not! Do you know what my father is? Have you forgotten that Lord Saxmundham is Bodger[2] the whisky man? Do you remember how we implored the County Council to stop him from writing Bodger's Whisky in letters of fire against the sky; so that the poor drinkruined creatures on the embankment could not wake up from their snatches of sleep without being reminded of their deadly thirst by that wicked sky sign? Do you know that the worst thing I have had to fight here is not the devil, but Bodger, Bodger, Bodger, with his whisky, his distilleries, and his tied houses? Are you going to make our shelter another tied house for him, and ask me to keep it?

BILL   Rotten drunken whisky it is too.

MRS BAINES   Dear Barbara: Lord Saxmundham has a soul to be saved like any of us. If heaven has found the way to make a good use of his money, are we to set ourselves up against the answer to our prayers?

BARBARA   I know he has a soul to be saved. Let him come down here; and I'll do my best to help him to his salvation. But he wants to send his cheque down to buy us, and go on being as wicked as ever.

UNDERSHAFT   (*with a reasonableness which Cusins alone perceives to be ironical*) My dear Barbara: alcohol is a very necessary article. It heals the sick—

BARBARA   It does nothing of the sort.

UNDERSHAFT   Well, it assists the doctor: that is perhaps a less questionable way of putting it. It makes life bearable to millions of people who could not endure their existence if they were quite sober. It enables Parliament to do things at eleven at night that no sane person would do at eleven in the morning. Is it Bodger's fault that this inestimable[3] gift is deplorably abused by less than one per cent of the poor? (*He turns *again to the table; signs the cheque; and crosses it).*

MRS BRINES Barbara: will there be less drinking or more if all those poor souls we are saving come to-morrow and find the doors of our shelters shut in their faces? Lord Saxmundham gives us the money to stop drinking—to take his own business from him.

CUSINS (*impishly*) Pure self-sacrifice on Bodger's part, clearly! Bless dear Bodger! (*Barbara almost breaks down as Adolpbus, too, fails her*).

UNDERSHAFT (*tearing out the cheque and pocketing the book as be rises and goes past Cusins to Mrs Baines*) I also, Mrs Baines, may claim a little disinterestedness. Think of my business! think of the widows and orphans! the men and lads torn to pieces with shrapnel[4] and poisoned with lyddite (*Mrs Baines shrinks; but he goes on remorselessly*)! the oceans of blood, not one drop of which is shed in a really just cause! the ravaged[5] crops! The peaceful peasants forced, women and men, to till their fields under the fire of opposing armies on pain of starvation! the bad blood of the fierce little cowards at home who egg on others to fight for the gratification[6] of their national vanity! All this makes money for me: I am never richer, never busier than when the papers are full of it. Well, it is your work to preach peace on earth and goodwill to men.

(*Mrs Baines's face lights up again*).

Every convert you make is a vote against war. (*Her lips move in prayer*). Yet I give you this money to help you to hasten my own commercial ruin. (*He gives her the cheque*).

CUSINS (*mounting the form in an ecstasy of mischief*) The millennium will be inaugurated by the unselfishness of Undershaft and Bodger. Oh be joyful! (*He takes the drumsticks from his pockets and flourishes them*).

MRS BAINES (*taking the cheque*) The longer I live the more proof I see that there is an Infinite Goodness that turns everything to the work of salvation sooner or later. Who would have thought that any good could have come out of war and drink? And yet their profits are brought today to the feet of salvation to do its blessed work. (*She is affected to tears*).

JENNY (*running to Mrs Baines and throwing her arms round her*) Oh dear! how blessed, how glorious it all is!

CUSINS (*in a convulsion of irony*) Let us seize this unspeakable moment. Let us march to the great meeting at once. Excuse me just an instant. (*He rushes into the shelter. Jenny takes her tambourine from the drum head*).

MRS BAINES Mr Undershaft: have you ever seen a thousand people fall on their knees with one impulse and pray? Come with us to the meeting. Barbara shall tell them that the Army is saved, and saved through you.

CUSINS (*returning impetuously from the shelter with a flag and a trombone,* *and coming between Mrs Baines and Undershaft*) You shall carry the flag down the first street, Mrs Baines (*he gives her the flag*). Mr Undershaft is a gifted trombonist: he shall intone an Olympian diapason to the West Ham Salvation March. (*Aside to Undershaft, as he forces the trombone on him*) Blow, Machiavelli, blow.

UNDERSHAFT   (*aside to him, as he takes the trombone*) The trumpet in Zion! (*Cusins rushes to the drum, which he takes up and puts on. Undershaft continues, aloud*) I will do my best. I could vamp a bass if I knew the tune.

CUSINS   It is a wedding chorus from one of Donizetti's operas; but we have converted it. We convert everything to good here, including Bodger. You remember the chorus. "For thee immense rejoicing—immenso giubilo—immenso giubilo." (*With drum obbligato*) Rum tum ti tum tum, tum tum ti ta—

BARBARA   Dolly: you are breaking my heart.

CUSINS   What is a broken heart more or less here? Dionysos Undershaft has descended. I am possessed.

MRS BRINES   Come, Barbara: I must have my dear Major to carry the flag with me.

JENNY   Yes, yes, Major darling.

CUSINS   (*snatches the tambourine out of Jenny's hand and mutely offers it to Barbara*).

BARBARA   (*coming forward a little as she puts the offer behind her with a shudder, whilst Cusins recklessly tosses the tambourine[7] back to Jenny and goes to the gate*) I can't come.

JENNY   Not come!

MRS BAINES   (*with tears in her eyes*) Barbara: do you think I am wrong to take the money?

BARBARA   (*impulsively going to her and kissing her*) No, no: God help you, dear, you must: you are saving the Army. Go; and may you have a great meeting!

JENNY   But aren't you coming?

BARBARA   No. (*She begins taking off the silver brooch from her collar*).

MRS BAINES   Barbara: what are you doing?

JENNY   Why are you taking your badge off? You can't be going to leave us, Major.

BARBARA   (*quietly*) Father: come here.

UNDERSHAFT   (*coming to her*) My dear! (*Seeing that she is going to pin the badge on his collar, he retreats to the penthouse in some alarm*).

BARBARA   (*following him*) Don't be frightened. (*She pins the badge on and steps back towards the table, showing him to the others*) There! It's not much for 5000 pounds is it?

MRS BAINES   Barbara: if you won't come and pray with us, promise me you will pray for us.

BARBARA I can't pray now. Perhaps I shall never pray again.

MRS BAINES Barbara!

JENNY Major!

BARBARA (*almost delirious*) I can't bear any more. Quick march!

CUSINS (*calling to the procession in the street outside*) Off we go. Play up, there! Immenso giubilo. (*He gives the time with his drum; and the band strikes up the march, which rapidly becomes more distant as the procession moves briskly away*).

MRS BAINES I must go, dear. You're overworked: you will be all right tomorrow. We'll never lose you. Now Jenny: step out with the old flag. Blood and Fire! (*She marches out through the gate with her flag*).

JENNY Glory Hallelujah! (*flourishing her tambourine and marching*).

UNDERSHAFT (*to Cusins, as he marches out past him easing the slide of his trombone*) "My ducats[8] and my daughter"!

CUSINS (*following him out*) Money and gunpowder!

BARBARA Drunkenness and Murder! My God: why hast thou forsaken me?

She sinks on the form with her face buried in her hands. The march passes away into silence. Bill Walker steals across to her.

【注释】

1. Major Barbara is a three act play by George Bernard Shaw, written and premiered in 1905 and first published in 1907. 《芭芭拉上校》是肖伯纳的三幕剧，写于1905，1907年出版

2. Lord Saxmundham is Bodger: He symblizes the liquor industrialist in this drama much as Undershaft does the millionaire munitions capitalist. 他代表了剧中因经营酒业获利的资本家

3. inestimable: a thing of inestimable value. 无法体量的

4. shrapnel: shell containing lead pellets that explodes in flight. 弹片

5. ravaged: having been robbed and destroyed by force and violence. 被掠夺

6. gratification: state of being gratified; great satisfaction. 十分满意

7. tambourine: a shallow drum with a single drumhead and with metallic disks in the sides. 手鼓

8. ducats: formerly a gold coin of various European countries. 达克特（以前欧洲许多国家通用的金币）

Questions for discussion:

1. How do you understand the conflicts between Barbara and her father Andrew Undershaft from the extracts?

2. In what ways does George Bernard Shaw portray the character of Major Barbara?

名言摘录

1. A day's work is a day's work, neither more nor less, and the man who does it needs a day's sustenance, a night's repose and due leisure, whether he be painter or ploughman.

2. A fashion is nothing but an induced epidemic.

3. A fool's brain digests philosophy into folly, science into superstition, and art into pedantry. Hence University education.

7 Riders to the Sea

J. M. Synge

A PLAY IN ONE ACT

SCENE. —*An Island off the West of Ireland.* (*Cottage kitchen, with nets, oilskins, spinning wheel, some new boards standing by the wall, etc. Cathleen[1], a girl of about twenty, finishes kneading cake, and puts it down in the pot-oven by the fire; then wipes her hands, and begins to spin at the wheel. NORA, a young girl, puts her head in at the door.*)

NORA: (*In a low voice.*) Where is she?

CATHLEEN: She's lying down, God help her, and may be sleeping, if she's able.

(*Nora comes in softly, and takes a bundle from under her shawl[2].*)

CATHLEEN: (*Spinning the wheel rapidly.*) What is it you have?

NORA: The young priest is after bringing them. It's a shirt and a plain stocking were got off a drowned man in Donegal.

(*Cathleen stops her wheel with a sudden movement, and leans out to listen.*)

NORA: We're to find out if it's Michael's they are, some time herself will be down looking by the sea.

CATHLEEN: How would they be Michael's, Nora. How would he go the length of that way to the far north?

NORA: The young priest says he's known the like of it. "If it's Michael's they are," says he, "you can tell herself he's got a clean burial by the grace of God, and if they're not his, let no one say a word about them, for she'll be getting her death," says he, "with crying and lamenting."

(*The door which Nora half closed is blown open by a gust of wind.*)

CATHLEEN: (*Looking out anxiously.*) Did you ask him would he stop Bartley going this day with the horses to the Galway fair?

NORA: "I won't stop him," says he, "but let you not be afraid. Herself does be saying prayers half through the night, and the Almighty God won't leave her destitute," says he, "with no son living."

CATHLEEN: Is the sea bad by the white rocks, Nora?

NORA: Middling bad, God help us. There's a great roaring in the west, and it's worse it'll be getting when the tide's turned to the wind.

(*She goes over to the table with the bundle.*) Shall I open it now?

CATHLEEN: Maybe she'd wake up on us, and come in before we'd done. (*Coming to the table.*) It's a long time we'll be, and the two of us crying.

NORA: (*Goes to the inner door and listens.*) She's moving about on the bed. She'll be coming in a minute.

CATHLEEN: Give me the ladder, and I'll put them up in the turf-loft, the way she won't know of them at all, and maybe when the tide turns she'll be going down to see would he be floating from the east.

(*They put the ladder against the gable of the chimney; Cathleen goes up a few steps and hides the bundle in the turf-loft. Maurya comes from the inner room.*)

MAURYA: (*Looking up at Cathleen and speaking querulously.*) Isn't it turf enough you have for this day and evening?

CATHLEEN: There's a cake baking at the fire for a short space. (*Throwing down the turf*) and Bartley will want it when the tide turns if he goes to Connemara[3].

(*Nora picks up the turf and puts it round the pot-oven.*)

MAURYA: (*Sitting down on a stool at the fire.*) He won't go this day with the wind rising from the south and west. He won't go this day, for the young priest will stop him surely.

NORA: He'll not stop him, mother, and I heard Eamon Simon and Stephen Pheety and Colum Shawn saying he would go.

MAURYA: Where is he itself?

NORA: He went down to see would there be another boat sailing in the week, and I'm thinking it won't be long till he's here now, for the tide's turning at the green head, and the hooker' tacking from the east.

CATHLEEN: I hear some one passing the big stones.

NORA: (*Looking out.*) He's coming now, and he's in a hurry.

BARTLEY: (*Comes in and looks round the room. Speaking sadly and quietly.*) Where is the bit of new rope, Cathleen, was bought in Connemara?

CATHLEEN: (*Coming down.*) Give it to him, Nora; it's on a nail by the white boards. I hung it up this morning, for the pig with the black feet was eating it.

NORA: (*Giving him a rope.*) Is that it, Bartley?

MAURYA: You'd do right to leave that rope, Bartley, hanging by the boards (*Bartley takes the rope*). It will be wanting in this place, I'm telling you, if Michael is washed up to-morrow morning, or the next morning, or any morning in the week, for it's a deep grave we'll make him by the grace of God.

BARTLEY: (*Beginning to work with the rope.*) I've no halter[4] the way I can ride down on the mare[5], and I must go now quickly. This is the one boat going for two weeks or beyond it, and the fair will be a good fair for horses I heard them saying below.

MAURYA: It's a hard thing they'll be saying below if the body is washed up and there's no man in it to make the coffin[6], and I after giving a big price for the finest white boards you'd find in Connemara.

(*She looks round at the boards.*)

BARTLEY: How would it be washed up, and we after looking each day for nine days, and a strong wind blowing a while back from the west and south?

MAURYA: If it wasn't found itself, that wind is raising the sea, and there was a star up against the moon, and it rising in the night. If it was a hundred horses, or a thousand horses you had itself, what is the price of a thousand horses against a son where there is one son only?

BARTLEY: (*Working at the halter, to Cathleen.*) Let you go down each day, and see the sheep aren't jumping in on the rye, and if the jobber comes you can sell the pig with the black feet if there is a good price going.

MAURYA: How would the like of her get a good price for a pig?

BARTLEY: (*To Cathleen*) If the west wind holds with the last bit of the moon let you and Nora get up weed enough for another cock for the kelp. It's hard set we'll be from this day with no one in it but one man to work.

MAURYA: It's hard set we'll be surely the day you're drownd'd with the rest. What way will I live and the girls with me, and I an old woman looking for the grave?

(*Bartley lays down the halter, takes off his old coat, and puts on a newer one of the same flannel.*)

BARTLEY: (*To Nora.*) Is she coming to the pier?

NORA: (*Looking out.*) She's passing the green head and letting fall her sails.

BARTLEY: (*Getting his purse and tobacco.*) I'll have half an hour to go down, and you'll see me coming again in two days, or in three days, or maybe in four days if the wind is bad.

MAURYA: (*Turning round to the fire, and putting her shawl over her head.*) Isn't it a hard and cruel man won't hear a word from an old woman, and she holding him from the sea?

CATHLEEN: It's the life of a young man to be going on the sea, and who would listen to an old woman with one thing and she saying it over?

BARTLEY: (*Taking the halter.*) I must go now quickly. I'll ride down on the red mare, and the gray pony'll run behind me. The blessing of God on you.

(*He goes out.*)

MAURYA: (*Crying out as he is in the door.*) He's gone now, God spare us, and we'll not see him again. He's gone now, and when the black night is falling I'll have no son left me in the world.

CATHLEEN: Why wouldn't you give him your blessing and he looking round in the door? Isn't it sorrow enough is on every one in this house without your sending him out with an unlucky word behind him, and a hard word in his ear?

(*Maurya takes up the tongs and begins raking the fire aimlessly without looking round.*)

NORA: (*Turning towards her.*) You're taking away the turf from the cake.

CATHLEEN: (*Crying out.*) The Son of God forgive us, Nora, we're after forgetting his bit of bread.

(*She comes over to the fire.*)

NORA: And it's destroyed he'll be going till dark night, and he after eating nothing since the sun went up.

CATHLEEN: (*Turning the cake out of the oven.*) It's destroyed he'll be, surely. There's no sense left on any person in a house where an old woman will be talking for ever.

(*Maurya sways herself on her stool.*)

CATHLEEN: (*Cutting off some of the bread and rolling it in a cloth; to Maurya.*) Let you go down now to the spring well and give him this and he passing. You'll see him then and the dark word will be broken, and you can say "God speed you," the way he'll be easy in his mind.

MAURYA: (*Taking the bread.*) Will I be in it as soon as himself?

CATHLEEN: If you go now quickly.

MAURYA: (*Standing up unsteadily.*) It's hard set I am to walk.

CATHLEEN: (*Looking at her anxiously.*) Give her the stick, Nora, or maybe she'll slip on the big stones.

NORA: What stick?

CATHLEEN: The stick Michael brought from Connemara.

MAURYA: (*Taking a stick Nora gives her.*) In the big world the old people do be leaving things after them for their sons and children, but in this place it is the young men do be leaving things behind for them that do be old.

(*She goes out slowly. Nora goes over to the ladder.*)

CATHLEEN: Wait, Nora, maybe she'd turn back quickly. She's that sorry, God help her, you wouldn't know the thing she'd do.

NORA: Is she gone round by the bush?

CATHLEEN: (*Looking out.*) She's gone now. Throw it down quickly, for the Lord knows when she'll be out of it again.

NORA: (*Getting the bundle from the loft.*) The young priest said he'd be passing to-morrow, and we might go down and speak to him below if it's Michael's they are surely.

CATHLEEN: (*Taking the bundle.*) Did he say what way they were found?

NORA: (*Coming down.*) "There were two men," says he, "and they rowing round with poteen[⑦] before the cocks crowed, and the oar of one of them caught the body, and they passing the black cliffs of the north."

CATHLEEN: (*Trying to open the bundle.*) Give me a knife, Nora, the string's perished with the salt water, and there's a black knot on it you wouldn't loosen in a week.

NORA: (*Giving her a knife.*) I've heard tell it was a long way to Donegal.

CATHLEEN: (*Cutting the string.*) It is surely. There was a man in here a while ago—the man sold us that knife—and he said if you set off walking from the rocks beyond, it would be seven days you'd be in Donegal.

NORA: And what time would a man take, and he floating?

(*Cathleen opens the bundle and takes out a bit of a stocking. They look at them eagerly.*)

CATHLEEN: (*In a low voice.*) The Lord spare us, Nora! isn't it a queer hard thing to say if it's his they are surely?

NORA: I'll get his shirt off the hook the way we can put the one flannel on the other (*she looks through some clothes hanging in the corner.*) It's not with them, Cathleen, and where will it be?

CATHLEEN: I'm thinking Bartley put it on him in the morning, for his own shirt was heavy with the salt in it (*pointing to the corner*). There's a bit of a sleeve was of the same stuff. Give me that and it will do.

(*Nora brings it to her and they compare the flannel.*)

CATHLEEN: It's the same stuff, Nora; but if it is itself aren't there great rolls of it in the shops of Galway, and isn't it many another man may have a shirt of it as well as Michael himself?

NORA: (*Who has taken up the stocking and counted the stitches, crying out.*)

It's Michael, Cathleen, it's Michael; God spare his soul, and what will herself say when she hears this story, and Bartley on the sea?

CATHLEEN: (*Taking the stocking.*) It's a plain stocking.

NORA: It's the second one of the third pair I knitted, and I put up three score stitches, and I dropped four of them.

CATHLEEN: (*Counts the stitches.*) It's that number is in it (*crying out.*) Ah, Nora, isn't it a bitter thing to think of him floating that way to the far north[8], and no one to keen him but the black hags[9] that do be flying on the sea?

NORA: (*Swinging herself round, and throwing out her arms on the clothes.*) And isn't it a pitiful thing when there is nothing left of a man who was a great rower and fisher, but a bit of an old shirt and a plain stocking?

CATHLEEN: (*After an instant.*) Tell me is herself coming, Nora? I hear a little sound on the path.

NORA: (*Looking out.*) She is, Cathleen. She's coming up to the door.

CATHLEEN: Put these things away before she'll come in. Maybe it's easier she'll be after giving her blessing to Bartley, and we won't let on we've heard anything the time he's on the sea.

NORA: (*Helping Cathleen to close the bundle.*) We'll put them here in the corner.

(*They put them into a hole in the chimney corner. Cathleen goes back to the spinning-wheel.*)

NORA: Will she see it was crying I was?

CATHLEEN: Keep your back to the door the way the light'll not be on you.

(*Nora sits down at the chimney corner, with her back to the door. Maurya comes in very slowly, without looking at the girls, and goes over to her stool at the other side of the fire. The cloth with the bread is still in her hand. The girls look at each other, and Nora points to the bundle of bread.*)

CATHLEEN: (*After spinning for a moment.*) You didn't give him his bit of bread?

(*Maurya begins to keen softly, without turning round.*)

CATHLEEN: Did you see him riding down?

(*Maurya goes on keening.*)

CATHLEEN: (*A little impatiently.*) God forgive you; isn"t it a better thing to raise your voice and tell what you seen, than to be making lamentation for a thing that's done? Did you see Bartley, I'm saying to you?

MAURYA: (*With a weak voice.*) My heart's broken from this day.

CATHLEEN: (*As before.*) Did you see Bartley?

MAURYA: I seen the fearfulest thing.

CATHLEEN: (*Leaves her wheel and looks out.*) God forgive you; he's riding the mare now over the green head, and the gray pony behind him.

MAURYA: (*Starts, so that her shawl falls back from her head and shows her white tossed hair. With a frightened voice.*) The gray pony behind him.

CATHLEEN: (*Coming to the fire.*) What is it ails you, at all?

MAURYA: (*Speaking very slowly.*) I've seen the fearfulest thing any person has seen, since the day Bride Dara seen the dead man with the child in his arms.

CATHLEEN & NORA: UAH.

(*They crouch down in front of the old woman at the fire.*)

NORA: Tell us what it is you seen. (*They crouch down in front of the old woman at the fire.*)

NORA: Tell us what it is you seen.

MAURYA: I went down to the spring well, and I stood there saying a prayer to myself. Then Bartley came along, and he riding on the red mare[8] with the gray pony behind him (*she puts up her hands, as if to hide something from her eyes.*) The Son of God spare us, Nora!

CATHLEEN: What is it you seen.

MAURYA: I seen Michael himself.

CATHLEEN: (*Speaking softly.*) You did not, mother; it wasn't Michael you seen, for his body is after being found in the far north, and he's got a clean burial by the grace of God.

MAURYA: (*A little defiantly.*) I'm after seeing him this day, and he riding and galloping. Bartley came first on the red mare; and I tried to say "God speed you," but something choked the words in my throat. He went by quickly; and "the blessing of God on you," says he, and I could say nothing. I looked up then, and I crying, at the gray pony, and there was Michael upon it—with fine clothes on him, and new shoes on his feet.

CATHLEEN: (*Begins to keen.*) It's destroyed we are from this day. It's destroyed, surely.

NORA: Didn't the young priest say the Almighty God wouldn't leave her destitute with no son living?

MAURYA: (*In a low voice, but clearly.*) It's little the like of him knows of the sea. Bartley will be lost now, and let you call in Eamon and make me a good coffin out of the white boards, for I won't live after them. I've had a husband, and a husband's father, and six sons in this house—six fine men, though it was a hard birth I had with every one of them and they coming to the world—and some of them were found and some of them were not found, but they're gone now the lot of them... There were Stephen, and Shawn, were lost in the great wind, and found after in the Bay of Gregory of the Golden Mouth, and carried up the two of them on the one plank, and in by that door.

(*She pauses for a moment, the girls start as if they heard something through the door that is half open behind them.*)

NORA: (*In a whisper.*) Did you hear that, Cathleen? Did you hear a noise in the north-east?

CATHLEEN: (*In a whisper.*) There's some one after crying out by the seashore.

MAURYA: (*Continues without hearing anything.*) There was Sheamus and his father, and his own father again, were lost in a dark night, and not a stick or sign was seen of them when the sun went up. There was Patch after was drowned out of a curagh[10] that turned over. I was sitting here with Bartley, and he a baby, lying on my two knees, and I seen two women, and three women, and four women coming in, and they crossing themselves, and not saying a word. I looked out then, and there were men coming after them, and they holding a thing in the half of a red sail, and water dripping out of it—it was a dry day, Nora—and leaving a track to the door.

(*She pauses again with her hand stretched out towards the door. It opens softly and old women begin to come in, crossing themselves on the threshold, and kneeling down in front of the stage with red petticoats over their heads.*)

MAURYA: (*Half in a dream, to Cathleen.*) Is it Patch, or Michael, or what is it at all?

CATHLEEN: Michael is after being found in the far north[11], and when he is found there how could he be here in this place?

MAURYA: There does be a power of young men floating round in the sea, and what way would they know if it was Michael they had, or another man like him, for when a man is nine days in the sea, and the wind blowing, it's hard set his own mother would be to say what man was it.

CATHLEEN: It's Michael, God spare him, for they're after sending us a bit of his clothes from the far north.

(*She reaches out and hands Maurya the clothes that belonged to Michael. Maurya stands up slowly, and takes them into her hands. NORA looks out.*)

NORA: They're carrying a thing among them and there's water dripping out of it and leaving a track by the big stones.

CATHLEEN: (*In a whisper to the women who have come in.*) Is it Bartley it is?

ONE OF THE WOMEN: It is surely, God rest his soul.

(*Two younger women come in and pull out the table. Then men carry in the body of Bartley, laid on a plank, with a bit of a sail over it, and lay it on the table.*)

CATHLEEN: (*To the women, as they are doing so.*) What way was he drowned?

ONE OF THE WOMEN: The gray pony knocked him into the sea, and he was washed out where there is a great surf on the white rocks.

(*Maurya has gone over and knelt down at the head of the table. The women are keening softly and swaying themselves with a slow movement. Cathleen and Nora kneel at the other end of the table. The men kneel near the door.*)

MAURYA: (*Raising her head and speaking as if she did not see the people around her.*) They're all gone now, and there isn't anything more the sea can do to me… I'll have no call now to be up crying and praying when the wind breaks from the south, and you can hear the surf is in the east, and the surf is in the west, making a great stir with the two noises, and they hitting one on the other. I'll have no call now to be going down and getting Holy Water in the dark nights after Samhain[11], and I won't care what way the sea is when the other women will be keening. (*To Nora.*) Give me the Holy Water, Nora, there's a small sup still on the dresser.

(*Nora gives it to her.*)

MAURYA: (*Drops Michael's clothes across Bartley's feet, and sprinkles[12] the Holy Water over him.*) It isn't that I haven't prayed for you, Bartley, to the Almighty God. It isn't that I haven't said prayers in the dark night till you wouldn't know what I'd be saying; but it's a great rest I'll have now, and it's time surely. It's a great rest I'll have now, and great sleeping in the long nights after Samhain, if it's only a bit of wet flour we do have to eat, and maybe a fish that would be stinking.

(*She kneels down again, crossing herself, and saying prayers under her breath.*)

CATHLEEN: (*To an old man.*) Maybe yourself and Eamon would make a coffin when the sun rises. We have fine white boards herself bought, God help her, thinking Michael would be found, and I have a new cake you can eat while you'll be working.

THE OLD MAN: (*Looking at the boards.*) Are there nails with them?

CATHLEEN: There are not, Colum; we didn't think of the nails.

ANOTHER MAN: It's a great wonder she wouldn't think of the nails, and all the coffins she's seen made already.

CATHLEEN: It's getting old she is, and broken.

(*Maurya stands up again very slowly and spreads out the pieces of Michael's clothes beside the body, sprinkling them with the last of the Holy Water.*)

NORA: (*In a whisper to Cathleen.*) She's quiet now and easy; but the day Michael was drowned you could hear her crying out from this to the spring well. It's fonder she was of Michael, and would any one have thought that?

CATHLEEN: (*Slowly and clearly.*) An old woman will be soon tired with anything she will do, and isn't it nine days herself is after crying and keening, and making great sorrow in the house?

MAURYA: (*Puts the empty cup mouth downwards on the table, and lays her hands together on Bartley's feet.*) They're all together this time, and the end is come. May the Almighty God have mercy on Bartley's soul, and on Michael's soul, and on the souls of Sheamus and Patch, and Stephen and Shawn (*bending her head*); and may He have mercy on my soul, Nora, and on the soul of every one is left living in the world.

(*She pauses, and the keen rises a little more loudly from the women, then sinks away.*)

MAURYA: (*Continuing.*) Michael has a clean burial in the far north, by the grace of the Almighty God. Bartley will have a fine coffin out of the white boards, and a deep grave surely. What more can we want than that? No man at all can be living for ever, and we must be satisfied.

(*She kneels down again and the curtain falls slowly.*)

【注释】

1. Cathleen: daughter of Maurya. Nora is her sister, and Bartley, her brother. 剧中人物 Maurya 是母亲，Cathleen 和 Nora 是她的女儿，Bartley 是她的小儿子。

2. shawl: cloak consisting of an oblong piece of cloth used to cover the head and shoulders. 披肩

3. Connemara: a mountainous region in County Galway, W Ireland, on the Atlantic coast. 爱尔兰地名

4. halter: rope or canvas headgear for a horse, with a rope for leading. 缰绳

5. mare: female equine animal. 母马

6. coffin: box in which a corpse is buried or cremated. 棺材
7. poteen: illicitly distilled whiskey. 私酿威士忌
8. the far north: refers to one point of the compass.
9. hags: birds. 鸟
10. curagh: a small boat with a hide or tarpaulin covered frame. 小船
11. Samhain: Feast of All Saints, November 1. 凯尔特人的萨温节，11 月 1 日开始
12. sprinkle: distribute loosely. 撒

Questions for discussion:

1. Is there any conflict in "Riders to the Sea"? If so, between whom and what?
2. What is the theme of the play?
3. Is this play romantic? Is it realistic? Is it poetic? Have a discussion.
4. What role does fate play in this tragedy?
5. Does the play have a plot? How is the situation developed?

名言摘录

If it was a hundred horses, or a thousand horses you had itself, what is the price of a thousand horses against a son where there is one son only?

8 Waiting for Godot

Samuel Beckett

A country road. A tree.
Evening.
Estragon, sitting on a low mound, is trying to take off his boot. He pulls at it with both hands, panting. He gives up, exhausted, rests, tries again.
As before.
Enter Vladimir.

ESTRAGON: (*giving up again*). Nothing to be done.

VLADIMIR: (*advancing with short, stiff strides, legs wide apart*). I'm beginning to come round to that opinion. All my life I've tried to put it from me, saying Vladimir, be reasonable, you haven't yet tried everything. And I resumed the struggle. (*He broods, musing on the struggle. Turning to Estragon.*) So there you are again.

ESTRAGON: Am I?

VLADIMIR: I'm glad to see you back. I thought you were gone forever.

ESTRAGON: Me too.

VLADIMIR: Together again at last! We'll have to celebrate this. But how? (*He reflects.*) Get up till I embrace you.

ESTRAGON: (*irritably*). Not now, not now.

VLADIMIR: (*hurt, coldly*). May one inquire where His Highness spent the night?

ESTRAGON: In a ditch.

VLADIMIR: (*admiringly*). A ditch! Where?

ESTRAGON: (*without gesture*). Over there.

VLADIMIR: And they didn't beat you?

ESTRAGON: Beat me? Certainly they beat me.

VLADIMIR: The same lot as usual?

ESTRAGON: The same? I don't know.

VLADIMIR: When I think of it ... all these years ... but for me ... where would you be ... (*Decisively.*) You'd be nothing more than a little heap of bones at the present minute, no doubt about it.

ESTRAGON: And what of it?

VLADIMIR: (*gloomily*). It's too much for one man. (*Pause. Cheerfully.*) On the other hand what's the good of losing heart now, that's what I say. We should have thought of it a million years ago, in the nineties.[1]

ESTRAGON: Ah stop blathering and help me off with this bloody thing.

VLADIMIR: Hand in hand from the top of the Eiffel Tower, among the first. We were respectable in those days. Now it's too late. They wouldn't even let us up. (*Estragon tears at his boot.*) What are you doing?

ESTRAGON: Taking off my boot. Did that never happen to you?

VLADIMIR: Boots must be taken off every day, I'm tired telling you that. Why don't you listen to me?

ESTRAGON: (*feebly*). Help me!

VLADIMIR: It hurts?

ESTRAGON: (*angrily*). Hurts! He wants to know if it hurts!

VLADIMIR: (*angrily*). No one ever suffers but you. I don't count. I'd like to hear what you'd say if you had what I have.

ESTRAGON: It hurts?

VLADIMIR: (*angrily*). Hurts! He wants to know if it hurts!

ESTRAGON: (*pointing*). You might button it all the same.

VLADIMIR: (*stooping*). True. (*He buttons his fly.*) Never neglect the little things of life.

ESTRAGON: What do you expect, you always wait till the last moment.

VLADIMIR: (*musingly*). The last moment ... (*He meditates.*) Hope deferred[2] maketh the something sick, who said that?

ESTRAGON: Why don't you help me?

VLADIMIR: Sometimes I feel it coming all the same. Then I go all queer. (*He takes off his hat, peers inside it, feels about inside it, shakes it, puts it on again.*) How shall I say? Relieved and at the same time ... (*he searches for the word*) ... appalled. (*With emphasis.*) AP-PALLED. (*He takes off his hat again, peers inside it.*) Funny. (*He knocks on the crown as though to dislodge a foreign body, peers into it again, puts it on again.*) Nothing to be done. (*Estragon with a supreme effort succeeds in pulling off his boot. He peers inside it, feels about inside it, turns it upside down, shakes it, looks on the ground to see if anything has fallen out, finds nothing, feels inside it again, staring sightlessly before him.*) Well?

ESTRAGON: Nothing.

VLADIMIR: Show me.

ESTRAGON: There's nothing to show.

VLADIMIR: Try and put it on again.

ESTRAGON: (*examining his foot*). I'll air it for a bit.

VLADIMIR: There's man all over for you, blaming on his boots the faults of his feet. (*He takes off his hat again, peers inside it, feels about inside it, knocks on the crown, blows into it, puts it on again.*) This is getting alarming. (*Silence. Vladimir* *deep in thought, Estragon pulling at his toes.*) One of the thieves was saved. (*Pause.*) It's a reasonable percentage. (*Pause.*) Gogo.

ESTRAGON: What?

VLADIMIR: Suppose we repented.

ESTRAGON: Repented what?

VLADIMIR: Oh ... (*He reflects.*) We wouldn't have to go into the details.

ESTRAGON: Our being born?

Vladimir breaks into a hearty laugh which he immediately stifles, his hand pressed to his pubis, his face contorted.

VLADIMIR: One daren't even laugh any more.

ESTRAGON: Dreadful privation.

VLADIMIR: Merely smile. (*He smiles suddenly from ear to ear, keeps smiling, ceases as suddenly.*) It's not the same thing. Nothing to be done. (*Pause.*) Gogo.

ESTRAGON: (*irritably*). What is it?

VLADIMIR: Did you ever read the Bible?

ESTRAGON: The Bible ... (*He reflects.*) I must have taken a look at it.

VLADIMIR: Do you remember the Gospels?

ESTRAGON: I remember the maps of the Holy Land. Coloured they were. Very pretty. The Dead Sea was pale blue. The very look of it made me thirsty. That's where we'll go, I used to say, that's where we'll go for our honeymoon. We'll swim. We'll be happy.

VLADIMIR: You should have been a poet.

ESTRAGON: I was. (*Gesture towards his rags.*) Isn't that obvious?

Silence.

VLADIMIR: Where was I ... How's your foot?

ESTRAGON: Swelling visibly.

VLADIMIR: Ah yes, the two thieves. Do you remember the story?

ESTRAGON: No.

VLADIMIR: Shall I tell it to you?

ESTRAGON: No.

VLADIMIR: It'll pass the time. (*Pause.*) Two thieves, crucified at the same time as our Saviour. One—

ESTRAGON: Our what?

VLADIMIR: Our Saviour. Two thieves. One is supposed to have been saved and the other ... (*he searches for the contrary of saved*) ... damned.

ESTRAGON: Saved from what?

VLADIMIR: Hell.

ESTRAGON: I'm going.

He does not move.

VLADIMIR: And yet ... (pause) ... how is it—this is not boring you I hope—how is it that of the four Evangelists[3] only one speaks of a thief being saved. The four of them were there—or thereabouts—and only one speaks of a thief being saved. (*Pause.*) Come on, Gogo, return the ball[4], can't you, once in a while?

ESTRAGON: (*with exaggerated enthusiasm*). I find this really most extraordinarily interesting.

VLADIMIR: One out of four. Of the other three, two don't mention any thieves at all and the third says that both of them abused him.

ESTRAGON: Who?

VLADIMIR: What?

ESTRAGON: What's all this about? Abused who?

VLADIMIR: The Saviour.

ESTRAGON: Why?

VLADIMIR: Because he wouldn't save them.

ESTRAGON: From hell?

VLADIMIR: Imbecile! From death.

ESTRAGON: I thought you said hell.

VLADIMIR: From death, from death.

ESTRAGON: Well what of it?

VLADIMIR: Then the two of them must have been damned.

ESTRAGON: And why not?

VLADIMIR: But one of the four says that one of the two was saved.

ESTRAGON: Well? They don't agree and that's all there is to it.

VLADIMIR: But all four were there. And only one speaks of a thief being saved. Why believe him rather than the others?

ESTRAGON: Who believes him?

VLADIMIR: Everybody. It's the only version they know.

ESTRAGON: People are bloody ignorant apes.

He rises painfully, goes limping to extreme left, halts, gazes into distance off with his hand screening his eyes, turns, goes to extreme right, gazes into distance. Vladimir watches him, then goes and picks up the boot, peers into it, drops it hastily.

VLADIMIR: Pah!

He spits. Estragon moves to center, halts with his back to auditorium.

ESTRAGON: Charming spot. (*He turns, advances to front, halts facing auditorium.*) Inspiring prospects. (*He turns to Vladimir.*) Let's go.

VLADIMIR: We can't.

ESTRAGON: Why not?

VLADIMIR: We're waiting for Godot.

ESTRAGON: (*despairingly*). Ah! (*Pause.*) You're sure it was here?

VLADIMIR: What?

ESTRAGON: That we were to wait.

VLADIMIR: He said by the tree. (*They look at the tree.*) Do you see any others?

ESTRAGON: What is it?

VLADIMIR: I don't know. A willow.

ESTRAGON: Where are the leaves?

VLADIMIR: It must be dead.

ESTRAGON: No more weeping.

VLADIMIR: Or perhaps it's not the season.

ESTRAGON: Looks to me more like a bush.

VLADIMIR: A shrub.

ESTRAGON: A bush.

VLADIMIR: A—. What are you insinuating? That we've come to the wrong place?

ESTRAGON: He should be here.

VLADIMIR: He didn't say for sure he'd come.

ESTRAGON: And if he doesn't come?

VLADIMIR: We'll come back tomorrow.

ESTRAGON: And then the day after tomorrow.

VLADIMIR: Possibly.

ESTRAGON: And so on.

VLADIMIR: The point is—

ESTRAGON: Until he comes.

VLADIMIR: You're merciless.

ESTRAGON: We came here yesterday.

VLADIMIR: Ah no, there you're mistaken.

ESTRAGON: What did we do yesterday?

VLADIMIR: What did we do yesterday?

ESTRAGON: Yes.

VLADIMIR: Why ... (*Angrily.*) Nothing is certain when you're about.

ESTRAGON: In my opinion we were here.

VLADIMIR: (*looking round*). You recognize the place?

ESTRAGON: I didn't say that.

VLADIMIR: Well?

ESTRAGON: That makes no difference.

VLADIMIR: All the same ... that tree ... (*turning towards auditorium*) that bog ...

ESTRAGON: You're sure it was this evening?

VLADIMIR: What?

ESTRAGON: That we were to wait.

VLADIMIR: He said Saturday. (*Pause.*) I think.

ESTRAGON: You think.

VLADIMIR: I must have made a note of it. (*He fumbles in his pockets, bursting with miscellaneous rubbish.*)

ESTRAGON: (*very insidious*). But what Saturday? And is it Saturday? Is it not rather Sunday? (*Pause.*) Or Monday? (*Pause.*) Or Friday?

VLADIMIR: (*looking wildly about him, as though the date was inscribed in the landscape*). It's not possible!

ESTRAGON: Or Thursday?

VLADIMIR: What'll we do?

ESTRAGON: If he came yesterday and we weren't here you may be sure he won't come again today.

VLADIMIR: But you say we were here yesterday.

ESTRAGON: I may be mistaken. (*Pause.*) Let's stop talking for a minute, do you mind?

VLADIMIR: (*feebly*). All right. (*Estragon sits down on the mound. Vladimir paces agitatedly to and fro, halting from time to time to gaze into distance off. Estragon falls asleep. Vladimir halts finally before Estragon.*) Gogo! ... Gogo! ... GOGO!

Estragon wakes with a start.

ESTRAGON: (*restored to the horror of his situation*). I was asleep! (*Despairingly.*) Why will you never let me sleep?

VLADIMIR: I felt lonely.

ESTRAGON: I had a dream.

VLADIMIR: Don't tell me!

ESTRAGON: I dreamt that—

VLADIMIR: DON'T TELL ME!

ESTRAGON: (*gesture toward the universe*). This one is enough for you? (*Silence.*) It's not nice of you, Didi. Who am I to tell my private nightmares to if I can't tell them to you?

VLADIMIR: Let them remain private. You know I can't bear that.

ESTRAGON: (*coldly.*) There are times when I wonder if it wouldn't be better for us to part.

VLADIMIR: You wouldn't go far.

ESTRAGON: That would be too bad, really too bad. (*Pause.*) Wouldn't it, Didi, be really too bad? (*Pause.*) When you think of the beauty of the way. (*Pause.*) And the goodness of the wayfarers. (*Pause. Wheedling.*) Wouldn't it, Didi?

【注释】

1. We should have thought of it a million years age, in the nineties: According to the context, Vladimir is saying that they should have committed suicide long ago. 根据文本，弗拉基米尔意指他们应很久以前自杀

2. Hope deferred: Hope delayed. 希望被延迟，无法实现

3. the four Evangelists: referring to the four of Jesus Cbrist's disciples who wrote the four Gospels. They were St. Matthew, St. Mark, St. Luke, and St. John. 四位福音传教士，分别是马太、马哥、路加和约翰

4. return the ball: anwer me. 回答我

Questions for discussion:

1. What do you think the relationship between Vladimir and Estragon? In the scene, they have suggested several times to leave, but they keep staying together, why?

2. Who is Godot? What does Godot symbolize? What is implied by his failure to appear?

3. What are the boots, hats, leash, and tree intended to symbolize?

名言摘录

1. Every word is like an unnecessary stain on silence and nothingness.

2. We are all born mad. Some remain so.

3. The fact is, it seems, that the most you can hope is to be a little less, in the end, the creature you were in the beginning, and the middle.

9 Look Back in Anger

John Osborne

Act I

(... *At rise of curtain, Jimmy and Cliff are seated in the two armchairs R. and L., respectively. All that we can see of either of them is two pairs of legs, sprawled way out beyond the newspapers, which hide the rest of them from sight. They are both reading. Beside them, and between them, is a jungle of newspapers and weeklies. When we do eventually see them, we find that Jimmy is a tall, thin young man about twenty-five, wearing a very worn tweed jacket and flannels. Clouds of smoke fill the room from the pipe he is smoking. He is a disconcerting mixture of sincerity and cheerful malice, of tenderness and free-booting cruelty; restless, importunate, full of pride, a combination which alienates the sensitive and insensitive alike. Blistering honesty, or apparent honesty, like his, makes few friends. To many he may seem sensitive to the point of vulgarity. To others, he is simply a loudmouth. To be as vehement as he is is to be almost noncommittal. Cliff is the same age, short, dark, big-boned, wearing a pullover and grey, new, but very creased trousers. He is easy and relaxed, almost to lethargy, with the rather sad, natural intelligence of the self-taught.*

If Jimmy alienates love, Cliff seems to exact it—demonstrations of it, at least, even from the cautious. He is soothing, natural counterpoint to Jimmy. Standing L., below the food cupboard, is Alison. She is leaning over an ironing board. Beside her is a pile of clothes. Here is the most elusive personality to catch in the uneasy polyphony of these three people. She is tuned in a different key, a key of well-bred malaise that is often frowned in the robust orchestration of the two. Hanging over the grubby, but expensive, skirt she is wearing is a cheery red shirt of Jimmy's, but she manages somehow to look quite elegant in it. She is roughly the same age as the men. Somehow, their combined physical oddity makes her beauty more striking than it really is. She is tall, slim, dark. The bones of her face are long and delicate. There is a surprising reservation about her eyes, which are so large and deep they should make equivocation impossible. The room is still, smoke-filled. The only sound is the occasional thud of Alison's iron on the board. It is one of those chilly Spring evenings, all cloud and shadows. Presently, Jimmy throws his paper down.)

JIM: Why do I do this evening Sunday? Even the book reviews seem to be the same as last week's. Different books—same reviews. Have you finished that one yet?

CLI: not yet.

JIM: I've just read three whole columns on the English Novel. Half of it's in French. Do the Sunday papers make you feel ignorant?

CLI: Not 'arf.

JIM: Well, you *are* ignorant. You're just a peasant. (*To Alison*) What about you? You're not a peasant are you?

ALI (*Absently*): What's that?

JIM: I said do the papers make you feel you're not so brilliant after all?

Alison: Oh—I haven't read them yet.

Jim: I didn't ask you that. I said—

CLI: Leave the poor girlie alone. She's busy.

JIM: Well, she can talk, can't she? You can talk, can't you? You can express an opinion. Or does the White Woman's Burden make it impossible to think?[1]

ALI: I'm sorry. I wasn't listening properly.

JIM: You bet you weren't listening. Old Porter talks, and everyone turns over and goes to sleep. And Mrs. Porter gets' em all going with the first yawn.

CLI: Leave her alone, I said.

JIM: Why do you bother? You can't understand a word of it.

CLI: Uh huh.

JIM: You're too ignorant.

CLI: Yes, and uneducated. Now shut up, will you?

JIM: Why don't you get my wife to explain it to you? She's educated. (*To her.*) That's right, isn't it?

CLI: (*Kicking out at him from behind his paper*). Leave her alone, I said.

JIM: Do that again, you Welsh ruffian, and I'll put your ears off. (*He bangs Cliff's paper out of his hands.*)

CLI: (*Leaning forward*): Listen—I'm trying to better myself. Let me get on with it, you big, horrible man. Give it me. (*Puts his hand out for paper*)

ALI: Oh, give it to him, Jimmy, for heaven's sake! I can't think!

CLI: Yes, come on, give me the paper. She can't think.

JIM: Can't think! (*Throws the paper back at him*) She hasn't had a thought for years! Have you?

ALI: No.

JIM: (*Picks up a weekly.*) I'm getting hungry.

ALI: Oh, no, not already!

CLI: He's a bloody pig.

JIM: I'm not a pig. I just like food—this' all.

CLI: Like it! You're like a sexual maniac—only with you it's food. You'll end up in the News of the World, boy, you wait. James Porter, aged twenty-five, was bound over last week after pleading guilty to interfering with a small cabbage and two tins of beans on his way home from "The Builder's Arms." The accused said he hadn't been feeling well for some time, and had been having black-outs. He asked for his good record as an air-raid warden, second class, to be taken into account.

JIM (*Grins*): Oh, yes, yes, yes. I like to eat. I'd like to live too. Do you mind?

CLI: Don't see any use in your eating at all. You never get any fatter.

JIM: People like me don't get fat. I've tried to tell you before. We just burn everything up. Now shut up while I read. You can make me some more tea.

CLI: Good God, you've just had a great potful! I only had one cup.

JIM: Like hell! Make some more.

CLI: (*To Alison*): Isn't that right? Didn't I only have one cup?

ALI (*Without looking up*): That's right.

CLI: There you are. And she only had one cup too. I saw her. You guzzled the lot.

JIM (*Reading his weekly*): Put the kettle on.

CLI: Put it on yourself. You've creased up my paper.

JIM: I'm the only one who knows how to treat a paper, or anything else, in this house. (*Picks up another paper*) Girl here wants to whether her boy friend will lose all respect for her if she gives him what he asks for. Stupid bitch.

CLI: Just let me get at her, that's all.

JIM: Who buys this damned thing? (*Throws it down*) Haven't you read the other posh[2] paper yet?

CLI: Which?

JIM: Well, There are only two posh papers on a Sunday[3]—the one you're reading, and this one. Come on, let me have that one, and you take this.

CLI: Oh, all right. (*They exchange*) I was only reading the Bishop of Bromley. (*Puts out his hand to Alison*) How are you, dullin'?

ALI: All right, thank you, dear.

CLI: (*Grasping her hand*): Why don't you leave all that, and sit down for a bit?

ALI (*Smiling*): I haven't much more to do.

CLI: (*Kisses her hand, and puts her fingers in his mouth*): She's a beautiful girl, isn't she?

JIM: That's what they all tell me. (*His eyes meet hers*)

CLI: It's a lovely, delicious paw you've got. Ummmmm. I'm going to bite it off.

ALI: Don't! I'll burn his shirt.

JIM: Give her finger back, and don't be so sickening. What's the Bishop of Bromley say?

CLI: (*Letting go of Alison*): Oh, it says here that he makes a very moving appeal to all Christians to do all they can to assist in the manufacture of the h-Bomb.

JIM: Yes, well, that's quite moving, I suppose. (*To Alison*) Are you moved, my darling?

ALI: Well, naturally.

JIM: There you are: even my wife is moved. I ought to send the Bishop a subscription. Let's see. What else does he say. Dumdidumdidumdidum. Ah, yes. He's upset because someone has suggested that he support the rich against the poor. He says he denies the difference of class distinctions. "This idea has been persistently and wickedly fostered by—the working classes!" Well!

(*He looks up at both of them for reaction, but Cliff is reading, and Alison is intent on her ironing*)

JIM (*To Cliff*): Did you read that bit?

CLI: Um?

(*He has lost them, and he knows it, but he won't leave it*)

JIM (*To Alison*): You don't suppose your father could have written it, do you?

ALI: Written what?

JIM: What I just read out, of course.

ALI: Why should my father have written it?

JIM: Sounds rather like Daddy, don't you think?

ALI: Does it?

JIM: Is the Bishop of Bromley his nom de plume[4], do you think?

CLI: Don't take any notice of him. He's being offensive. And it's so easy for him.

JIM (*Quickly*): Did you read about the woman who went to the mass meeting of a certain American evangelist at Earls Court? She went forward, to declare herself for love or whatever it is, and, in the rush of converts to get to the front, she broke four ribs and got kicked in the head. She was yelling her head off agony, but with 50,000 people putting all they'd got into "Onward Christian Soldiers," nobody even knew she was there. (*He looks up sharply for a response; but here isn't any*) Sometimes, I wonder if here isn't something wrong with me. What about that tea?

CLI: (*Still behind paper*): What tea?

JIM: Put the kettle on. (*Alison looks up at him*)

ALI: Do you want some more tea?

JIM: I don't know. No, I don't think so.

ALI: Do you want some, Cliff?

JIM: No, he doesn't. How much longer will you be doing that?

ALI: Won't be long.

JIM: God, how I hate Sundays! It's always so depressing, always the same. We never seem to get any further, do we? Always the same ritual. Reading the papers, drinking tea, ironing. A few more hours, and another week gone. Our youth is slipping away. Do you know that?

CLI: (*Throws down paper*): What's that?

JIM (*Casually*): Oh, nothing, nothing. Damn you, damn both of you, damn them all.

CLI: Let's go to the pictures. (*To Alison*) What do you say, lovely?

ALI: I don't think I'll be able to. Perhaps Jimmy would like to go. (*To Jimmy*) Would you like to?

JIM: And have my enjoyment ruined by the Sunday night yobs[5] in the front row. No, thank you. (*Pause*) Did you read Priestley's[6] piece this week? Why on earth I ask, I don't know. I know damned well you haven't. Why do I spend ninepence on that damned paper every week? Nobody reads it except me. Nobody can be bothered. No one can raise themselves out of their delicious sloth. You two will drive me round the bend soon—I know it, as sure as I'm sitting here. I know you're going to drive me mad. Oh, heavens, how I long for a little ordinary human enthusiasm. Just enthusiasm—that's all. I want to hear a warm, thrilling voice cry out Hallelujah! (*He bangs his breast theatrically*) Hallelujah! I'm alive! I've an idea. Why don't we have a little game? Let's pretend that we're human beings, and that we're actually alive. Just for a while. What do you say? Let's pretend we're human. (*He looks from one to the other*) Oh, brother, it's such a long time since I was with anyone who got enthusiastic about anything.

CLI: What did he say?

JIM (*Resentful of being dragged away from his pursuit of Alison*): What did who say?

CLI: Mr. Priestly.

JIM: What he always says, I suppose. He's like Daddy—still casting well-set glances back to the Edwardian twilight from his comfortable, disenfranchised wilderness. What the devil have you done to those trousers?

CLI: Done?

JIM: Are they the ones you bought last weekend? Look at them. Do you see what he's done to those new trousers?

ALI: You are naughty, Cliff. They look dreadful.

JIM: You spend good money on a new pair of trousers, and then sprawl about in them like a savage. What do you think you're going to do when I'm not around to look after you? Well, what are you going to do? Tell me?

CLI: (*Grinning*): I don't know. (*To Alison*) What am I going to do, lovely?

ALI: You'd better take them off.

JIM: Yes, go on. Take 'em off. And I'll kick your behind for you.

ALI: I'll give them a press while I've got the iron on.

CLI: O. K. (*Starts taking them off*) I'll just empty the pockets. (*Takes out keys, matches, handkerchief*)

JIM: Give me those matches, will you?

CLI: Oh, you're not going to start up that old pipe again, are you? It stinks the place out. (*To Alison*) Doesn't it smell awful?

(*Jimmy grabs the matches, and lights up*)

ALI: I don't mind it. I've got used to it.

JIM: She's a great one for getting used to things. If she were to die, and wake up in paradise—after the first five minutes, she'd have got used to it.

CLI: (*Hands her the trousers*): Thank you, lovely. Give me a cigarette, will you?

JIM: Don't give him one.

CLI: I can't stand the stink of that old pipe any longer. I must have a cigarette.

JIM: I thought the doctor no cigarettes?

CLI: Oh, why doesn't he shut up?

JIM: All right. They're your ulcers[7]. Go ahead, and have a bellyache, if that's what you want. I give up. I give up. I'm sick of doing things for people. And all for what?

(*Alison gives Cliff a cigarette. They both light up, and she goes on with her ironing*)

JIM: Nobody thinks, nobody cares, no beliefs, no convictions and no enthusiasm. Just another Sunday evening.

(*Cliff sits down again, in his pullover and shorts*)

JIM: Perhaps there's a concert on. (*Picks up Radio Times*) Ah. (*Nudges Cliff with his foot*) Make some more tea.

(*Cliff grunts, He is reading again*)

JIM: Oh, yes. There's Vaughan Williams[8]. Well, that's something, anyway. Something strong, something simple, something English. I suppose people like me aren't supposed to be very patriotic. Somebody[9] said—what was it—we get our cooking from Paris (that's a laugh), our politics from Moscow, and our morals from Port Said[10]. Something like that, anyway. I hate to admit it, but I think I can understand how her Daddy must have felt when he came back from India, after all those years away. The old Edwardian brigade do make their brief little world look pretty tempting. All homemade cakes and croquet, bright ideas, bright uniforms, always the same picture: high summer, the long days in the sun, slim volumes of verse, crisp linen, the smell of starch. What a romantic picture. Phony, too, of course. It must have rained sometimes. Still, even I regret it somehow, phony or not. If you've no world of your own. It's rather pleasant to regret the passing of someone else's. I must be getting sentimental. But I must say it's pretty dreary living in the American Age—unless you're an American, of course. Perhaps all our children will be Americans. That's a thought, isn't it? (*He gives Cliff a kick, and shouts at him*) I said that's a thought!

CLI: You did?

JIM: You sit there like a lump of dough. I thought you were going to make me some tea. (*Cliff groans. Jimmy turns to Alison*) Is your friend Webster coming tonight?

ALI: He might drop in. you know what he is.

JIM: Well, I hope he doesn't. I don't think I could take Webster tonight.

ALI: I thought you said he was the only person who spoke your language.

JIM: So he is. Different dialect but same language. I like him. He's got bite, edge, drive—

ALI: Enthusiasm.

JIM: You've got it. When he comes here, I begin to feel exhilarated. He doesn't like me, but he gives me something, which is more than I get from most people. Not since—

ALI: Yes, we know. Not since you were living with Madeline. (*She folds some of the clothes she has already ironed, and crosses to the bed with them*)

CLI: (*Behind paper again*): Who's Madeline?

ALI: Oh, wake up, dear. You've heard about Madeline enough times. She was his mistress. Remember? When he was fourteen. Or was it thirteen?

JIM: Eighteen.

ALI: He owes just about everything to Madeline.

CLI: I get mixed up with all your women. Was she the one all those years older than you?

JIM: Ten years.

CLI: Proper little Marchbanks[11], you are!

JIM: What time's that concert on? (*Checks paper*)

CLI: (*Yawns*): Oh, I feel so sleepy. Don't feel like standing behind that blinking sweet-stall[12] again tomorrow. Why don't you do it on your own, and let me sleep in?

JIM: I've got to be at the factory first thing, to get some more stock, so you'll have to put it up on your own. Another five minutes.

(*Alison had returned to her ironing board. She stands with her arms folded, smoking, staring thoughtfully*)

JIM: She had more animation in her little finger that you two put together.

CLI: Who did?

ALI: Madeline.

JIM: Her curiosity about things, and about people was staggering. It wasn't just a naïve nosiness. With her, it was simply the delight of being awake, and watching.

(*Alison starts to press Cliff's trousers*)

CLI (*Behind paper*): Perhaps I will make some tea, after all.

JIM (*Quietly*): Just to be with her was an adventure. Even to sit on the top of a bus with her was liking setting out with Ulysses.

CLI: Wouldn't have said Webster was much like Ulysses. He's an ugly little devil.

JIM: I'm not talking about Webster, stupid. He's all right though, in his way. A sort of female Emily Bronte. He's the only one of your friends (*to Alison*) who's worth tuppence, anyway. I'm surprised you get on with him.

ALI: So is he, I think.

JIM: (*Rising to window R., and looking out*). He's not only got guts, but sensitivity as well. That's about the rarest combination I can think of. None of your other friends have got either.

ALI (*Very quietly and earnestly*): Jimmy, please—don't go on.

(*He turns and looks at her. The tired appeal in her voice has pulled him up suddenly. But soon gathers himself for a new assault. He walks C., behind Cliff, and stands, looking down at his head*)

CLI: (*Mumbling*). Dry up. Let her get on with my trousers.

JIM: (*Musingly*). Don't think I could provoke her. Nothing I could do would provoke her. Not even if I were to drop dead.

CLI: Then drop dead.

JIM: They're either militant like her Mummy and Daddy. Militant, arrogant, and full of malice. Or vague. She's somewhere between the two.

CLI: Why don't you listen to that concert of yours? And don't stand behind me. That blooming droning on behind me gives me a funny feeling down the spine.

(*Jimmy gives his ears a twist and Cliff roars with pain. Jimmy grins back at him.*)

JIM: (*Moving in between them*). Have you ever seen her brother? Brother Nigel? The straight-backed, chinless wonder from Sandhurst[13]? I only met him once myself. He asked me to step outside when I told his mother she was evil minded.

CLI: And did you?

JIM: Certainly not. He's a big chap. Well, you've never heard so many well-bred commonplaces come from beneath the same bowler hat. The Platitude from Outer Space—that's Brother Nigel. He'll end up in the Cabinet one day, make no mistake. But somewhere at the back of that mind is the vague knowledge that he and his pals have been plundering and fooling everybody for generations. (*Going upstage, and turning*) Now Nigel is just about as vague as you can get without being actually invisible. And invisible politicians aren't much use to anyone—not even to his supporters! And nothing is more vague about Nigel than his knowledge. His knowledge of life and ordinary human beings is so hazy, he really deserves some sort of decoration for it—a medal inscribed "For Vaguery in the Field." But it wouldn't do for him to be troubled by any stabs of conscience, however vague. (*Moving down again*) Besides, he's a patriot and an Englishman, and he doesn't like the idea that he may have been selling out his countrymen all these years, so what does he do? They only thing he can do—seek sanctuary in his own supidity. The only way to keep things as much like they always have been as possible, is to make any alternative too much for your poor, tiny brain to grasp. It takes some doing nowadays. It really does. But they knew all about character building at Nigel's school, and he'll make it all right. Don't you worry, he'll make it. And, what's more, he'll do it better than anybody else!

(*There is no sound, only the plod of Alison's iron. Her eyes are fixed on what she is doing. Cliff stares at the floor. His cheerfulness has deserted him for the moment. Jimmy is rather shakily triumphant. He cannot allow himself to look at either of them to catch their response to his rhetoric, so he moves across to the window, to recover himself, and look out*)

JIM: It's started to rain. That's all it needs. This room and the rain. (*He's been cheated out of his response, but he's got to draw blood somehow. Conversationally*) Yes, that's the little woman's family. You know Mummy and Daddy, of course. And don't let the Marquess of Queensberry manner[14] fool you. They'll kick you in the groin while you're handing your hat to the maid. As for Nigel and Alison— (*In a reverent, Stuart Hibberd[15] voice*) Nigel and Alison. They're what they sound like: sycophantic, phlegmatic, and pusillanimous.

CLI: I'll bet that concerts started by now. Shall I put it on?

JIM: I looked up that word the other day. It's one of those words I've never been quite sure of, but always thought I knew.

CLI: What was that?

JIM: I told you—pusillanimous. Do you know what it means?

(*Cliff shakes his head*)

JIM: Neither did I really. All this time, I have been married to this woman, this monument to non-attachment, and suddenly I discover that there is actually a word that sums her up. Not just an adjective in the English language to describe her with—it's her name! Pusillanimous! It sounds like some fleshy Roman matron, doesn't it? The lady Pusillanimous seen here with her husband Sextus! If he were put into a Hollywood film, he's so unimpressive, they'd make some poor British actor play the part. He doesn't know it, but those beefcake Christians will make off with his wife in the wonder of stereophonic sound before the picture's over. (*Alison leans against the board, and closes her eyes*) The Lady Pusillanimous has been promised a brighter easier world than old Sextus can ever offer her. Ili, Pusey! What say we get the hell down to the Arena, and maybe feed ourselves to a couple of lions, huh?

ALI: God help me, if he doesn't stop, I'll go out of my mind in a minute.

JIM: Why don't you? That would be something, anyway. (*Crosses to chest of drawers R.*) But I haven't told you what it means yet, have I? (*Picks up dictionary*) I don't have to tell her she knows. In fact, if my pronunciation is at fault, she'll probably wait for a suitably public moment to correct it. Here it is. I quote: Pusillanimous.

Adjective. Wanting of firmness of mind, of small courage, having a little mind, mean-spirited, cowardly, timid of mind. From the Latin *pusillus*, very little, and *anumus*, the mind. (*Slams the book shut*) That's my wife! That's her, isn't it? Behold the lady Pusillanimous. (*Shouting hoarsely*) Hi, Pusey! When's your next picture?

(*Jimmy watches her, waiting for her to break. For no more than a flash. Alison's face seems to contort, and it looks as though she might throw her head back, and scream. But it passes in a moment. She is used to these carefully rehearsed attacks, and it doesn't look as though he will get his triumph tonight. She carries on with her ironing. Jimmy crosses, and switches on the radio. The Vaughan Williams concert has started. He goes back to his chair, leans back in it, and closes his eyes*)

ALI: (*Handing Cliff his trousers*) There you are, dear. They're not very good, but they'll do for now.

(*Cliff gets up and puts them on*)

ALI: Oh, that's lovely.

CLI: Thank you, you beautiful, darling girl. (*He puts his arms round her waist, and kisses her. She smiles, and gives his nose a tug. Jimmy watches from his chair*)

ALI (*To Cliff*): Let's have a cigarette, shall we?

CLI: That's a good idea. Where are they?

ALI: On the stove. Do you want one, Jimmy?

JIM: No, thank you, I'm trying to listen. Do you mind?

CLI: Sorry, your lordship.

(*He puts a cigarette in Alison's mouth, and one in his own, and lights up. Cliff sits down, and picks up his paper. Alison goes back to her board. Cliff throws down paper, picks up another, and thumbs through that*)

JIM: Do you have to make all that racket?

CLI: Oh, sorry.

JIM: It's quite a simple thing, you know—turning over a page, anyway, that's my paper. (*Snatches it away*)

CLI: Oh, don't be so mean!

JIM: Price nine-pence, obtainable from any news-agent's. Now let me hear the music, for God's sake. (*Pause. To Alison*) Are you going to be much longer doing that?

ALI: Why?

JIM: Perhaps you haven't noticed it, but it's interfering with the radio.

ALI: I'm sorry. I shan't be much longer.

(*A pause. The iron mingles with the music. Cliff shifts restlessly in his chair. Jimmy watches Alison, his foot beginning to twitch dangerously. Presently, he gets up quickly, crossing below Alison to be the radio and turns it off*)

ALI: What did you do that for?

JIM: I wanted to listen to the concert, that's all.

ALI: Well, what's stopping you?

JIM: Everyone's making such a din—that's what's stopping me.

ALI: Well, I'm very sorry, but I can't stop everything because you want to listen to music.

JIM: Why not?

ALI: Really, Jimmy, you're like a child.

JIM: Don't try and patronize me. (*Turning to Cliff*) She's so clumsy. I watch for her to do the same things every night. The way she jumps on the bed, as she were stamping on someone's face, and draws the curtains back with a great clatter, in that casually destructive way of hers. It's like someone launching a battleship. Have you ever noticed how noisy women are? (*Crosses below chairs to L. C.*) Have you? The way they kick the floor about, simply walking over it? Or have you watched them sitting at their dressing tables, dropping their weapons and banging down their hits of boxes and brushes and lipsticks? (*He faces her dressing table*) I've watched her doing it night after night. When you seen a woman in front of her bedroom mirror, you realize what a refined sort of a butcher she is. (*Turns in*) Did you ever see some dirty old Arab, sticking his fingers into some mess of lamb fat and gristle? Well, she's just like that. Thank God they don't have many women surgeons! Those primitive hands would have your guts out in no time. Flip! Out it comes, like the powder out of its box. Flop! Back it does, like the powder puff on the table.

CLI: (*Grimacing cheerfully*): Ugh! Stop it!

JIM (*Moving upstage*): She'd drop your guts like hair clips and fluff all over the floor. You've got to be fundamentally insensitive to be as noisy and as clumsy as that. (*He moves C., and leans against the table*) I had a flat underneath a couple of girls once. You heard every damned thing those bastards did, all day and night. The most simple, everyday actions were a sort of assault course on your sensibilities. I used to plead with them. I even got to screaming the most ingenious obscenities I could think of, up the stairs at them. But nothing, nothing, would move them. With those two, even a simple visit to the lavatory sounded like a medieval siege. Oh, they beat me in the end—I had to go. I expect they're still at it. Or they're probably married by now, and driving some other poor devils out of their minds. Slamming their doors, stamping their high heels, banging their irons and saucepans—the eternal flaming racket of the female.

(*Church bells start ringing outside*)

JIM: Oh, hell! Now the bloody bells have started! (*He rushes to the window*) Wrap it up, will you? Stop ringing those bells! There's somebody going crazy in here! I don't want to hear them!

ALI: Stop shouting! (*Recovering immediately*) You'll have Miss Drury up here.

JIM: I don't give a damn about Miss Drury—that mild old gentlewoman doesn't fool me, even if she takes in you two. She's an old robber. She gets more than enough out of us for this place every week. Anyway, she's probably in church. (*Points to the window*) Swinging on those bloody bells! (*Cliff goes to the window and closes it*)

CLI: Come on, now, be a good boy. I'll take us all out, and we'll have a drink.

JIM: They're not open yet. It's Sunday. Remember? Anyway, it's raining.

CLI: Well, shall we dance? (*He pushes Jimmy round the floor, who is past the mood for this kind of fooling*) Do you come here often?

JIM: Only in the mating season. All right, all right, very funny. (*He tries to escape, but Cliff holds him like a vise*) Let me go.

CLI: Not until you've apologized for being nasty to everyone. Do you think bosoms will be in or out, this year?

JIM: Your teeth will be out in a minute, if you don't let go!

(*He makes a great effort to wrench himself free, but Cliff hangs on. They collapse to the floor C., below the table, struggle. Alison carries on with her ironing. This is routine, but she is getting close to breaking point, all the same. Cliff manages to break away, and finds himself in front of the ironing board. Jimmy springs up. They grapple*)

ALI: Look out, for heaven sake! Oh, it's more like a zoo every day!

(*Jimmy makes a frantic, deliberate effort, and manages to push Cliff on to the ironing board, and into Alison. The board collapses. Cliff falls against her, and they end up in a heap on the floor. Alison cries out in pain. Jimmy looks down at them, dazed and breathless*)

CLI: (*Picking himself up*): She's hurt. Are you all right?

ALI: Well, does it look like it!

CLI: She's burnt her arm on the iron.

JIM: Darling, I'm sorry.

ALI: Get out!

JIM: I'm sorry, believe me. You think I did it on pur—

ALI: (*Her head shaking helplessly*) Clear out of sight!

(*He stares at her uncertainly. Cliff nods to him, and he turns and goes out of the door*)

CLI: Come and sit down. (*He leads her to the armchair R.*) You look a bit white. Are you all right?

ALI: Yes. I'm all right now.

CLI: Let's have a look at your arm. (*Examines it*) Yes, it's quite red. That's going to be painful. What should I do with it?

ALI: Oh, it's nothing much. A bit of soap on it will do. I never can remember what you do with burns.

CLI: I'll just pop down to the bathroom and get some. Are you sure you're all right?

ALI: Yes.

CLI: (*Crossing to door*): Won't be a minute. (*Exit*)

(*She leans back in the chair, and looks up at the ceiling. She breathes in deeply, and bring her hands up to her face. She winces as she feels the pain in her arm, and she lets it fall. She runs her hand through her hair*)

ALI (*In a clenched whisper*): Oh, God!

(*Cliff re-enters with a bar of soap*)

CLI: It's this scented muck. Do you think it'll be allright?

(*She nods*) You're a brave girl.

ALI: I don't feel very brave. (*Tears harshening her voice*) I really don't, Cliff. I don't think I can take much more. (*Turns her head away*) I think I feel rather sick.

CLI: All over now. (*Puts the soap down*) Would you like me to get you something? (*She shakes her head. He sits on the arm of the chair, and puts his arm round her. She leans her head back on him*) Don't upset yourself, lovely. (*He manages the back of her neck, and she lets her head fall forward*)

ALI: Where is he?

CLI: In my room.

ALI: What's he doing?

CLI: Lying on the bed. Reading, I think. (*Stroking her neck*) That better?

(*She leans back, and closes her eyes again*)

ALI: Bless you.

(*He kisses the top of her head*)

CLI: I don't think I'd have the courage to live on my own again—in spite of everything. I'm pretty rough, and pretty ordinary really, and I'd seem worse on my own. And you get fond of people too, worse luck.

ALI: I don't think I want anything more to do with love. Any more I can't take it on.

CLI: You're too young to start giving up. Too young, and too lovely. Perhaps I'd better put a bandage on that—do you think so?

ALI: There's some on my dressing table.

(*Cliff crosses to the dressing table R.*)

ALI: I keep looking back, as far as I remember, and I can't think what it was to feel young, really young. Jimmy said the same thing to me the other day. I pretended not be listening—because I knew that would hurt him, I suppose. And—of course—he got savage, like tonight. But I knew just what he meant. I suppose it would have been so easy to say, "Yes, darling, I know just what you mean. I know what you're feeling." (*Shrugs*) It's those easy things that seem to be so impossible with us.

(*Cliff stands down R., holding the bandage, his back to her*)

CLI: I'm wondering how much longer I can go on watching you two tearing the insides out of each other. It looks pretty ugly, sometimes.

ALI: You wouldn't seriously think of leaving us, would you?

CLI: I suppose not. (*Crosses to her*)

ALI: I think I'm frightened. If only I knew what was going to happen.

CLI: (*Kneeling on the arm of her chair*): Give it here. (*She holds out her arm*) Yell out if I hurt you. (*He bandages it for her*)

ALI: (*Staring at her outstretched arm*) Cliff—

CLI: Um? (*Slight pause*) What is it, lovely?

ALI: Nothing.

CLI: I said: what is it?

ALI: You see— (*Hesitates*) I'm pregnant.

CLI: (*After a few moments*) I'll need some scissors.

ALI: They're over there.

CLI: (*Crossing to the dressing table*) That is something, isn't it? When did you find this out?

ALI: Few days ago. It was a bit of a shock.

CLI: Yes, I dare say.

ALI: After three years of married life, I have to get caught out now.

CLI: None of us infallible, I suppose. (*Crosses to her*) Must say I'm surprised, though.

ALI: It's always been out of the question. What with—this place, and no money, and oh—everything. He's resented it, I know. What can you do?

CLI: You haven't told him yet.

ALI: Not yet.

CLI: What are you going to do?

ALI: I've no idea.

CLI: (*Having cut her bandage, he starts trying it*): That's too tight?

ALI: Fine, thank you. (*She rises, goes to the ironing board, folds it up, and leans it against the food cupboard R.*)

CLI: Is it ... Is it ...?

ALI: Too late to avert the situation? (*Places the iron on the rack of the stove*) I'm not certain yet. Maybe not. If not, there won't be any problem, will there?

CLI: And if it is too late?

(*Her face is turned away from him. She simply shakes her head*)

CLI: Why don't you tell him now?

(*She kneels down to pick up the clothes on the floor, and folds them up*)

CLI: After all, he does love you. You don't need me to tell you that.

ALI: Can't you see? He'll suspect my motives at once. He never stops telling himself that I know how vulnerable he is. Tonight it might be all right—we'd make love. But later, we'd both lie awake, watching for the light to come through that little window, and dreading it. In the morning, he'd feel hoaxed, as if I were trying to kill him in the worst way of all. He'd watch me growing bigger every day, and I wouldn't dare to look at him.

CLI: You may have to face it, lovely.

ALI: Jimmy's got his own private morality, as you know. What my mother calls "loose". It is pretty free, of course, but it's very harsh too. You know, it's funny, but we never slept together before we were married.

CLI: It certainly is—knowing him!

ALI: We knew each other such a short time, everything moved at such a pace, we didn't have much opportunity. And, afterwards, he actually taunted me with my virginity. He was quite angry about it, as if I had deceived him in some strange way. He seemed to think an untouched woman would defile him.

CLI: I've never heard you talking like this about him. He's be quite pleased.

ALI: Yes, he would. (*She gets up, the clothes folded over her arm*) Do you think he's right?

CLI: About what?

ALI: Oh—everything.

CLI: Well, I suppose he and I think the same about a lot of things, because we're alike in some ways. We both come from working people, if you like. Oh, I know some of his mother's relatives are pretty posh, but he hates them as much as he hates yours. I'm common. (*Grins*) Common as dirt, that's me.

(*She puts her hand on his head, and strokes it thoughtfully*)

ALI: You think I should tell him about the baby?

(*He gets up, and puts his arm round her*)

CLI: It'll be all right—you see. Tell him.

……

【注释】

1. The term "White Man's Burden" was coined in 1899 by Rudyard Kipling, an English author, to refer to the white people's obligation to manage the affairs of the supposed backward non-white people in English colonies. Here Jimmy coins a similar term.

2. posh: smart, elegant. 聪明的，优雅的

3. The two papers are *The Times* and *The Observer*. 两份报刊分别为《泰晤士报》和《观察者》

4. nom de plume: pen name. 笔名

5. yobs: slow-thinking foolish fellows. 弱智

6. Priestley: John Boynton Priestley, English author. 约翰·波因顿·普里斯利，英国作家

7. ulcers: a sore area on the outside of the body or the surface of an organ inside the body which is painful and may bleed or produce a poisonous substance. 溃疡

8. Vaughan Williams: an English composer. 英国作曲家

9. Here "somebody" refers to George Orwell, an English author. 指乔治·奥威尔，英国作家

10. Port Said: a port in Egypt. 埃及塞得港

11. Marchbanks: a character in Bernard Shaw's *Candida*, who, at the age of eighteen, falls in love with the thirty-three-year-old Candida. 肖伯纳戏剧《康蒂妲》中的一名角色

12. Sweet-stall: candy stand. 糖果摊

13. Sandhurst: the site of the Royal Military College. 英国皇家军事学院所在地

14. the Marquess of Queensberry manner: rules for boxing drawn by the Marquess of Queensberry in 1867. 拳击的规则，1867年由昆斯伯里侯爵创立

15. Stuart Hibberd: a BBC news commentator. 一名BBC新闻评论员

Questions for discussion:

1. What is Jimmy angry about?
2. Describe the relationship between Jimmy and Alison and analyze its cause.
3. Who is Cliff? What is his function in the play?
4. What are the major significances of *Look Back in Anger* in the history of British drama?

名言摘录

The heaviest, strongest creatures in this world seem to be the loneliest.

戏 剧 术 语

1. **Character**: Character is another important aspect of drama. Aristotle places it immediately after plot for in his analysis plot is character in action. Similar to other literary forms such as fiction and novel, character in drama can be portrayed in four ways. First, character is described by appearance. Actors' physical appearance can usually give audiences a direct and immediate impression of what kind of person the character is. Second, character is revealed by speech. Third, character is established by action. A character's external actions give readers clues to his or her emotions. Sometimes, the playwright may create a misleading or ambiguous impression of a character at the beginning of the play and then gradually reveal the truth as the play progresses. Sometimes, the playwright will deliberately leave audiences in a state of confusion of what kind of person the character is. But the more usual practice of most dramatists is to dispose the genuine nature and background of character through the speech of others.

2. **Comedy**: In the most common literary application, a comedy is a fictional work in which the materials are selected and managed primarily in order to interest and amuse us: the characters and their discomfitures engage our pleasurable attention rather than our profound concern; we are made to feel confident that no great disaster will occur, and usually the action turns out happily for the chief characters.

3. **Diction**: Diction refers to the language of the play, the words which the actors speak. Dramatists usually have utilitarian requirements for the discourse they employ in a play. First, the dialogue must be simple, concise and interesting, for the words must be immediately understood by audiences. Second, it should capture the spirit of time. For example, the diction in Shakespeare's plays represent the trend of history at that period. Third, it must be appropriate both for the character and the situation. Fourth, it should be dynamic enough to reveal the characters' relationship to each other, to indicate what is happening inside the character and thus to reflect the progression of the action. Finally, good dramatic language must be suited for oral speaking, for in the theater, there is no turning back the page and no pause to weigh and consider a line before continuing to the next.

4. **Drama**: The form of composition designed for performance in the theater, in which actors take the roles of the characters, perform the indicated action, and utter the written dialogue. (The common alternative name for a dramatic composition is a play.)

In poetic drama the dialogue is written in verse, which in English is usually blank verse. Almost all the heroic dramas of the English Restoration Period, however, were written in heroic couplets (iambic pentameter lines rhyming in pairs). A closet drama is written in dramatic form, with dialogue, indicated settings, and stage directions, but is intended by the author to be read rather than to be performed.

5. **Melodrama**: The term melodrama refers to a dramatic work that puts characters in a lot of danger in order to appeal to the emotions. It may also refer to the genre which includes such works, or to language, behavior, or events which resemble them. It is based around having the same character in every scene, often a hero, damsel in distress, a villain. It is also used in scholarly and historical musical contexts to refer to dramas of the 18th and 19th centuries in which orchestral music or song was used to accompany the action.

6. **Music**: Music refers to all of the auditory aspect of a play, including sound effects and the tonal pattern of the spoken word. Many great playwrights are expert in making use of the sound to enhance the effect of a play. For instance, in Eugene O'Neill's *The Emperor Jones*, the sound of the African drama throughout the play not only intensifies the sense of fear but also assumes the role of an invisible force throughout the play.

7. **Plot**: Aristotle places plot foremost in his list of ingredients that composes drama, for it provides the basic framework of the action. "Plot" is basically another term for structure, the things that happen in the play and the ways in which those incidents connects. Traditionally, a typical dramatic plot consists of five parts: (1) the exposition, i. e., the exposing of facts, the presentation and definition of the established situation from which the play takes rise; (2) the rising action, in which the plottings and counterplottings, accumulation of incidents and development of characters complicate the original situation; (3) the climax or rising point, which reverses the emotional tone and direction of the action and after which nothing new can be added; (4) the falling action, in which the various complications begin to find their resolution; and (5) the conclusion or denouement, which establishes a new situation to end the play.

8. **Protagonist**: The main character in a drama or other literary work.

9. **Spectacle**: Spectalce concerns all of the visual aspects of a play: the scenery, light effect, blocking, costume, make-up, etc. They make drama on stage quite impressive to audiences. For example, in Act I, Scene II of *Hamlet*, when the Queen

asks Hamlet to "cast thy nighted color off", Hamlet should obviously be dressed in black. Hamlet dressed in black in this scene is a typical example of how a playwright can invent a striking stage effect through character's costume: Hamlet enters at the beginning of the scene with the king, the Queen, and the courtiers, who all dress in gaudery. However, he is dressed in black, which shows that he is silent and isolated from the other figures. The stage picture has an effect which is very striking in performance.

10. **Thought**: Thought in drama may include the following two layers of meanings. Firstly, it refers to the rationale of individual characters in a play. Characters in drama will make subjective decisions or will be caught in conflicting emotional entanglement, which will all be reflected as their thought. Secondly, thought also concerns a play's theme which summarizes the moral and indicates the symbolic meaning of the play as a whole.

11. **Tragedy**: The term is broadly applied to literary, and especially to dramatic, representations of serious actions which eventuate in a disastrous conclusion for the protagonist (the chief character).

12. **Tragicomedy**: A type of Elizabethan and Jacobean drama which intermingled both the standard characters and subject matter and the standard plot-forms of tragedy and comedy. Tragicomedy represented a serious action which threatened a tragic disaster to the protagonist, yet, by an abrupt reversal of circumstance, turned out happily.

13. **History play**: The Elizabethan chronicle plays are sometimes called history plays. This latter term, however, is often applied more broadly to any drama based mainly on historical materials, such as Shakespeare's Roman plays *Julius Caesar* and *Antony and Cleopatra*.